Overwhelmed By The Grace of God

Jeffrey M. Rifkin

ISBN 978-1-64299-528-2 (paperback)
ISBN 978-1-64299-529-9 (digital)

Copyright © 2019 by Jeffrey M. Rifkin

All rights reserved. No part of this publication may be reproduced, distributed, or transmitted in any form or by any means, including photocopying, recording, or other electronic or mechanical methods without the prior written permission of the publisher. For permission requests, solicit the publisher via the address below.

Christian Faith Publishing, Inc.
832 Park Avenue
Meadville, PA 16335
www.christianfaithpublishing.com

Printed in the United States of America

Acknowledgments

This book has evolved over the past sixteen years. It was born from my reactions and fears to initially learning that I had inherited the gene that causes polycystic kidney disease. This disease had taken my mother's life, as well as the lives of her sister and father.

As my disease progressed, my marriage ran a strange and painful parallel course. My wife and I became more estranged. I had tried desperately to shorten the distance between us until I had little energy to do anything. My entire life focused on surviving the debilitating effects of my end-stage renal disease.

Although I felt abandoned and alone in my marriage, my children's love carried me through the terrifying ordeal. I would like to express my love and appreciation to my children, who demonstrated their unconditional love and care while I was at my worst.

To Cyndi and Rachel, my eldest daughters: I love you both for your expression of your love and concern through prayer and encouragement.

To London, not only did you tirelessly prepare each meal for me when I was on dialysis, you did extensive research to learn what I could and could not eat. You continue to be an enormous light in my life. Your artistic and scholastic talents are only surpassed by your enormous capacity to love.

To my son, Matthew, who saw to my every need each and every night while I was on dialysis: I love you for your bravery and service. Despite being so fearful that I would die, you refused to run to protect your heart, but stayed to watch over and protect me. One day, you will be a fine soldier.

When I felt frightened for my life, my children and God were there to walk this craggy, jagged road with me. No man had greater comfort in his time of sickness and trouble.

I wish to express my love for my sisters, Lori and Rosetta. I love you both with all of my heart! Lori, your family's caretaking and hospitality, both before and after my transplant, were heart-felt. You were bright lights in my darkness. My rapid recovery from surgery was largely due to all that you all have done for me.

To my cousins, Joyce and Alex: Thank God we have been there for one another when each of us had to cope with polycystic kidney disease and the uncertainties it brought. Our shared struggles with this dreaded disease claimed our mothers. As we sought refuge from our own fears of death, your many prayers and words of encouragement gave me the courage to press on.

Corky and Sharon: Although you were spared from this family curse, your support and love were so appreciated.

Dr. Vincent Casingal, how do I begin to thank you for your operating room expertise? I prayed that God would guide your hands and use your skills to save my life. Neither of you disappointed me.

I would like to thank all of my nephrologists, nurses, and lab technicians at Metrolina Nephrology Associates, especially Dr. Peale Chuang, Dr. Benjamin Hippen, Dr. Chris Fotiadis, and Dr. Kimberly Yates for your gracious follow-up care.

My gratitude to the lab technicians at Metrolina Nephrology Associates will never be forgotten. I must give a special *shout-out* to Bev, my lab tech, who drew my blood with gentle and tender hands. She gave me great comfort through her bright smile, exuding personality, and huge supply of Bob Marley tunes.

To Dr. Rebecca Panuski, who has been my primary physician since relocating to North Carolina: You gave me hope in the midst of my fears.

To all of my colleagues at Lakeside Family Physicians: I must thank you for your continued prayers and the warm welcome you gave me upon my return to work.

I have had the wonderful fortune of finding my editor, Kimberly Brouillette, who has worked tirelessly to bring this book to fruition. Thank you for all of your suggestions and corrections to my manuscript.

To Tess Rifkin, my beloved mother: Although you now dwell in heaven, your guidance, encouragement and persistence continue to influence my life. I love you with all of my heart.

To Shar Rifkin: When I had completely given up on finding love, not only did God send you to me, He supplied the perfect woman for me. You are strong, intelligent, successful, warm, affectionate, caring, and deeply committed to your walk with Jesus. Your external beauty is only surpassed by what God has fashioned within you. Your past struggles with your health give us a battleground to support each other through unconditional love, sacrifice, prayer, understanding, and mutual care. It is my deepest wish that God will grant us the grace to spend many years together as husband and wife and to be an example of Christ-like love for friends, family, and strangers alike.

To my brother, Jay: You were taken from my life so quickly and with you went many of my dreams. I take tremendous consolation in knowing that we will spend eternity together.

Most of all, I wish to express my deepest respect and acknowledgment to Almighty God. Were it not for your grace and mercy, this book could never have been written. Not only did you save my life, you have given me a testimony that will hopefully be shared with millions of people. I am truly blessed to be alive and well, and most of all, saved.

Jeffrey M. Rifkin

*"I will bring back your health
and heal your injuries,"* says the Lord.
—Jeremiah 30:17

Prologue

In the early morning of November 22, 2011, I opened my eyes to familiar sounds that slowly pulled me out of a deep sleep. I lay there feeling completely lethargic and disoriented, trying to become acquainted with my surroundings. The constant beeping and low murmurs coming from the hallway droned on continuously with no signs of ceasing. Suddenly, a nurse entered the room, stood beside my bed, and adjusted my catheter.

"Good morning, Mr. Rifkin. You're out of surgery and in the intensive care unit."

As much as I wanted to respond, I was unable to form any words with my mouth. Anesthesia from the surgery still overwhelmed my mind, as my memories slowly trickled back to me. Only five hours earlier, I had been intensely praying. Thoughts ran rapidly through my mind as I considered that I could awaken into eternity in only moments. My quiet contemplation was interrupted by my nurse's soft voice.

"Mr. Rifkin, can you hear me?"

I nodded my head and slurred, "Yes, but I feel so disoriented."

"That's normal. It will take you a little time to fully awaken. Meanwhile, I want to congratulate you on your transplant. Your surgeon said that everything went exceptionally well!" she replied as she ambled to the other side of my bed. She thoroughly checked the leads and wires running from my body to the monitors above my bed. "This might be one of the best Thanksgivings you'll ever have!" My nurse flashed another smile before leaving to check on her next patient.

Thankfulness enveloped me as I pondered the truth of her statement. I was filled with gratitude, which permeated from the depth of my soul. Despite being confused, this one thought was very lucid. *God, how can I begin to thank you for this transplant?*

At that moment, my younger sister by five years came into view. Lori had faithfully cared for me as I lived in her home during the previous four months. Throughout that time, she faithfully demonstrated her unconditional love for me.

"How are you feeling?" Lori asked as she lovingly touched my feet, which were snugly tucked beneath the hospital bed sheets and blanket.

"I'm still very groggy, but I'm relieved it's over. The nightmare is finally over."

"You have a lot to be thankful for. By the way, I heard from one of the nurses. Millie is doing well and recovering in another room."

Tears streamed down my cheeks as a sense of joy filled me completely. I was extremely grateful for the gift of life, but was even more appreciative of the sacrifice that Millie had made. At risk to her own health, she had donated her kidney to me. I was so relieved to learn that she was recovering without complications also.

Even through my blurry eyes, I could clearly see the exhaustion on Lori's face. We had both awakened early at 4:30 a.m. to make the half-hour drive from her home to Carolinas Medical Center in Charlotte.

"I hope you don't mind, but I need to leave for a few hours. I'm exhausted and could use a nap. Plus, your surgery took more than four hours!"

Attempting a smile, I assured her, "Not at all. Please get some rest. I'll be fine."

"I'll return later this evening. Until then, I'll stay in touch with the nurses to make sure you're okay. Do you need anything?"

My lower lip quivered as I said, "Nope. I'm good. Thank you for everything." I could not stop my eyes from welling up with tears.

Lori bent over and kissed my cheek. Since childhood, my younger sister had never felt very comfortable with any display of emotion. This was especially true whenever others would cry.

"Stop it. I'll see you later. I'll call Miranda and the kids to let them know how you're doing."

It comforted me for Lori to offer to let my wife and teenage kids know about my surgery outcome. Her follow-up was reassuring as I had only begun my recovery, especially since I was in a difficult situation in my marriage and family life.

My wife, Miranda, and I had been separated since August. At that time, she suddenly informed me that she wanted a divorce. It saddened me when our teenage kids, London and Matthew, lived with Miranda. I was resigned to take up residence with Lori, her husband, Peter, and their teenage daughter, Steffani.

I listened to Lori's steps as they faded away down the ICU hallway. Within seconds, I was alone with my thoughts. *Lord, how do I begin to thank you for giving me another chance at living out my life? Father, I am completely overwhelmed by your grace. Thank you, Abba. Thank you so much!* I wanted nothing more than to continue praising God for rescuing me from certain death. It was not enough to simply thank Him for keeping His promise to find me a donated kidney.

As I prayed, my nurse returned and interrupted my quiet reverie. She brought a small cup close to my face and gently placed the straw into my mouth, instructing me to drink some water.

"Dr. Casingal wants to make sure you drink a lot of fluids, Mr. Rifkin. You can have as much as you want. I bet you're happy for that!"

"Oh, God, yes!"

Eagerly, I drank the entire cup of water within seconds and asked for more. Downing a second cup, I smiled and thanked her. It had been nearly eleven months since I had begun dialysis, and therefore I had been severely restricted in my fluid intake.

"Mr. Rifkin, Dr. Casingal inserted a catheter so that we can measure the outflow of your urine.

"The outflow?"

"We need to be sure that your new kidney is working sufficiently, and the best way is for us to measure your urine output."

Although it was not a pleasant thought, it was a small price for ensuring that my new kidney was functioning well.

I began noticing several IV lines going into my hand and arm.

"Nurse? What are these IVs for?"

She came over to my bed and touched my left hand. "This line is bringing saline and some antibiotics, and the other is your morphine drip. It should keep you comfortable as your body heals from your surgery."

Quite honestly, I was not feeling any pain whatsoever. The morphine was doing an exceptional job.

As I scanned the large room filled with other intensive care patients, I wondered why each of them was there. All of them were adult males, many in their forties or older. Before I could finish studying each one, my curtains were drawn by my nurse. She immediately began to measure my urine outflow before emptying my catheter bag. Upon finding the results, she smiled as she wrote down the numbers in my chart. Seeing her expression, I assumed she was pleased. I do not remember much more, because I drifted in and out of sleep most of the remainder of the day.

Lori and Peter came to visit me that evening, but their stay was brief. Even though I sincerely wanted to spend time with them, I could not stay awake long enough, and so they headed home. The moments in my dreams, as well as when I was lucid, were extraordinary. I felt as though I had fallen in love with life. Nothing, not even feeling abandoned by Miranda, could shake my new appreciation for living.

The same God who had performed miracles of healing and salvation during biblical times, answered my cries for help. With the transplant behind me, my suffering with polycystic kidney disease and end-stage renal failure had been halted, thankfully.

God's compassion was greater than the progression of the horrible genetic disease. If the Creator of the heavens and earth considered my plight and even made provision for a special miracle, then how could I allow myself to be discouraged or fearful? This is the story of how I was overwhelmed by the grace of God.

Chapter 1

I kicked off my covers with excitement, not wasting a moment before both of my little legs hit the floor. We lived in the housing projects on Stone Avenue, located within the much-maligned borough of Brooklyn.

For as long as I could remember, this small two-bedroom apartment was my home for all of my four years. When my brother, Jay, was born six weeks before, my life took on an enthusiasm that I could barely contain. Playing with him became my obsession, and each day with him was better than a week at Steeplechase Park in Coney Island.

My pace to his crib quickened with each step. Stepping quietly into my mom and dad's bedroom, I immediately saw Jay's crib. It puzzled me when I felt a chilly draft flow through the room, so I looked over to one of the windows only a few feet behind his crib. It was open, in spite of the fact that it was a chilly November morning.

Unwilling to wait until everyone awoke, I renewed my desire to play with Jay. Before bending down to touch his small hands, I leaned over his crib, unable to fully comprehend what I saw. Suddenly, I gasped for air, as the reality of the situation overwhelmed me.

Blood was coming out of his nose and mouth. His inanimate body seemed suspended in time, lying in the crib with his arms outstretched on the small mattress. The moment lasted an eternity, as a million questions raced through my mind.

Without wasting another moment, I ran to my mother's side of the bed and shook her violently. "Mom! Mom!"

"What? What's wrong?"

"It's Jay! Mom, please come!"

My mother rushed out of bed and ran to Jay's crib. I stumbled after her, and as she saw his lifeless body, my mother began to scream. "Oh my God!"

Without wasting a moment, she pinched his tiny nose and began breathing into his small mouth. Immediately, Dad jumped up and joined her in the futile vigil. Mom's steadfast attempts were broken only by her screams and sobs.

I stood there, terrified by this surreal scene, my chest and throat tightening with each fruitless attempt to awaken my baby brother. My dad broke in with words my mom and I refused to believe.

"Tess, stop! He's gone. I am calling the hospital."

Mom picked Jay up and held him to her chest, weeping uncontrollably. Her tears dripped onto his face and forehead. She looked up at me with a vacant stare. Blood appeared to completely drain from her face. She staggered slightly. As she desperately tried to catch her breath, I waited for her to say something, anything to alleviate my anxieties and fear.

Finally, she spoke. "Jeffrey, go and wait in the living room."

"But, Mommy," I protested.

"Go! Go now!" Mom ordered with wet trails streaming down her cheeks.

I slowly obeyed her and made my way into our living room. Sitting on the couch, I tried to make any sense out of what I had just witnessed. As I sat there, the vision of that open window continued to haunt me. It seems like an eternity as I waited quietly in the faintly lit room, until I was suddenly startled by a knock at the door. I saw my dad walk to the door, and upon opening it, two men walked in, one of whom was carrying a long black bag.

My dad spoke in a subdued voice, "He's back here. Follow me."

All three men walked to my parents' bedroom, as I sat completely still on the couch. My young eyes remained transfixed on a small spot on the opposite wall. I held my breath, not knowing what to expect.

Suddenly, the two strangers reentered the living room and walked toward the front door. I was so confused as I saw them carrying my baby brother, Jay, inside the black body bag. A deep sadness overwhelmed me, and I felt completely alone. Remaining frozen on the couch, I was afraid to move for fear that something out of my control could happen to my parents or me.

From the moment that my brother's small body was carried out of the house, my days seemed to pass by like in a dream. To this day, I still cannot remember anything else that happened that day. It seemed as though the two men crammed all of my hopes and dreams for a normal, fun-filled, and healthy life into the black body bag with my baby brother's lifeless body.

Not long after that fateful November morning, I began to have discussions with God in order to understand the meaning and purpose of life. I was searching for some logical explanation that made any sense. In hindsight, some of my experiences were quite supernatural.

One night, I was awakened for no apparent reason. As I opened my eyes and found clarity, I got out of bed and stared up at the stars through my bedroom window. Their beauty inspired me, and I tried to imagine the world before God created the universe.

Suddenly and unexpectedly, a tremendous peace overtook me. As I crawled back into bed, I smiled and sank back into my pillow, experiencing a comfort I had not known before. Even after that, I had many more similar occurrences in my room in which I felt God's presence. They only enhanced my desire to know Him and His ways more intimately.

* * * * *

I never discussed Jay's death or the impact it had upon my family until I was almost fifty-one years old. That fateful day in November 1951, when I lost my brother, was the most traumatizing event of my life. It not only defined me; it set the course of my life.

Even now, as I share this with you, I mourn for my loss. Although I have mentally processed and worked through this unforgettable trauma, I often think about the lifetime of memories I did not have the chance to make. I never had the opportunity to experience brotherly camaraderie, countless mischievous adventures, and shared secrets.

Most people wonder why afflictions and death visit the most innocent of us. I spent hundreds of hours contemplating those thoughts as a child. Throughout my life, I frequently pondered the meaning and purpose of life. I desired to know God, because I believed that I would understand many of life's mysteries through Him.

In doing so, I have found tremendous comfort in trusting God, even in the midst of not understanding why these painful events occur. I am thankful for the life that God has given to me, although there have been many challenges, losses, and some regrets. All of the events of my life have made me into the man I am.

Most of all, I am deeply humbled and thankful to God for providing an atoning and redemptive sacrifice in the person of Jesus. Without Him, my life would lose all meaning and joy. He is the one who has helped me make it through the enormous challenges of my extremely difficult circumstances.

Chapter 2

Although Jay's death was largely unspoken of, the reality of it still hit our family in the face every day. In the midst of our overwhelming grief, we had to still function from day to day. The toll of it on my parents could be easily seen, and became very real to me.

My father became distant and more of a peripheral member of our family. He had difficulty with expressing anything other than anger, and certainly did not ever talk about his youngest son's sudden death.

As I look back upon my mother's behavior during that painful time, her means to find hope and healing was to become pregnant with another child almost immediately. She also focused most of her attention upon me. It became her lifelong preoccupation to raise me into a man who would garner respect, admiration, and love from everyone.

My mother's idolatrous love for me only served to increase my dad's alienation from both her and me. He began to gamble, shooting craps with his friends after work. Dad would spend hours in the dimly lit alleyway behind the Welbilt plant where he worked. As a result, my parents began to argue on a regular basis, and their fights became more virulent and contentious by the day.

* * * * *

My sister Lori was born on September, 1952. I remember being so fearful that she would die like my baby brother. After my mom returned from the hospital with Lori, I constantly worried about my new baby sister. As time went on, I finally became more secure in believing and trusting that she would not suffer the same fate as Jay.

While there were many fun moments in our home, the disagreements between my parents continued. Almost daily, their fights were mainly centered on our lack of adequate food and clothing, largely due to my dad's problem with gambling.

My dad's lack of education and ambition made matters even worse. My parents had married when my dad was only twenty-two and my mom was twenty. After I was born, my father was ill-prepared and too immature to provide for a family.

There were many days when we had nothing to eat. During those times, my mom would boil water on the stove so that neighbors would think she was cooking dinner whenever they dropped by. When they left, Mom would turn off the stove and make us peanut butter and jelly sandwiches.

I remember one specific incident during breakfast when they began to argue vehemently. Within minutes, they were screaming at each other.

"I am totally sick of your gambling!" my mother yelled and threw her breakfast toward my father's chest. "You're a pathetic husband and father!"

Covered with eggs and ketchup, my dad lunged toward my mother. Her jaw was clenched tightly as she picked up a butter knife from the table. With her face twisted with fury, she yelled, "Come closer, you bastard!"

My dad screamed back, "Shut up! I hate you!"

While sitting in my seat quietly, I was overwhelmed with the desire to disappear. Suddenly, my dad swung his arm toward a container of milk near me, knocking it over. The milk spilled all over the table and dripped repeatedly onto the floor.

Startled and shocked by my dad's violent and impulsive display of rage, I remained completely still. I avoided any chance of negative attention and focused on the steady drip of the beads of milk as they rhythmically hit the floor. All of the screaming faded into background. I silently pleaded, "God, please make the screaming stop! Please, God!"

I don't know how long the violent screaming continued, but when I finally came back to reality, the first thing I noticed was Lori crying. My mother, obviously still very upset, was doing her best to console my baby sister.

As I scanned the kitchen, my dad was nowhere to be seen. I slowly arose from the table to search for him. My mom told me that my father had slammed the door to our apartment as he left.

Several hours later, my father returned and sat silently on our couch. The entire time while Lori and I watched cartoons, our father's eyes were constantly fixed on the television. He did this without uttering a word or acknowledging our presence.

After hearing my dad come through the front door, my mom came into living room. Within minutes, the angry discourse resumed.

"So, you finally decided to come home? Where have you been!"

Without looking away from the television, Dad wasted no time in responding. "I went for a walk. Is that okay with you?"

"I really don't give a shit what you do. But, it's nice of you to come home to your children!" Mom shouted and then left the room.

Lori and I continued to watch one of our favorite shows, but we were both clearly agitated and uncomfortable with what we had witnessed. I continued to watch, but did not dare move. I was afraid that my mother would use my obvious discomfort as a reason to recommence the clash with my father. These arguments occurred quite frequently, making it difficult to fully enjoy family life. My primary place of refuge was found in my relationship with God.

Chapter 3

Not long after Lori's birth, I developed a severe case of asthma. I was required to take medications daily, but it wasn't always enough to prevent an attack. I often found myself being rushed to the local emergency room in order to get an injection of adrenaline to open my air passageways.

My pediatrician gave specific instructions that I must not be allowed to exert myself. Therefore, my parents prohibited me from performing any type of exercise. I couldn't even run in and around the buildings on my block like a normal boy.

One day in particular, I remember playing punch ball and having no problems breathing at all. I walked home with my head held high, so proud of my newfound athletic ability. Feeling like a normal child for once, I hurried through the door and exclaimed my achievement to my parents.

Instead of celebrating with me, my dad berated me. "I told you, you are too fragile to play ball!"

My dad was obviously worried about me; however, I would not let him discourage me. "Dad, I'm fine. I just want to be like the other kids. I'm going to play."

From that day, I did not let asthma stop me from experiencing the joy of athletic competition or having fun with my cousins and friends. In fact, my newly found determination laid the foundation for me to excel in many areas of my life. Whenever anyone told me I could not do something, my response was, "Watch me!"

In spite of my positive attitude, my health became very frail. Whenever I was ill, it was not unusual for me to run very high fevers, sometimes reaching as high as 105 degrees. Every time, my mom would put me in a cold bath until my fever subsided. I still remember experiencing hallucinations.

Later in life, my mother told me that I had contracted several life-threatening diseases. I find it amazing how God obviously had plans for me that I could not imagine. I'm still discovering what those plans are.

* * * * *

In 1955, I found my mother crying in our kitchen. I slowly approached her and placed my hand on her side. "Mommy, why are you crying?"

My mom did her best to compose herself, but her efforts were inadequate. "My sister, Rosetta, is dying. Aunt Rosetta is dying, Jeffrey."

I hugged my mom and clung on to her tightly. My young heart broke with empathy as I watched her sobbing into a handkerchief. Immediately, the immense grief she expressed brought me back to the morning of Jay's death.

While it was very painful to witness my mom's sorrow, my heart had an alien sense of relief at being able to grieve *with* her. I did my best to try to comfort her. "Mommy, I'm so sorry."

During those moments, Mom lay her weary head upon mine while holding me. My little arms clung tightly around her waist, as I heard her sobs fill my ears. My heart ached for her turmoil and loss.

After the death of a beloved relative, it is very common in Jewish families to name a child in honor of that person. Soon thereafter, couples often commit to conceiving a child in order to accomplish this goal.

Within months, my mom was pregnant again. She was determined to have another daughter. In fact, she would often say, "If God is good to me, he'll give me another little girl." Almost one year later, my sister Rosetta was born soon after Aunt Rosetta died from leukemia.

* * * * *

Although my parents' marital difficulties continued to plague our home in those early years of my life, there were still many moments that were fun and exciting. Every Sunday morning, it became the family ritual for my parents to "wrestle" in bed.

Within minutes of starting, I would hear my mom's voice calling for me. "Jeffrey, help me beat up Daddy."

My favorite part was running into their room where they were wrestling. The first thing I'd do was jump on Dad on their bed. He'd always feign being knocked unconscious by my devastating attack, giving me a weekly victory to be proud of.

One particular Sunday morning, I heard my mom's usual plaintive cry for help. After putting on my new boxing gloves, I enthusiastically ran into their room. Running directly toward my dad, I punched him in the temple. He immediately fell backward onto the bed.

Pretending to be serious, Mom quickly turned to me and yelled, "Jeffrey, run! I think you really knocked Daddy out!"

I ran as fast as I could and huddled in a dark corner of my room. I tried to be as quiet as possible. A minute later, my dad strode in cautiously searching for me.

Upon finding me, he smiled and said, "Jeff, you have a big punch! You really almost knocked me out!" I wasn't sure how to respond at first, but Dad's smile told me he was not angry at me.

Dad was raised in the tough Brownsville neighborhood of Brooklyn, New York. As a result, he had great respect for a man's ability to defend himself and others. He was naturally proud of my boxing prowess, which did come in handy at times.

While living in the projects, a neighborhood kid hit Lori. I quickly ran to her defense and began fighting with the kid, who was at least a year older than me. Although I got a few good licks in, he clearly won the fight. I managed to hurry Lori back to our apartment, only to be met by my dad's astonished face looking down on me.

"What the hell happened to you? You look like you got your ass kicked!"

"Daddy, a boy hit Lori, and I did my best to fight him off," I replied, wiping trickles of blood from my nose while shuffling my feet uneasily.

My father continued to stare down at me, which served to amplify my embarrassment. I was hoping that he would compliment me on my valor. My dad seemed annoyed as he said, "Well, I hope you hit him back! I will take you to see with Uncle Georgie. He can teach you how to box so that this crap never happens again."

Georgie Small was Dad's best friend from childhood. He happened to be a top-notch fighter in the middleweight division, so my dad had Uncle Georgie give me boxing lessons. The effort paid off.

Several months later, the same boy hit Lori again. I still remember his taunting smiling, as if to prod me into a fight. *What are you going to do about it?* This time, the outcome was very different.

I let loose on the boy's right eye with several punches, and even bloodied his nose. I must have made a big impression, because after that, he and I became good friends and never fought again.

Like my father, I quickly learned the rules of the mean streets of Brooklyn. I found out that when you stand up while being intimidated by a bully, the threat usually shrinks and diminishes quickly. Bullies want to pick on easier prey rather than take on someone who will fight back.

Chapter 4

As the years progressed, my parents' marriage worsened. In order to distance myself from their continual arguing, I focused my attention on other things. My passion for sports grew, as did my love for learning. Recognizing my desire to understand so many subjects, Mom spent many hours trying to encourage me in my studies. Unfortunately, I was often bored at school, because it did not challenge me.

One day, my parents told me that we had been asked to meet with my elementary school principal. I was nervous and somewhat anxious, not knowing what I must have done for the principal to request the meeting.

After we arrived at my school, we sat in the principal's office. He lit up his pipe and leaned forward in his chair. "Mr. and Mrs. Rifkin, your son does not belong in this school. Although he is only in the fourth grade, his reading level is nearly that of a high school student. In order to keep him interested in being here every day, his teacher often sends him on errands."

My mom looked back at him, barely able to hide a proud smile. "What do you suggest that we do?"

My principal took a puff from his pipe, and a cloud of sweet-smelling smoke filled the small space around us. "There is a school in Manhattan that specializes in teaching genius children. I suggest you enroll him there. We cannot challenge him enough to help him to move forward in his scholastic development."

I couldn't quite comprehend what was being said or how my principal's recommendation would affect me. I was too relieved that I was not in trouble to care. I didn't have a clue as to the magnitude of the upcoming changes that would take place.

My mom made the decision to not send me to the school in Manhattan for "genius children" but chose to send me to the yeshiva instead. The yeshiva was a Jewish parochial school that gave me training in Hebrew studies, as well as the standard education found in public schools. While this decision did not excite me in the least, it did excite me that the school was located only one block from my maternal grandparents' apartment on Eastern Parkway in Brooklyn.

Throughout my entire childhood, my grandparents lived nearby. Whenever my family moved, they would find an apartment within a two-block radius of our home. I was closer to and had more love for my grandfather than I ever did for my own father.

While my parents looked for an apartment close to my new school, I was blessed to live with my grandparents for several months. Those months were the happiest days of my childhood. No longer did I have to constantly hear and witness violent arguments between my parents.

Instead, I would do my homework, and my grandparents and I would find our way to the living room to watch the local and world news. I learned so much about the world and politics that I often impressed my friends with my deft knowledge.

My grandparents were respectful and loving, and they provided a peaceful and joyful environment for me. My grandfather represented a wonderful model of how a man should love his wife. He adoringly referred to my grandma as "my princess." He would even go out of his way to ensure that her needs and wants were satisfied.

We would also enjoy shows such as *The Alex Miller Show* and *Lawrence Welk*. All three of us would join in and sing along, while enjoying Italian ice and other delicious treats.

Gramps had us bursting at the seams with laughter from his jokes, some of them somewhat bawdy. Laughter filled the two-bedroom apartment, and my emotional health blossomed. The joyous laughter quickly turned into tears upon hearing that my parents had found a new place for us to live.

When my parents found an apartment in the building adjacent to my grandparents, I was reintroduced to the family mayhem. Since I had been declared a "genius," the pressures I felt were enormous. It was so overwhelming that I developed shingles on my left forearm and my parents were taken aback when they were told that my shingles were the result of stress.

When it was time to rejoin my family, I returned to the dysfunctional cauldron, still boiling over with great fury. The fighting between my parents escalated right away, and my grades began to suffer greatly. The pressures of having to be a boy genius took a huge toll upon my psyche and physical well-being.

When my pediatrician told my mom that the outbreak was the result of stress, she blamed my father. While her intentions were to protect me, she unknowingly made my situation worse. It seemed that my mom's slim hopes of joy rested solely upon my abilities to succeed academically. This only angered my dad, who was obviously jealous of my mother's adoration and protection of me.

In an effort to relieve the pressures on my mom and the jealousy of my dad, I settled for average grades. I was no longer the child prodigy, the messiah child. As a result, Mom's expectations for me were more normalized, and my dad no longer had any need to envy me. At least, that was what I had hoped, because his criticisms of me were unrelenting.

That lasted until one of my teachers, who was leaving the yeshiva to teach at Einstein University, called me out of class. As I followed him into the hall, I was not prepared for this short discussion. "Jeffrey, you need to promise me that when you are older, you will go to college." He leaned closer to me in order to make his point. "Promise me."

"Yes, I will." I responded more quizzically than with the assurance and pride that most other kids my age would have possessed.

"You are far too brilliant to accept any level of mediocrity. Do you understand?"

"Yes, I think so," I replied.

My teacher smiled as he placed his hand on my shoulder and led me back to the classroom. Before leaving the yeshiva, he sent a letter to my parents essentially repeating our conversation. In spite of his encouragement, my need for emotional survival superseded my promise to my teacher, and my resolve to remain a mediocre student was steadfast. I continued on my quest to dash my mom's expectations of excellence. This was in an attempt to relieve myself of the pressures I faced by mitigating my dad's jealousy of mom's adoration of me. This strategy lasted for many years.

* * * * *

Life in Brownsville was both exciting and frightening at times. I formed a number of friendships with boys who lived on my street. We spent almost all of our free time playing various street sports such as punch ball, stoop ball, and stickball. We loved playing football, basketball, softball, and Little League baseball.

In addition to my other friends, I also enjoyed spending a lot of my time with my cousin Corky, who was two years older than me. His birthday was the day before mine, and we always celebrated together. Corky was a more accomplished athlete than me, and whenever I played any sports activity with him and his friends, my athletic abilities would excel.

My friend Gerald and I were both nine years old when we would often go roller-skating on Eastern Parkway, the busy street on which we both lived. While skating one day, I felt one of my skates loosening up as we rolled down on the pavement. As I bent down to use my skate key to tighten the clamps, a man ran up from the basement apartment, stared at me for what seemed like a lifetime, and sprinted down the street.

Several seconds later, another man staggered up from that same apartment with a large knife protruding from his back. My efforts to tighten my skate came to an abrupt halt as the man fell dead only several feet away from me. As a result, I became an eyewitness to the murder, and fearful for my own safety. Luckily, no one ever questioned me, and I never saw the murderer again. However, I was still frightened that he would return one day when I least expected.

On another day some many months later, I was playing with Gerald when we heard that one of our neighbors had jumped from her window. As Gerald and I ran to the courtyard, which separated my building from the building where my grandparents lived, we saw her lifeless and twisted body sprawled upon the bloody pavement. Gerald and I exchanged fleeting glances as we pondered her reasons for jumping from her fifth-story window.

I immediately thought, "God, why do I have to see so much death? Why did my brother have to die? He would have been my best friend and teammate for life." I didn't receive any answers to these questions; in fact, the calamities of my life only continued to escalate into an exploding crescendo.

During a week of particularly hateful and virulent fighting between my parents, my dad asked me to come into the bathroom one evening. This request seemed very strange and unusual. I was even more surprised when I saw my mom waiting there for me with him.

"Jeff, Dad will be moving out and living with Grandpa and Bubby," she told me cautiously.

"What! Why!" I asked them, hoping to hear that it was a practical joke.

"Well, you know, Dad and I fight all the time, and we think it's best for him to live somewhere else."

It became quickly evident that they were not teasing me at all. As I hung my head in sadness, I began wheezing from asthma. Mom pulled me to her chest and held me. Dad tried to comfort me by touching my shoulder; however, my mother would not allow him.

"Get your freaking hands off him!" she yelled.

Before I knew it, my dad disappeared into the bedroom. After several minutes, he came back out with a pillowcase stuffed with many of his belongings and stood by the door.

"Bye, Daddy."

My sisters, Lori and Rosetta, joined me at the door as Mom went into the kitchen to prepare dinner. We sobbed heavily as Dad hugged each of us one by one.

"I'll see you guys on Sunday," he said as he walked out the door and disappeared into the Brooklyn night.

The epic changes in my life had an immediate and big impact on me. In my innocence I blamed myself for the breakup of my family. It also affected Lori and Rosetta. In particular, my sever-year-old sister, Lori, began exhibiting anxiety symptoms, such as constantly twirling her hair. She did it so incessantly that it caused some bald spots to form on her scalp.

We visited my dad regularly at his parents' apartment two blocks from our apartment house. Although I missed him, I relished the peace and quiet we all experienced.

For the first few months of their separation, my dad would ask both Lori and I to speak to Mom and convince her to allow him to come home. This request made me extremely uncomfortable because it placed their reconciliation squarely upon my young shoulders. Nevertheless, I gave in to the pressure and asked Mom before dinner one evening.

"Mom, can Dad move back in?" I asked in a disingenuous tone that was obvious to my mother.

"You know how much happier I am without him. Why are you asking that? Did Daddy put you up to this?"

I nervously shifted my weight and placed my arm onto the kitchen table. "Um . . . No. Why?"

"He did, didn't he? It's not your place to ask me that question. Now go and get your sisters. Dinner is almost ready."

I apologized to my mother and never did my dad's bidding again. Whenever he asked, I told him I would talk to Mom again. Each time I saw him, I'd make up one excuse after another until he stopped asking altogether.

In order to become self-sufficient, my mom started searching for a job. Within a few weeks, she found one at the local bingo hall. It wasn't long before we had more food in our home than ever before because Dad wasn't gambling the money away.

Our evenings were spent watching television and listening to music on our hi-fi stereo. I also began preparing for my Bar Mitzvah. My mom even hired a rabbi to teach me how to read the Torah and Haftorah sections. I already had a fairly good head start from my training in reading Hebrew at my yeshiva. I met with the rabbi several times each week. Like most Bar Mitzvah boys, I was both excited and frightened.

The Bar Mitzvah is the traditional coming-of-age ritual for all thirteen-year-old Jewish boys who are stepping into manhood. "Bar" is an Aramaic word which means "son." "Mitzvah" is a Hebrew word which means "commandment." Together, Bar Mitzvah would connote that the boy would be obligated to follow the Commandments.

According to rabbinical law, once I had my Bar Mitzvah, I would be held accountable for my actions. While I savored the thought of becoming a man, I was also frightened and awed by this responsibility. While I felt as though there was nothing I could possibly do to earn my dad's love and approval, my love and deep respect for God drove me to become the boy-man who would win God's approval. I studied diligently while the music of Sam Cooke, the Everly Brothers, the Drifters, and Elvis blared through the walls of our apartment.

My Bar Mitzvah was quickly arriving, and I knew that I would take my oath seriously. In preparation to finally become the man of the household, I felt some responsibility for our home. Before going to sleep each night, I prayed fervently for every member of my family, asking God to protect and comfort us.

Chapter 5

Soon before my Bar Mitzvah, my mom secured a position in Howard Schultz Insurance Company in Manhattan. She was happier than ever and was successful in her new job. Due to her new work schedule, my sisters and I ate dinner every weeknight with our grandparents.

I finished my first year at Walt Whitman Junior High School in the Flatbush section of Brooklyn. This required that I take two city buses to and from school every day, because my school was not within my regular district. I was able to attend that school because my mom was dating the school's dean, so they spent many evenings together. Eventually, they fell in love, and there was talk of potential marriage. Of course, this made any reconciliation with my father impossible.

I continued to work on my preparations for my Bar Mitzvah and felt extremely confident about the recitations of my Torah and Haftorah sections. All I needed to do was to memorize my speech for when it would come time to address my family and friends at the end of the ceremony. I was scared to death, since public speaking was never a skill I excelled at. The anticipation of a great deal of tension between my mom and dad, as well as their respective families, heightened my concerns.

The evening of my Bar Mitzvah arrived on July 15, 1960, and I was dressed in my white tuxedo. My apartment was buzzing with the sounds of my mom and sisters donning their beautiful dresses. I paced back and forth in the two-bedroom apartment, worrying about my impending speech. *God, I hope I won't make any mistakes or forget my lines.* This worrisome thought occupied my mind all evening until the ceremony ended.

Seeing my anxious state, my mom wrapped her arms around me and hugged me tightly. Kissing my cheek, she reassured me, "Jeffrey, I am so proud of you! I love you!"

Peering into my eyes, she noticed my discomfort and fear. "What's wrong? Are you that nervous about your speech?" Without waiting for my answer, she placed both hands upon my cheeks. "You can read your speech instead of worrying about remembering it. Okay?"

Mom's simple solution lifted a huge load off of my shoulders, and I smiled broadly. "Thanks, Mom!"

The evening went without any incidents, although the tension was palpable. Before the ceremony began, my mother presented me with a *tallit* and yarmulke to wear during my religious ceremony. The *tallit* is a woolen prayer shawl, and I felt so proud to have it around my shoulders.

As my Bar Mitzvah formal ceremony was concluding, I turned to face everyone and began to recite my speech. "As the children of Israel fled from impending doom into the desert …" My mind suddenly went blank.

I looked at my mom, who smiled and gestured toward the paper in my hand. I picked the paper up and began to read it. Within minutes, my speech was finished, and the celebration began. A band played and sang popular music as everyone celebrated with dancing and drinking.

After cutting the *challah* to bless the food and give thanks to God, we began to light the candles. My mom had designated important friends and family members to each light a candle as a way of honoring them.

My Bar Mitzvah party lasted until midnight. Unfortunately, not before my mom and dad shared a few harsh words. Thankfully, only a few of my family members were privy to this brief, yet very tense interaction.

As a Bar Mitzvah, I was accountable to God for all of my actions. The weight of that responsibility was not taken lightly. My prayer life intensified, and I purposed to follow the Ten Commandments as best I could. Every day I failed, my guilt grew heavier. I didn't understand how I could meet the expectations that I was to take on. The only thing I knew to do was to pray to God for help.

Chapter 6

My mother continued to be diligent at work, and she was doing well in her job. The very next year, we were even able to move from the tenement building in Brownsville to a duplex apartment in the middle-class neighborhood of East Flatbush. My grandparents moved two blocks from our new home so we could live close together.

It wasn't long before I was finishing my eighth-grade classes at Walt Whitman. I nervously tried to prepare for high school and meet the next challenges I would face. I wasn't sure if I was ready for this big change in my life. Little did I know that more changes were about to take place.

One evening, I was sitting on my bed, listening to my new transistor radio, a graduation present from my grandparents. Cousin Bruce Morrow's resonant voice filled my small bedroom, which was located in the front side of our home. I often had my blinds open at night, allowing the stars to flicker and glitter, amplifying my mystic muses. This night was no different.

As Cousin Brucie served up "Roses Are Red" by Bobby Vinton, my mom ambled into my room and sat beside me. "Jeffrey, I need to talk to you for a few minutes." She seemed uncomfortable, and I wondered if anything had happened to either of my grandparents.

"What happened? Is there anything wrong?"

"Dad and I have decided to get back together. We're going to look for a house to buy next weekend."

"Really?" I was somewhat bewildered by her decision, despite the fact that my mom and her boyfriend had broken up when he decided to marry another woman. My mom had been devastated by his betrayal and often spent her nights crying herself to sleep.

"Yes, I feel it is better for you and your sisters to live together as a family again. I love you very much, Jeff." My mom hugged me tightly and stood up from my bed. I was soon alone with only the company of the moon and stars illuminating my room through a window. I lay down upon my bed and focused my eyes on the night sky.

Cousin Brucie's voice was now muffled in thoughts as I pondered the surprising news I had just been told. I wondered how my parents' reconciliation would impact our lives. I imagined the excitement and happiness that would inhabit the faces of my sisters.

I had both doubts and fears about my parents' abilities to create a harmonious home, especially since my mom had hoped to marry the love of her life only months earlier. *This is not what I need right now. I am starting high school at the end of summer, and I have enough stress in my life.* I closed my eyes, as if attempting to rid any thoughts of my immediate family living under one roof again.

The next morning, my sisters' laughter and shouting awakened me. As I gathered my thoughts, I could hear my mom preparing breakfast. "Crap. They found out," I said to myself. "I better get up and join them."

I felt much divided for wanting to warn them against being so happy. I also wanted to tell my mother how reckless her decision was. It was not because my dad was such a bad guy but that they were so incredibly ill-matched. That caused my dad to feel inadequate and my mom to disrespect him.

I took on a steely bearing as I jumped out of bed and strode through the living room on my way to the kitchen. *You better make believe you're happy.* I did an excellent job at camouflaging my true feelings.

The following Saturday, we met our father at the door, and we all drove to Canarsie to look at model homes. My parents decided upon a three-story duplex house, which had an adjoining apartment downstairs. Our home was built by the time school began in the fall, when I was enrolled at Samuel J. Tilden High School.

Our family lived upstairs on the second floor, and my grandparents rented the apartment on the first floor. My mom used an interior decorator from Manhattan. Soon, our home was filled with expensive furniture and Italian mosaic tiles on the first floor.

For the next three years, I would find my way downstairs to my grandparents' apartment after finishing my homework. My dad drove a truck for a bakery and worked when the rest of us were asleep. Therefore, he napped during the day and awakened to prepare dinner.

My mom worked in the bustling Wall Street district in Manhattan. Upon arriving home in the evenings, she would visit with her parents for a few brief minutes. Afterward, she and I would make our way through a stairway connecting my grandparents' apartment to our home upstairs.

After dinner, I routinely spent my evenings with Grandma and Gramps by watching television, making jokes, and playing gin, which always involved Mom. During those times when my grandma requested either of her favorite Brooklyn delicacies, pizza or Italian ice, I would accompany Gramps without exception. My love for him was so strong and unconditional that when it was time for me to graduate and go off to college, it was a painstaking decision.

* * * * *

Before asthma affected and interrupted some aspects of my life, all of my family spent the summers in a bungalow colony in the Catskill Mountains in upstate New York. Our vacations even included my cousins, their parents, and my grandparents. Those were magical years for all of us, especially Corky and I.

We spent hours exploring the woods and creating imaginary wars and battling countless numbers of space aliens, foreign soldiers, and feral animals. It all came to a screeching halt after we learned that I was highly allergic to the pollen, which infiltrated the country air. From that time on, our summers were spent in Brooklyn and on the beach at Jacob Riis Park.

My junior and senior years in high school were rife with doctor's visits and trips to the emergency room. The bouts of my asthma attacks grew in intensity and frequency. Having earned a Regents

Scholarship, I had planned on attending Brooklyn College, which was located only four miles from our home.

Much to my surprise in June of 1965, I had a follow-up visit with my doctor, and he strongly advised my mom to send me to school in Arizona. Most physicians believed that the dry climate was beneficial to many asthmatics. So, we immediately called the registrar's office at Arizona State University, and I completed the requisite application forms within days of receiving it.

By the end of July, I received my acceptance letter in the mail. Mom and I had to scurry fiendishly to finalize my preparations to leave my hometown for a school 2,500 miles away. To make matters worse, I had learned that there were no dorm rooms available. My mom booked a room at the Hotel Tempe and trusted that a room would open after the first semester or that I would find other suitable living arrangements.

My day of departure approached more quickly than I had anticipated. I was very anxious about leaving my familiar surroundings; after all, I had never been more than one hundred miles from Brooklyn. My parents, sisters, grandparents, and cousin Joel drove their cars into the parking garage at JFK International Airport.

As we made our way to the TWA terminal, I felt my stomach reeling from nervousness and fear. My mom grabbed my hand just as she did when I was a little boy crossing the street. Her tight grip gave me a familiar, yet strange comfort.

As an eighteen-year-old young man, I had hoped I would face my first airline flight to college with a sense of excitement and adventure. However, I was frightened and insecure. Not only was I concerned about my maiden plane ride, but I was not certain of how long it would take to find permanent housing. Plus, Arizona seemed like a foreign country to a Brooklyn Jew.

When it was time for me to board, everyone took turns hugging and kissing me. My eyes locked onto those of my Gramps, whose eyes were filled with tears of love which fell upon his rugged cheeks. "*Boyala*, be good and do well." He quickly wiped them away with a white handkerchief that he snatched from his pocket. Next, he turned his strong, squat body away from me.

My mother saved her goodbyes for last. She hugged me tightly and wept. "Jeffrey, I love you so much. It is so difficult for me to let you go so far away, but thank God I'll be seeing you next month." (My mom had planned a surprise fiftieth wedding anniversary party for my grandparents, and I would be flying back for it.) She became unglued with a deep sorrow of separation, yet I knew how proud she was. I was the first and only person in my entire family to apply and be accepted into college.

"I love you, Mom. I'll call you once I get to my hotel room."

Finally, I walked to the boarding entrance, using my sleeve to absorb my tears. I quickly boarded the plane, found my seat, and buckled up. I closed my eyes and began to silently recite the Shema, the declaration of faith. "*Shema Yisrael, Adonai Eloheinu. Adonai echad.* Hear, O Israel, the Lord our God; the Lord is One."

I learned this prayer while at the yeshiva and recited it often as it brought a wonderful sense of solace and peace to me. Customarily, it is the first prayer that a Jewish child learns, and it is from Deuteronomy 6:4–9. I ended my prayer with a petition of safety. "God, please have me arrive safely in Phoenix so that I can begin this new phase of my life. Amen."

The moment I disembarked the plane and went outside, the dry heat hit me like a blast furnace. I found a taxi to take me to my hotel. For the first time in my life, I felt so grown-up, like a world traveler. The driver put my suitcases into the trunk and politely asked where I was going.

I wasted no time in responding. "Please, take me to the Hotel Tempe."

"The Hotel Tempe? Never heard of it. Let me call on the radio and find out where this is. Must be a very small place."

Suddenly, my heart began beating wildly. "This can't be a good sign if the cab driver has never heard of this place!" I thought. "Why the heck did Mom put me here?" My mind raced with thoughts of having to sleep on the street. I was scared to death.

We finally found my hotel, which was a small place within walking distance of the university and tucked away in the downtown section of Tempe. I placed a collect call to my mom and informed her that I had arrived in one piece, albeit frightfully. After going to my room, I set my suitcases down on the linoleum floor and picked one of the two beds as my own.

I quickly fell asleep and was finally awakened sometime after by the sound of someone walking into my room. Startled, I shot up out of bed as I saw a familiar face, a guy who I had known in high school and the older brother of Lori's friend, Johnny.

"Freddy. Is that you?" I said with a dumbfounded voice.

Freddy looked at me, his face looking as surprised as mine. "Jeff, is that you? Holy crap!"

I smiled and wondered if God had anything to do with this fortuitous event. After all, what were the odds that I would meet up with a friend from high school, in the same hotel, on the same day, and 2,500 miles from home? I'm sure the odds were significantly against it.

Chapter 7

It was only a matter of days before Freddy and I met two other freshman students at our hotel that we clicked with right away. In order to save money, the four of us found a two-bedroom apartment that we rented for the first semester. Our new *home away from home* was located within walking distance from Arizona State, where we all attended.

I was extremely excited to begin my new life as a student at the university. I would have an opportunity of being an independent person, and I was ready to prove that I could discipline myself to study, eat healthily, attend classes, and do my laundry regularly. I also relished the idea of finding who I really was and what I believed apart from my parents.

My parents put a great deal of emphasis on raising their children to be professionals. In fact, before leaving for college, my mom actually drafted a list of the professions that I could select from. Almost every profession involved being a physician; however, the last item on her list was an *attorney*. It was my choice to select to either become a general practitioner or a specialist.

"But, it's your choice, Jeffrey," she would say.

So, I decided to major in pre-dental so that I could maintain some modicum of self-respect and not give into my mom's well-intentioned control.

I did fairly well my first semester, despite the fact that I failed chemistry. I never took it in high school and was completely unprepared for that difficult course. Knowing that I would be required to take additional chemistry classes, I switched my major to political science.

* * * * *

Freddy and I became dorm-mates when a room finally opened up on campus. One of the exciting aspects of living in a dorm was that I got to meet many people from all over the country. While there were a few from states like Montana and California that I became friendly with, I gravitated toward several Jewish guys named Hank and Freddie, who were from the Philadelphia area. Other than our religious background, we had a lot in common. I spent most of my time with them, as well as a few freshman football players who were from New Jersey and Pennsylvania.

In spite of the fact that Freddy and I got along quite well, I moved out of his room and into the room of another friend named George, who would be the starting football center the following year. George was a good friend of Hank and Freddie.

All of us began hanging out together every day after class and even on the weekends. Due to the fact that we were Jews from the Northeast, we shared many of the same values, insights, experiences, and interests. This made us seem as though we were family, which cemented our friendships even more. My friendship with Hank and Freddie became so close that we decided we would share an apartment when classes resumed in the fall. Freddie's friend David also moved in with us.

To my friends, I was given the nickname Cat, as the result of wrestling a former high school wrestler in the dorm. All of my friends watched as the wrestler bet me I could not take him to the ground.

"Man, you did better than I thought you could. There was no way that I believed you'd be able to get that guy to the ground. We're going to call you the Cat now," George declared. From that time on, no one ever referred to me as Jeff again.

* * * * *

In October, I flew home for the first time since going away to college. My mom was there at the airport waiting to greet me on that overcast and chilly day. I was so excited to be back and see everyone, I could hardly stand it. My mother and Aunt Sylvie had planned this surprise fiftieth wedding anniversary party, and I would not miss this celebration despite the long plane ride home for the weekend.

As we parked the car upon returning to my grandparents' apartment, the first person I saw was my grandmother, who was dropping a bag of trash into the plastic bin. Her eyes widened with shock and surprise and dropped the bag of garbage upon the pavement. Placing her hand onto her chest, she yelled, "Jeffrey!" I hurried out of the car and over to her immediately, giving her a hug and kiss. She kissed me on the cheek and took my arm as we walked inside.

As we walked in the door, Grandma announced, "Ralph, Jeffrey has come home for our party! Your grandson is here!"

As soon as Gramps saw me, his expression was priceless. With tears welling up in his eyes, Gramps exclaimed, "I can't believe it!" He reached in his back pocket for his handkerchief and dabbed the tears. Not wanting to come across as too sentimental, Gramps stood up and went into the bathroom to compose himself.

In order to have both Grandma and Gramps be suitably dressed for their gala evening, Mom had to tell them a week in advance. Mom told me that Grandma and Gramps sobbed upon finding out about the effort and sacrifice that was made to honor them. My grandparents showed unconditional love and respect for each other their entire lives. It was their love that had brought sunlight to my sometimes dark and gloomy life.

When my grandparents entered the banquet hall, all of our relatives and longtime friends greeted them with love and honor. The party was a festive, merry, and joyous occasion. After it ended, I had conflicting emotions about returning to school. While I was excited to return to school and my friends, it was not an easy task to leave my family and grandparents again. In fact, as I prepared to fly back the very next day, I secretly wept as my eyes closed for the night.

Despite the fact that my parents had financed all of my expenses for college, I felt very independent and more self-assured. I looked forward to living my life apart from my mother's controlling affection and my father's criticisms. The very next day, I boarded my plane bound for Phoenix.

My freshman year ended, and I was disappointed in my academic performance. However, I was elated by my experience in my first year of college. I fully relished the friendships that I formed and took full advantage of campus life. I attended every Arizona State Sun Devils home football game and went to all of the other major sporting events.

I had dated several coeds, and my confidence began to swell. I was no longer the shy introvert. I was transforming into a more outgoing, young adult and was pleasantly surprised to find myself quite popular with many girls.

Before heading to New York for the summer, Freddie, Hank, and I made solid plans for sharing an apartment together in the fall. I was excited about returning the following school year, but I missed my family and looked forward to spending my summer vacation with them.

Chapter 8

My sophomore year was exciting, and sometimes even exhilarating. We all lived in a luxury apartment in Scottsdale, Arizona, a wealthy town just north of Tempe. Our tight-knit group became very friendly with a couple of guys named Norman and Michael, who were twin brothers from Skokie, a predominantly Jewish suburb of Chicago. Since each of us had our own car, it was an easy jaunt to school. After classes were done, we would all gather around our pool to study and soak up the rays. It wasn't unusual for us to spend hours hanging out together.

It was during this time that the American culture began to radically shift. Discontentment with the war in Vietnam began to spread its way across campuses around the country. Peace protest demonstrations would spring up all the time demanding an end to the war. While our campus was comparatively conservative to those in New York, California, and Wisconsin, there were pockets of radicalism emerging.

Another major impact on my life was the introduction of marijuana. I especially enjoyed getting high with the music of the Beatles, the Who, Buffalo Springfield, and the Rolling Stones echoing our passionate sentiments about politics and the nation's future. We could really get into some deep and thought-provoking discussions.

As the fall semester came to a close, I received a call from my mom that Gramps was gravely ill with a kidney disease. Fear and anxiety overwhelmed my thoughts. My carefree college life was suddenly interrupted by the inevitability of losing my beloved Gramps.

I telephoned my mom several times each week for updates on Gramps's failing health. She explained that his doctors had him on dialysis, which was necessary to keep him alive. There were many calls between us in which no words were uttered. The agony of knowing we were about to lose the most important man in our lives made our cries and uncontrolled sobbing the only appropriate form of communication.

Several weeks later, Mom called to tell me that Gramps's health was failing rapidly and that his doctors did not expect him to live much longer.

"Jeffrey, Gramps is going to die soon, and I don't think it's a good idea for you to fly back for his funeral."

"Why? Why not!"

I was surprised and somewhat angered by my mother's refusal to have me there to grieve alongside my grandma and family.

"I want to know why I can't come, Mom!"

She replied, "Jeffrey, I know how you love him. You have no idea how much he has loved you since the day you had come into his life. He is so proud of you. However, I cannot risk you getting so upset to the point of ruining your academic year. I'm sorry, but please understand that this is the decision I've made as your mother."

I wanted to continue my protest, but knew my mother would not relent. While I would be unable to see him, I prayed for him daily.

Several months later, my mom called. Her voice cracked as she told me the crushing news that my Gramps had died. I wept and once again pleaded with my mom to fly me home for his funeral; however, she remained steadfast in her decision. I was devastated at the realization that I would never again experience the love, acceptance, and guidance from my beloved grandfather.

Marijuana helped to soothe my pain, but no drug or words of condolence could lessen the ache in my heart. Although my love for Gramps could not keep him alive, I could make sure that I graduated from college as I had promised him. I would not let him down.

During the spring semester, I met Bo, another Jewish guy from Long Beach, Long Island. He and I connected on a very profound level, not only because we were both New Yorkers, but he and I shared a longing for God that none of my other friends possessed. Bo also had a deep understanding and appreciation for music and poetry, and his knowledge began to infiltrate and affect my inner being.

When he and I smoked, our conversations centered more upon God and the arts, instead of politics. Our brotherly bond matured to the point that we had decided to get an apartment together in the fall. It all worked out easily, since Freddie and Hank had both decided that they wanted to live without roommates. We were able to still remain close friends and hang out regularly, because all of us secured apartments within a one-block radius of each other. There was a lot of confusion when we all packed our cars for the exodus to our new homes.

Bo and I made plans to hang out on the beach near his home for much of the summer. One day, we met one of Bo's friends who had some tabs of LSD that he wanted to sell. It wasn't long before we were sitting on the beach and "dropping acid" together.

As the effects began to intensify, we walked for hours upon the shoreline. The entire time, we shared spirited discussions about our supernatural experiences with God. Every object seemed to come alive. Colors pulsated and sparkled, as the ocean seemed to breathe and develop a consciousness of its own. Even though my desire to know God was at an apex, I was acutely aware that this altered experience was not something I wanted to do on a regular basis.

* * * * *

I began my junior year with a high expectation of academic success and spiritual growth. After dabbling in several majors at Arizona State, I settled on business administration with a minor in English. Bo and I continued to share our apartment in Scottsdale, just below the apartment that Hank had rented. Freddie lived with another friend several blocks away. Norman and Michael lived one block from us.

Bo and I formed close relationships with both Norman and Michael. While Bo and I shared strong spiritual and literary interests, Norman and I were both very politically active. We frequently took part in on-campus and off-campus demonstrations protesting our military involvement in Vietnam. All of us congregated at the twins' apartment nearly every weekend to smoke weed, listen to music, and engage in deep discussions. In spite of the fact that marijuana was as much an integral part of my lifestyle and persona as my long black hair, my thirst for a personal experience and relationship with God was not being satisfied.

One evening, I was lying in my bed pondering the reasons and purposes for my life. I finally came to the conclusion that I was not fulfilling them, whatever they were supposed to be. I found myself longing for those supernatural experiences I had as a young child, because they filled me with wonder and awe of God's majesty.

As I continued in deep mediation, I remembered that I had an accounting class assignment that needed to be completed. Yet, I felt that this longing was far more pressing. My eyes began to focus beyond my mottled ceiling toward the desert sky and beyond. I felt so dissatisfied with my life that I began praying silently. *God, I feel lost and totally alone without you. Please help me.*

Suddenly, a vision came into my mind. I saw a man with dark olive skin, and very dark eyes peering at me. I quickly blinked, thinking my mind was inventing this vision. As I opened my eyes again, his black hair and beard came into view. The man was smiling at me.

I looked into his eyes and found pools of pure compassion inviting me to allow him to unconditionally love me. The more I focused upon his eyes, the more he smiled. Warmth filled my heart and began radiating throughout my entire body. I found it difficult to comprehend what I was seeing, yet this vision was reminiscent of many others I had in my early childhood. I remained motionless, concerned that any movement could interrupt this extraordinary spiritual encounter.

"I am the Messiah, the Moshiach promised from the beginning of time. You no longer have to feel alone in your pain and suffering. Follow me and allow me to heal you. Let me pour my love into you. Let my shalom fill you."

Even though it was a surreal experience, I was not surprised by his declaration. It was as if my soul responded with, "I knew that." I was more shocked at my aloof response to his invitation.

When I told my friends about my experience, they simply laughed and made some inane joke about having smoked too much marijuana. Their ridicule pressured me to not follow Jesus. I did not want to be branded as a *Jesus freak*. I also took into account my family's predictable reaction to following Jesus as a betrayal to Judaism. I also wanted to respect the memory of my family members who suffered and died in the Holocaust and the Russian pogrom.

Since Eastern mysticism began to grow in popularity, I took a path of least resistance. I fully believed that it would be far more difficult for them to accept me as a follower of Jesus than it would be for me to embrace yoga practices. I began reading books on yoga and meditation. No matter how much I studied these practices, I still felt a spiritual emptiness that I could not satisfy. The spiritual experience with Jesus stayed with me, despite my attempts to suppress it with a countercultural cocktail of sex, drugs, and rock and roll.

I had even become a vegetarian. This change was not borne strictly from a spiritual conviction. I had eaten ten cheeseburgers on a dare and a bet, and I could never imagine eating meat again.

At this point in my life, I was engrossed in the exciting new adventure of reinventing myself. I took on a new identity that was completely foreign to the one I had worn since childhood. Yet, Jesus's visitation nagged at me with a consistency that I could not shake.

Although I was a Jewish man, born and raised in Brooklyn, I could not deny what I had seen. That epiphany had deeply shaken my insulated world to its core. The decision to not follow Him was one of the deepest regrets I have ever had.

* * * * *

After my junior year ended, I made my journey back to New York. My long ride home was rife with ambivalent excitement. I could not empty my mind of the words Jesus had spoken to me. However, I was looking forward to travelling along a new road, which included a new world of meditative exploration and yogic discipline.

Being a hardcore vegetarian, my mom began researching some of the benefits and potential health risks of eschewing meat. She stocked many dietary staples to ensure that I would get sufficient protein, such as yogurt, cheeses, beans, rice, and tofu. She took joy in purchasing what my dad labeled as *weird food.*

That summer was very restorative, despite the fact that I continued to smoke marijuana on a daily basis. When I returned to school in the early fall, my diet and spiritual practices were so set in place that I found them easy to continue. Yet, my vision and short conversation with Jesus nagged at me. *How could I deny the unalterable fact that I rejected a direct invitation to follow the Messiah?*

Although these practices were very beneficial, they could not satisfy the deep longing I had for a personal relationship with God. Practicing yoga and meditation as replacements for Jesus was the equivalent of ripping a photo of a gourmet dinner from a magazine and eating it. It looked wonderful, yet did nothing to satisfy my hunger.

Marijuana was a useful tool in my denial process, and it remained an integral part of my life beyond my graduation from Arizona State University. In just a few short months, I would be embarking on my last year of college. Soon, my promises to Gramps and my yeshiva teacher would be fulfilled.

Chapter 9

Just prior to my senior year, Bo and I had rented an apartment just a few blocks from campus. We were not far from Norman and Micheal's rented house. Norman and I continued to invest our time and emotional energies into antiwar rallies. The opposition to the war was reaching its zenith, and our country seemed to be more divided than ever.

The year sped by, and all of our weekends were spent hanging out. We frequently attended many rock concerts in Phoenix. Bo and I saw two of our favorite British rock bands, Procol Harum and Led Zeppelin. We also learned that an extremely popular group from Long Island called the Rascals was coming to Phoenix for the very first time. Bo and I had touted them to all of our friends. While I played their latest album continuously on our turntable, I had an idea that might facilitate a meeting with our hometown heroes.

"Bo, how would you like to meet the Rascals?" I asked with a mischievous grin.

Bo looked up as "Whole Lotta Love" began to fill our two-bedroom apartment. "You've got to be kidding. How are you going to do that?" He chuckled derisively.

"Watch!"

I suddenly devised an evil plan which involved the Arizona State newspaper and the concert promoter. Quickly, I dialed the phone number to the newspaper editor.

"Hello. My name is Jeffrey Rifkin, and I've been asked by the promoter of the Rascals to write a story on the concert with the hopes of exposing our students to the New York rock sound."

"Okay. After you write the story, submit it, and I will determine if it's good enough for publication. Will that work for you?"

I really had no intention of writing the story, let alone submitting it for publication. "No problem. Thank you for the opportunity."

I hung up the phone and looked over at Bo, who looked fairly incredulous. "You're kidding me, right?"

I was too busy looking through the Yellow Pages searching for the promoter's phone number to answer. I shot a smile in Bo's direction, as I quickly dialed the phone again.

"Hello. My name Is Jeffrey Rifkin, and I am a student at Arizona State University, and I'm majoring in journalism."

The promoter listened as I plotted my scheme. "Since I have been a huge fan for their entire careers, the newspaper asked me to meet with the Rascals and write a story about them. They will be promoting the story before the concert takes place."

My heart was pounding as I waited for his response to my outrageous proposal. "That sounds like a great idea. Come to the stage door about an hour before the concert begins, and I'll have you meet with them backstage. I will also make sure that you have front-row tickets so that you can get some shots of them on stage."

I saw Bo get up from his chair and was standing next to me, apparently impressed by my chutzpah.

"That sounds great! I will be accompanied by my assistant, who is also my photographer. We'll see you there."

"No problem. Thanks for doing this. I will make sure that everything's arranged for you. Just let the stage people know who you are. Oh, and spell your name for me." After spelling my name for him, I hung up the phone and smiled boldly.

Bo slapped me on the back. "Holy crap! I can't believe you pulled this off, bro!"

The night of the concert went without a hitch. We were ushered into a huge room with tables piled high with delicious food. When the Rascals finally came in after finishing their final rehearsal, the lead singer, Felix Cavaliere, ambled to my side. "Who's the writer from the school newspaper?"

"That's me, Felix," I piped up.

Felix put his arm on my shoulder and smiled broadly. While I was a confident, ballsy young man, I did not find comfort in lying.

"Felix, I'm a huge fan. I've been following you guys and listening to your music since the beginning. I'm not really a journalist. I made up the story, because I really wanted to meet you."

He looked into my eyes and laughed quietly. He obviously appreciated my New York City "fear no one and nothing" attitude. We spoke about meditation and yoga. He even wrote down the telephone number of his personal spiritual guru, Swami Satchidananda, who had a studio in Manhattan. Our talk went on for about twenty minutes. Afterward, Bo and I watched the concert from the front row. No pictures were ever taken, and no story was ever written. However, we had a memorable story that we shared with Norman and Michael and that grew to mythical proportions. We used similar strategies to meet other rock legends, but before long, college graduation was upon us.

* * * * *

My parents made preparations for my graduation. They flew out to Phoenix and rented a hotel room in Scottsdale. They also booked rooms at the Riviera Hotel in Las Vegas, which was framed to be my graduation gift. The trip to Vegas was more of a gift to my parents for sacrificing their hard-earned money to fund my education.

Bo needed an additional year to graduate, and Michael had made a decision to not participate in this traditional, bourgeois exercise. My parents and I drove to Sun Devil Stadium where we soon found Norman. My mom looked deeply into my eyes and began to weep. "I wish Gramps were here to see you, Jeffrey. He would be so proud of you." Without hesitation, I quickly wiped my tears with my graduation gown sleeve, and Mom and I hugged tightly. My family made its way into the cavernous stands of the stadium to watch the finale of my education career. Norman and I took our place in our designated section; our long hair hung down from beneath our caps.

After spending several days in Las Vegas, which was a complete experience in boredom, we began our drive home to New York. During most of our car ride home, my mom and I shared all of the driving while my dad either sat quietly in the back seat or slept. One day, while driving on a beautifully clear day in New Mexico, my mom commented on how gorgeous God's handicraft was and used a good deal of poetic words in her description. As we exchanged our perspectives on beauty and our thoughts about God, I was taken by the depth of our conversation. We hadn't talked on this level for many years and my appreciation and respect for my mom's sensibilities and intelligence grew. As the conversation reached its denouement, for some reason I took the time to let my mom in on a secret. "Mom, I need to tell you something. I smuggled a pound of weed to bring home." She became rightfully alarmed. "What! Are you friggin' crazy?! Oh my God, where is it?" I told her that since my hair was so long, I was afraid to put it in my suitcase, lest the police stop us. "I put it in dad's suitcase before leaving the hotel." She had a very stunned look on her face, until I started laughing and shared a possible scenario of us being stopped and having my dad being handcuffed and put in a squad car. To my surprise, my mom appreciated my bizarre humor and added other possible scenarios. We laughed hysterically until our laughter awakened my father. "What's so damn funny?" he inquired from the back. "We were just laughing at a joke Jeff told. Just go back to sleep and we'll try to be less noisy." We both chuckled as my mom whispered, "Just be sure to get it out of his suitcase the moment we get home, you nut."

Chapter 10

After returning to Staten Island, I lived with my parents in their new home. I used my summer to work in my parents' garden and do all of the landscaping. The solitary moments in the sun gave me the time I needed to assess the direction I wanted to take with my life. I purchased a book on hatha yoga and began practicing the postures which were called *asanas*.

Doing yoga in the early morning brought relaxation and quiet to my restless soul and tense muscles. Even though I had earned my bachelor's degree in business administration, I was not motivated to secure a position in the business world. Instead, I made the decision to enroll in Long Island University's master's program in English. My classes included Russian literature, early American literature, and twentieth-century plays. I was elated.

My ambitions came to an abrupt halt when I suddenly became very ill. My skin took on a palette of yellows, oranges, and reds, and my eyes became very jaundiced. I ran a fever of 106, and our family doctor rushed to our home to diagnose and attempt to treat me.

Upon seeing my condition, he requested that I be taken to the hospital immediately. I spent one week in the hospital, still running an extremely high fever. Finally, my fever broke long enough for me to be discharged and sent home, my body exhausted and enervated.

I had contracted Hepatitis A; however, all of my doctors were not sure what the actual cause was. In fact, due to the enlargement of my spleen, they wondered if I was suffering from leukemia. Impatiently, I waited for the toxicology reports to return from the National Institute of Health. In the interim, I prayed to be spared from the disease that took my Aunt Rose's life.

The exhaustion I felt debilitated me, and therefore I dropped out of school. Within weeks, I learned that I had contracted toxoplasmosis, a parasitic disease primarily spread by cat feces. This confounded my physicians since I had never owned a cat, nor had I been in the presence of one. The only treatment they recommended was rest, and it took nearly two months to fully recover.

As the months progressed, I continued to smoke large amounts of marijuana. I felt hopeless and lost once again. After my bout with toxoplasmosis and Hepatitis A, my ambitions, aspirations, and enthusiasm for life disappeared. Soon, my body and soul became lifeless.

I felt as though my spirit was living in an uninhabitable and vacant building. I finally reached the point where I knew I needed help, so I asked my mother to find a psychiatrist. She made an appointment for the following week; however, an unforeseen event occurred which made that appointment no longer necessary or desired.

* * * * *

My cousin Corky was a partner in several record stores in New Jersey and had me managing the store in Princeton, which was adjacent to the university. I began to become very attracted to a young woman who was a practitioner of Transcendental Meditation, or TM.

TM was a form of meditation made famous by Maharishi Mahesh Yogi, who had many celebrity and well-known adherents, including the Beatles and the Beach Boys, among others. TM used a personalized mantra, or sound, that provided for deep relaxation. It was purported to create an experience where the practitioner transcended all thought.

I was in a desperate point in my life, and also knew that if I were going to capture this girl's heart, I needed to share this important piece of her life. She shared her experiences with me over dinner, and I agreed to attend a TM meeting with her. By the next week, I received my first instruction in TM and swore off all recreational drugs. I felt spiritually, emotionally, and physically rejuvenated.

I practiced TM faithfully twice daily and worked various jobs to maintain some degree of independence from my parents. I became enamored with my new lifestyle and made the decision to earn a living by becoming a TM teacher. That required that I attend a two-week intensive instructor's program with the Maharishi in northern California.

In order to earn the plane fare to fly to San Francisco, I worked in construction as a laborer. I saved enough money to fly there, but not enough to find my way home. My plan was to hitchhike home, which my parents found totally unacceptable. I was finally able to convince them to let me do it after I assured them that I would call daily to give them updates on my whereabouts. I was extremely excited about this adventure opportunity and was even impressed by my own bravery.

Chapter 11

My flight arrived in San Francisco, and I found my way to an inexpensive motel near the airport. I slept for a few hours before taking a cab to the Greyhound bus station, where my midnight bus ride to Eureka, California, was embarking. After arriving, I was assigned a room on the campus of Humboldt State College. My roommate was a guy about my age, who lived in northern New Jersey. To top it all off, I was served delicious vegetarian meals every day.

Our schedule included transcendental meditation and hatha yoga twice each day, as well as listening to the Maharishi talk every evening. The lectures were held in a large auditorium and were attended by hundreds of practitioners. Several celebrities also attended, including several of the Beach Boys and Billy Gibbons from ZZ Top.

Mark and I met two other guys from Corpus Christy, Texas, named Dudley and Gavin. During the conference, we spent most of our time together as a group. When it came to an end, our Texan friends invited us to travel with them. "Hey guys, let's hang out awhile and see some of the country before ya'll head back east."

Throughout this trip, we formed strong friendships. This was primarily based on our shared passion for TM and spiritual matters. As a result, our new Texas friends made a suggestion.

"Hey, guys, let's hang out awhile and see some of the country together before y'all head back east."

Dudley's invitation was immediately accepted by both of us. Not only would it make our way home more expeditious, we really enjoyed spending time with the guys.

Our trip was breathtaking and amazingly scenic. We drove through the Redwood Forest near Redding, California, and then drove east to Salt Lake City, Utah. When we arrived, we drove to the Salt Lake City Mormon Temple.

In the massive temple, we enjoyed gazing at the splendorous spires, beautiful architectural features, and ornate interior. I found a pew in the back and decided to meditate for a few minutes. I wanted to pay homage in the house of God.

While I knew little about the Mormon faith, I nonetheless believed that God bestowed his blessings on worshipers of all religions. Meditating in the temple was my way of experiencing the stillness within and around me. After we were done, we piled into the van and drove southeast. After nearly ten hours of driving, we finally reached the mystical, artistic city of Taos.

Taos is an amazing city nestled within the Sangre de Cristo mountain range. Our driver, Dudley, had been to Taos before and knew a lot about it already. He gave us a small tour of the city's history and luring sights.

He said, "This city has been inhabited by several Native American tribes, and therefore is very spiritual in nature. It is one of the longest continually inhabited cities in the country, and it has a number of mystical qualities."

I was intrigued by what Dudley shared and asked, "What mystical qualities are you talking about?" I moved closer to sit directly behind Dudley. I wanted to be able to hear what he had to say, and ask him some questions.

Dudley swung around to face me, happy that I had shown an interest. "Taos has a low-frequency humming sound that some people can hear. There is a lot of controversy about how it originated."

"Really? A humming sound?"

"Yeah. Some people say that it comes from the secret experiments done in Los Alamos. Others think it comes from electromagnetic vibrations emitted by the mountains. The most unusual theory is that the humming noise comes from low-flying alien spacecraft. Who knows why? But it's pretty cool."

I suggested, "After we get some dinner and park the van in a campground, let's meditate and try to hear it!" My excitement could not be contained, since I had always been drawn to life's mystical experiences.

We finally found the local grocery store and picked up tortillas, avocados, and cheddar cheese. After finding a peaceful spot in a pine forest just outside of the city, we ate our dinner. An hour later, I placed my sleeping bag on a soft grassy surface and meditated. To my disappointment, I heard nothing but the soft and melodious songs in the woods that emanated from the many species of birds.

We camped high above the small artist colony in the mountains. It wasn't long before I lay down and placed my head upon my rolled-up jean jacket. For several hours, I was mesmerized by the beauty of the environment. The sweet aroma of the trees filled the air. Taking it all in seemed more important than sleep.

As I watched the countless stars twinkle above me in the vast southwestern sky, I was amazed at how the sky was not invaded by any other light, except for the bright moon. I was overwhelmed with awe at the panoramic view above me. I realized that I was but a small piece in the much larger, grander picture of creation.

The experience gave me a sense of peacefulness and contentment. With a long, deep sigh, I thought, "I feel so amazingly relaxed and happy." Within minutes, my eyelids closed, and I drifted off to sleep.

We woke up at the crack of dawn as the morning sun arose. The air was brisk and chilly, and I was not in any rush to climb out of my sleeping bag. However, my desire for breakfast superseded my need to stay warm. I brushed my teeth and my hair quickly before we gathered by the van.

After eating sandwiches again, we left and traveled the hour-and-a-half trip to Santa Fe. We toured the extremely artistic city together for several hours. At the end of our excursion, we parted ways and promised to stay in touch with each other.

Mark and I waited for the van to drive off before putting our thumbs out to hitch a ride to Phoenix. It did not take us long before a car stopped to pick us up. We were fortunate to travel for nearly one hundred miles before it was time to exit with our backpacks. Once again, we appealed to strangers for rides that would bring us closer to Phoenix. Finally, we arrived after two days.

Upon arrival, I was unable to locate Bo, so we stayed in a friend's home for an entire day. However, I was fortunate to locate his sister, Judy, who put Mark and I up for the night. She explained that Bo had flown to Jamaica and had taken up a Rastafarian lifestyle, replete with smoking ganja and playing drums in several reggae bands.

Ready to leave, Mark and I awoke at the crack of dawn and set out for home. We were fortunate to find a ride fairly quickly, and rode for several hours. The driver told us all about his personal problems, which included divorce and substance abuse. However, when a police officer stopped the driver for having a broken taillight, the man dropped us off at an exit in the middle of the desert.

Mark and I were undaunted. We relished the adventure and had faith that God would supply us with a ride quickly. Minutes quickly turned into hours, and every car passed us by. Things went from bad to worse when I went to take a swig of water from my plastic canteen. I discovered that all of my water had drained out from a puncture in the bottom of my canteen.

Mark had little water of his own but was only willing to give me a small swallow. We remained in this same spot for most of the day, and both of us were parched and very worried about our situation. I looked up at the scorching sun and noticed some vultures flying above us.

"Mark, there are vultures up there! Do you think they sense that we are not getting out of here alive?"

My faith was now as dry as my canteen.

"I don't know. But, we have to figure something out, and quickly!"

I looked across the highway and could barely see a sign for a Mexican cantina. "Mark, look across the highway. Let's head over there and get some food and water."

"How are we going to get across a six-lane highway with all of this traffic and then walk all the way to that restaurant?"

I felt as though we needed to take whatever chance was necessary. I knew that our current strategy was not working. "Let's do it anyway. I can hardly breathe from all of this dry dust."

After timing our sprints across the highway and dodging the myriad of semis and cars, we finally staggered into the cantina. For over an hour, we filled up on pitchers of water and large quesadillas. Having satisfied our hunger and thirst, we ventured back to our spot heading east.

As we put our thumbs out, it began raining. Immediately, I began praying silently. *God, please help us to find a ride quickly!* I turned to Mark and confidently told him that the rain was a positive sign from God.

Mark was not so convinced. "Let's hope so."

Within moments, an old pickup truck slowed and pulled over for us to get in. As we placed our backpacks in the rear cab and piled into the front seat, I was immediately awed by our hosts. I sat next to a woman who appeared to be in her fifties. She possessed the clearest blue eyes I had ever seen. They were like pools of Jamaican water that I had seen in old travel guides. Her fiery red hair only further accented her gorgeous eyes.

She introduced the driver sitting next to her as her husband. She wasted little time to ask us any questions about our destination or how we had been stranded in the desert. I volunteered to be the spokesman and told her everything about our time with the Maharishi. Upon telling her that I was on my way home to Staten Island, she became very animated, and her eyes became almost iridescent.

"I'm from Manhattan," she said in a thick New York City accent. "I moved out here because I knew that God had intended me to marry a Native American man. So, I loaded up my car and met my soul mate." She gestured to her husband, who smiled broadly.

The magical nature of our conversation only further underlined my belief that God had intervened and sent this couple to assist us. We drove for approximately ninety minutes before they stopped to let us out. She even apologized for being unable to drive us further.

Our drive went without incident, until we were picked up by a pair of brothers in Texas. Both of the men had broken limbs in casts. The driver had a cast on his right arm, and his brother had one on his right leg.

I shot a quick look to Mark as we settled in the back seat. This odd sight made me worry about our safety, but fortunately they were friendly. My anxiety soon dissipated as they explained that they had been in an automobile accident a couple of weeks before.

Sensing concern in our reaction, the driver quickly attempted to alleviate our fears. "Don't worry, y'all. We were rear-ended by a pickup truck, and the driver was as drunk as a skunk. It wasn't our fault." He turned his head toward us and flashed a short, reassuring smile.

We finally made it to Pennsylvania, where Mark and I parted ways. I found a phone booth outside of a gas station and called my mom to tell her that I was relatively close to home. She seemed very relieved.

Near the end of the day, I approached the Goethals Bridge in New Jersey. Upon crossing the bridge, I would be finally back in Staten Island and no more than fifteen minutes from home. Suddenly, a police car stopped us.

The officer walked around the front of his vehicle and stood in front of me. "Son, do you know it's illegal to hitchhike across this bridge?" He leaned closer to me, waiting for my response.

"I didn't know that, Officer. I'm sorry. I've hitchhiked all the way from Arizona, and my family lives right across the bridge. Any chance, you could make an exception for me?"

The officer looked at me up and down. His eyes settled on my long hair, which was pulled back into a ponytail. "Nope. Sorry. I can't do that."

I was completely exhausted from my adventure and was eager to get home to rest and share my stories with my family. The exhaustion and anticipation of seeing my folks gave me a boldness that even took me by surprise. "Officer, can you give me a ride?"

He was shocked by my request. "Are you crazy? I'm not going to risk losing my job!" He stared into my eyes with disbelief at my audacity.

"I totally understand. How about I get into your back seat and duck down until we're across the bridge?"

The officer stood there in silence for several seconds and then gave me a wry grin and shook his head. "All right, get in. But don't let your hippie head come up until I tell you to. Okay?" The officer drove us across the bridge and then secretly let me out.

After weeks of studying and extensive traveling, I finally found my way home. Since it was a hot summer's day, it was no surprise to find every member of my family inside their home. Everyone, including my dad, wanted to hear all about my great adventure. Before my storytelling began, I silently thanked God for my safe passage home.

Chapter 12

After returning home from my sojourn in California and my hitch-hiking adventures, I received a phone call from my friend Jackie. He was a counselor in a sports camp in the Adirondack Mountains in upstate New York. He offered me a position as a camp counselor. Since I was not working at the time, plus I also loved to travel, go on adventures, and was a complete sports enthusiast, I unhesitatingly accepted the position.

I took the next bus to the small town near the camp. Jackie and a woman he had been dating at the camp came to meet me at the bus station. As they familiarized me with the duties of my position, I found myself getting excited about my new adventure. I settled in and met each of the young boys assigned to my bunkhouse. I awoke each morning at the crack of dawn and would sit outside and meditate. It was not long before the word got out that the *new guy* did some weird spiritual practice while sitting against a pine tree early each morning. I explained to all of them about my spiritual discipline and vegetarian diet. While most of the other counselors smoked marijuana and placed no dietary restrictions upon themselves, I became good friends with them.

While it was extremely fun working with young pre-adolescent boys, I was soon struck by a severe asthma attack. During my week-long stay in Glens Falls Hospital, a young nurse's aide took great interest in me. Nancy was nineteen years old and divorced, with a two-year-old daughter. Regularly, she would stop by and visit me in the hospital room that I shared with three other patients. She would charm me with her small-town smile and humor.

Upon returning to the camp, I was quite surprised when I received a letter from her within three days of my discharge. In it,

Nancy declared her attraction to me and stated that she felt we had a connection. She also asked if I were interested in dating her while I was still in the area.

As soon as I read the letter, I called her. She invited me to her parents' home in nearby Hudson Falls. After meeting her mother, stepfather, and her daughter, Megan, we walked around the four-acre property. Eventually, we found our way to the loft of the barn, where we spoke for many hours. Sometime between kissing and hours of in-depth discussion, we both acknowledged that something very special was growing between us. When we both began getting very sleepy, I knew it was time to leave, although I enjoyed our time together very much. Nancy and I made plans to see each other the very next night. I kissed her and made my way to the highway. Putting my thumb out, I hitched a ride back to the camp, just as I did to get to her home.

Nancy and I spent many wonderful moments at her parents' home in the idyllic Hudson Falls countryside. Nancy seemed so different from anyone else I had dated, because I was very used to going out with city girls.

As a country girl, Nancy was very innocent, witty, and well-read. She loved to tease me, which I found very endearing. She was also very beautiful and resembled a young Geena Davis. By the time I had to return to Staten Island, we were committed to being in a relationship.

Within a month, we had fallen deeply in love and had made plans to see each other despite the two hundred miles that separated us. We took turns riding the Greyhound bus to spend time with each other. As autumn came to a close, we decided to set up a home together in Staten Island and eventually marry.

It was a challenging time for all of us. In order to support my new family, I began a job as a door-to-door Fuller Brush salesman. Fortunately, I only worked at the job for several months. A friend of mine offered me a position working alongside him as a shipper for Lady Madonna, an upscale lady's clothing store in Manhattan. Meanwhile, Nancy had difficulty adjusting to living in the city. We often had discussions about moving back upstate.

Meagan, Nancy's young daughter, had her own adjustments. Sharing her mom with me often frustrated her. However, within a year, she and I had forged a close relationship, and she often referred to me as her *daddy*.

I found it hard to believe and comprehend the depth of my love for both Nancy and Meagan and was happy beyond my ability to comprehend. Despite our deep love, our relationship was marked by jealousy and insecurity. She frequently accused me of being interested in other females, and inasmuch as she was a very rebellious young woman, her method to evoke jealousy from me was to wear see-through blouses, sans bras. Her strategy worked well, and I often felt as though I could not trust her commitment. Her declarations of love were inconsistent with her behavior, which brought about insecurity and mistrust. In my protests, I declared my innocence. I also brought out that I had a problem with the way she seemed to elicit the attention of other guys.

We still talked about getting married, although we still had ongoing problems related to mutual insecurity. In spite of trying to work through these issues, they continued even after we moved to Hudson Falls. Nancy got her job back at Glens Falls Hospital, and I was hired as an orderly.

One day, as the weather began to grow colder, she took me by the hand and led me outside. She walked me out into the fields which stretched for hundreds of yards behind her parents' home. There, she made a bed out of our jackets, and we became intimate. While making passionate love, she made sure that I planted my seed.

Not ready to take that step in our relationship, I protested. "What are you doing? We never talked about getting pregnant!"

"Don't worry," she whispered in my ear. "I love you and want to spend my entire life with you."

Despite my initial reservations, I went along with her plan. It wasn't long before I learned I was going to be a father. I felt exhilarated! That sensation did not last long, because I learned that Nancy was spending a good deal of her free time with an old friend, who worked with her at the hospital. Despite her denials, she and Nick were becoming an item at the hospital.

I decided that the best way for me to cope with feeling so threatened by Nick was to befriend him. I did not want to come across as being a *jealous, insecure boyfriend*, but that was exactly how I felt.

I spoke with him on several occasions when he came over to our rented apartment, hoping to gain insight into their intentions. I listened and watched how they looked at each other. I even studied the tonality of the body language they displayed. Then one day, when Nancy and I both had the day off, she asked me to take a walk. An ominous feeling filled my ever-tightening chest cavity. My bronchial tubes were going into spasms, and I began wheezing.

Nancy wasted no time as she said, "I have feelings for Nick, and I want you to move out so I can pursue a relationship with him."

I was in shock. "But what about the baby you're carrying?" I was even less prepared for what was coming next.

"I'm going to abort it, and I'll need your financial help."

I pleaded with Nancy to not follow through on her plans for abortion and offered to raise the child on my own. Despite the fact that I supported a woman's reproductive rights in theory, I was aghast at the thought of ending our son's or daughter's life simply because our child did not fit into her future plans.

Nancy was unrelenting in her decision but tried to offer some comfort and reassurance. "I totally love you, but I don't think you offer me any financial security." She looked deeply into my eyes as she delivered this crippling, emasculating, *so-called reassuring* statement.

"I have a bachelor's degree, and your boyfriend Nick has no college experience, but you think he possesses a greater potential for supporting you and Meagan! Really?"

I became severely depressed but made a decision which would eventually have tremendous impact upon my future. Never again would a woman leave me because of perceived beliefs that I did not have the potential to provide for my family.

It did not take me long to pack up all of my belongings and find my way back to Staten Island. I became devastatingly despondent and overcome with anxiety. It took me a year to get over the immense pain of losing my child and the family I had worked so hard to love and support.

My grief was so powerful that I would often break down and weep, even while working in various jobs in several Manhattan companies. My lunch often consisted of a sandwich, along with many swigs of vodka graciously shared by one of my workmates. My mother was so hurt and angry to witness my suffering that she would break out in impromptu cussing. She called Nancy the most vile names. I knew that in order to heal, I needed a change.

* * * * *

In 1974, I decided to move to Boston. I contacted Nancy's best friend, Carol. I had met her on several occasions when Nancy and I were still together, and we became friends. Carol lived in a large communal house in Brookline. When we spoke on the phone, I asked Carol if there was room for me where she lived. She explained that she lived with six roommates and would have to run it by them before any decision could be made.

Within days, Carol told me that her roommates were open to having me join them, but I needed to pay my fair share of expenses. I agreed and made plans to take a train from Penn Station to the Back Bay station in Boston. I was met by Carol who drove me to my new home.

Although I was not upfront about my motivations for living in her home, my primary reason was to start a new life. I felt that living with Carol might help in any attempts to reconcile with Nancy. On the drive to Brookline, Carol wasted little time in telling me what she thought about my relationship with Nancy.

"Jeff, I hope that you and Nancy can work out your differences because you guys were prefect for each other!"

As a few tears trickled from my eyes, I replied, "Yes, we were, but it was very painful for me. Not only did she cheat on me, but then she aborted my child too. It was more than I could take."

"I know. However, in Nancy's first marriage, her husband cheated on her all of the time. I think she just got scared about how strong her love for you was becoming. She messed up, but hopefully, you can understand and forgive her."

I remained silent, but in my heart I knew that it would be very difficult to get over my deep wounds. I looked straight ahead and changed the subject by making inane comments about the architecture along Massachusetts Avenue.

After getting settled in my new home, I started looking for a job in many of Boston's prominent hospitals. One afternoon, I was coming out of Massachusetts General when I was approached by a young and beautiful woman named Maria. She smiled and introduced herself as the guidance counselor in the hospital's nursing program.

"Why are you here?" she inquired.

I smiled back at her and replied, "I'm here looking for work and was actually attempting to apply for a position as a neurosurgeon. I was told there were no openings."

She laughed at my wry, self-deprecating humor. "You're quite funny! I'd like to learn more about you, strictly from a professional point of view. Tell me about yourself."

After I told her that I had earned a bachelor of science degree from Arizona State University, she informed me about a new program she had begun with her nursing students.

"I am administering a vocational-interest test to my students, and I'd like you to take it. I think it will help you narrow your career choice focus."

"I'm happy to take the test, but to be honest, I'd rather go out with you. You are absolutely gorgeous!"

She smiled and wasted no time in reiterating her reason for approaching me. "My only reason for asking you to take this test is to add a larger pool of respondents to this test. However, I am very flattered."

Maria handed me the test and gave me instructions on how to respond to each question. I took it in my hand, but not before staring longingly into her eyes and smiling. I found her dark brown eyes and curly black hair very attractive. She smiled back at me and tilted her head to the side. Her face glistened in the fall sunlight, as it shone down from the sky. With the test in my hand, I continued to peer into her eyes, and fortunately for me, she did not look away from me.

I said, "I will take it home and bring it back as soon as I am done."

We exchanged smiles, which only encouraged my desire to date her. It was refreshing for me to see that a beautiful, professional woman had some interest in me, even though it was on a professional basis at that time.

Within two days, I finished the test. After taking the trolley and Red Line to the hospital, I smiled as I found Maria sitting in her office. She immediately stood up to greet me. After finishing our greetings, I handed her the test. She was both surprised and delighted at the speed with which I had finished it. After informing me that she would send it off to be scored, she invited me to sit down.

"Jeff, I can tell from your accent that you are not a native Bostonian. Are you from New York?"

"I am, but went off to Arizona State after high school and came back to New York upon graduating."

"Why did you decide to move to Boston?" she asked me.

I gave her the full rundown on my relationship with Nancy, not omitting any details. She rose from her chair and offered me a warm hug. As she held me tightly, I could not restrain my sobs any longer. She clearly empathized with me as she saw my eyes wet with tears. Softly, she told me how many women would give anything to have a man who was as tenderhearted as I was.

"One day, you'll make someone a wonderful husband."

I could tell from the tears welling up in her eyes and the sadness which was all too evident that she had experienced her own hurt, torment, and disappointment.

"Is there any chance that you would consider dating me, Maria?"

Maria glanced away from me for a moment before smiling. Gazing directly at me with her own big brown eyes, she replied, "Let's find out the results of your test first, okay? I will call you when the results and interpretation have come in."

A week passed before I heard back from Maria once again. We set a day and time for us to review my results. As I ambled into her office, Maria greeted me with a warm smile, once again. She handed me the test and asked me to have a seat.

As I perused the interpretations, I was very surprised to learn that based on my interests and skills, it was suggested that I return to school to study psychology. I imagined what my future might be like, with diplomas hanging on my office walls, and having deep discussions with patients.

I looked up from the test and shared my thoughts with her. "Psychology? Never in my wildest musings did I ever consider becoming a psychologist."

Maria perceived me to be a deep thinker and a man of great substance. She said, "I have thought about you a lot since we've met. You are very attractive, not only physically, but emotionally, as well. The truth is, I've been married once before and have a young child. However, the next time I marry, I want my husband to be a doctor. I no longer want to struggle financially."

Maria sensed my discomfort, given what she knew about Nancy's reason for terminating our relationship. She continued, "If things ever change for you and you decide to pursue a career in psychology, I would love to get to know you better. Also, please consider cutting your hair because not many professional women want to date a hippie!" She chuckled as she spoke, which helped to dilute my disappointment.

Maria called me on several occasions wanting to see me, but I was very busy trying to get back with Nancy. Although Nancy and I had tried twice to rekindle the love we had shared in the past, my heart had been broken, and I could no longer trust her. I finally told her to never contact me again, and finally made the decision to move on and not hold on to the pain I had shouldered.

Pain and hurt were choices, and I discovered that I had the power to choose to embrace joy and happiness, instead. Vodka was no longer the beverage which accompanied my lunch. I returned to using TM, and I quickly recovered my emotional and psychological equilibrium.

I was greatly indebted to Maria for her inspiration and encouragement. Her prodding had directed me back toward a better way of life. Although I was very attracted to her, we lost touch and never dated. However, I have often wondered if she ever found her *doctor*.

* * * * *

Within days, I found a job in the garment center in downtown Boston. Although it wasn't a position which utilized my intelligence, it did give me a weekly paycheck to support myself. My job in the garment center was extremely boring, and each day was agonizingly slow. It was so bad that I toyed with the idea of returning to school and earning a bachelor's degree in *nursing*.

Soon, I met with the Nursing Department's director at Boston University. As I sat across from her, she appeared to be impressed with my desire to pursue a nursing degree.

"Since you already have your bachelor's, give me two years of nursing courses, and you can earn a bachelor's in nursing. There is a considerable need for male nurses, and you should have no difficulty landing a position anywhere in the country."

I began to feel very hopeful about my future, especially since I had no direction whatsoever. "Really? Only two years? I know I can succeed and do well. I need a little time to think about it. I don't want to waste time or money, if I'm not totally committed to this program."

She smiled, quickly rose from her chair, and extended her hand. I thanked her and shook her hand gently.

"You are very kind to have taken time out of your busy schedule to meet with me. As soon as I know what I want to do, I will contact you. Will that be okay?"

"My pleasure. Best of luck in whatever course you choose."

* * * * *

Carol and I spent a good amount of time together, but most of my time was spent with Bobby. He was a schoolteacher, who was a practitioner of kundalini yoga. Bobby also attended classes at the yoga club on the Harvard University campus. After inviting me to attend the classes on many occasions, I finally agreed to tag along with him. I found the yoga to be very challenging and much more strenuous than hatha yoga.

Our kundalini yoga teacher had a full beard and was dressed in a white turban, along with a white flowing shirt and pants. My new instructor, Mahan Singh, was a member of the 3HO Foundation, which stood for Healthy, Happy, and Holy. He taught several meditations, which seemed to cause deeper sessions than transcendental meditation (TM), which I had continued to practice. I was so impressed that I decided to begin attending classes with Bobby each week. I even planned to awaken at 5:30 a.m. every day to practice yoga and meditation with him.

The yoga and meditations produced very profound experiences. After my sessions, it was not unusual for me to leave my body during my deep rest periods. I equated those experiences with divine and mystical encounters. I believed these experiences were finally bringing me closer to a direct experience with knowing God.

My desire to have a personal relationship with God was even more powerful and significant to me than my interest in TM. I was looking for a new lifestyle, where the search for God was the most predominant motivation in my life. My interest peaked when Bobby told me that he and his girlfriend, Karen, were going to 3HO's Annual Summer Solstice Celebration in Espanola, New Mexico.

"Jeff, you ought to go with us. We live in tents for the celebration and have a blast! Their guru, Yoga Bhajan, teaches tantric yoga every day. He'll even give you a spiritual name if you want."

"I have to see if I can get the time off. I would love to go back and visit the Southwest. It would be amazing to soak up all of that spiritual teaching! Let me think about it."

Bobby's face lit up almost as wide as his huge Afro. "Dude, it's not like you have an amazing job working as some professional. You can always get another job if they won't give you the time off."

* * * * *

Before sunrise on June 19, 1974, Karen, Bobby, and I began our trip. After driving for more than four days, we finally arrived in Espanola, New Mexico. The entire town was in a valley nestled between the Jemez and Sangre de Cristo mountain ranges.

We drove up a dusty, rocky road and found the 3HO campgrounds. The camp was inhabited by hundreds of American Sikh men and women, who were dressed in turbans and white clothing. We registered and found a site to pitch our tents in the midst of the multitude that was scattered everywhere.

While Karen decided to nap, Bobby and I took the opportunity to stroll around the campground. He acted as my tour guide, while I placated him. Soon, a booming voice sounded over a loudspeaker and announced that we would soon be blessed by Yogi Bhajan's presence. Right away, the Sikhs began scurrying to place their sheepskins upon the concrete slab located under a large aluminum roof.

We began walking to our tents to get our sheepskins, when a very familiar voice called out to me. "Cat! Is that you?"

As I looked in the direction of the voice, I quickly recognized the man with a long beard. Although his head was covered in a large turban, Norman's smile was unforgettable. Immediately, Norman and I exchanged hugs.

"Cat, what are you doing here?" Norman asked.

"Wait! What is happening here? Since when did you become a Sikh? And how bizarre is it for us to meet here?"

Although seeing Norman was a big relief due to our familiarity, meeting him in this unexpected location was quite unsettling. As a result, my expectations for the trip's benefit to me became temporarily diminished.

"I've been a Sikh for five years. You're going to love this, Cat!" Norman laid his right hand on my left shoulder. "Yogi Bhajan is the real deal. Practicing kundalini yoga will change your entire perspective on life. Your spiritual growth will accelerate beyond belief!"

My time in Espanola was everything Norman said it would be. Every day, we spent a lot of time together. When I met with Yogi Bhajan, he gave me a new spiritual name, Mukta, which was the Punjabi word for "liberation." It perfectly represented my insatiable desire for spiritual liberation and development. I adopted the new name with excitement and exhilaration.

As my visit drew to a close, I made a decision to jump into that lifestyle with commitment and purpose. Sikhs lived in communal homes called ashrams, and the ashram in Denver happened to announce that they needed more people.

I learned that they maintained two *family businesses*, which needed additional people to run them efficiently. The Golden Temple Conscious Cookery was a vegetarian restaurant, and their menu was comprised of dishes formulated by Yogi Bhajan, as well as those created by his secretaries and other accomplished cooks.

I looked forward to living in an environment which offered structure and discipline, as well as spiritual guidance. My soul was starving for intensified growth. I sensed there was so much more to God than what I experienced during my practice with TM, or while I was observing the Jewish feasts and holidays. I also lacked personal discipline and believed that living in a highly organized environment could give me the structure needed to *find God*.

With the Native American powwow concluding, Karen and Bobby decided to drive to the California coast for an extended vacation. However, I needed to go home and talk to my family about my new decisions. Once again, I placed my backpack by the side of the interstate and prayed that good people would help me travel way home. My prayers were answered, and I made my way safely across the country. Upon arriving at my parents' house, I shared my *good news* with them; however, they found little joy in my decision.

"When are you going to settle down and develop a career?" my mom asked. "Did we spend all of our money to educate you so that you can live in a commune and dress like a freak? AND you want us to now call you Mukta? Are you crazy!"

My mom's anger cut through me like a finely sharpened knife. I understood her criticism, but I didn't think she understood what I needed. She had no appreciation for my need for spiritual evolution. What I could not admit to her was that I was fearful of the responsibilities of adulthood.

I had mistakenly believed that once I graduated from college, I would be magically equipped with the emotional tools I needed to become an adult. Perhaps this was due to my dysfunctional family, or from the trauma I experienced during my early childhood; maybe it was from the years of abusing marijuana. Regardless of the reason, we hugged and kissed. As they said *goodbye* to Jeff, I embraced my new identity as Mukta. It was only a few days later that I found a ride to Denver to begin my new adventure.

Chapter 13

When I arrived in Denver, I felt highly insecure with my newly adopted lifestyle and religion. My identity was firmly established in Judaism, yet that personal relationship with the God of Abraham, Benjamin, and Jacob was sorely lacking. For me, Judaism was limited to celebrating the feasts and holidays. It was also a very strong cultural identity.

Jews have always been a persecuted people, who suffered greatly since the beginning of recorded history. We were also the *chosen people*, the *apple of God's eye*. So why was it that I had never felt the full weight of God's favor or love?

I experienced His presence, but I also experienced extensive emotional pain and trauma. In my desperation for a practical knowledge and experience of God, I was willing to travel down a path completely different from Judaism. I needed a practical, experiential relationship with God, and living in an ashram gave me some modicum of control in that quest. I had thought that if I inculcated discipline and ancient yogic practices, my desire to know God would be realized. I believed that if knowing God would be determined by my efforts and actions, success would definitely occur. I slowly began settling in among the other twenty-two Sikhs.

The ashram had two "family" businesses. The main source of income was a natural foods restaurant. In addition, there was also a landscaping business.

I became very excited about working in the restaurant since I was intrigued with natural foods as well as international cuisine. In addition, I wanted to learn as much as I could about the restaurant's business side, especially since I had graduated with a bachelor's degree in business administration.

Within months, I was asked to manage the restaurant, the Golden Temple Conscious Cookery. I took this responsibility with zeal and passion and saw the opportunity as an honor. I also felt it was an expression of their trust in my abilities to manage others, as well as recognition of my overall business understanding.

I was in charge of twenty people, most of whom knew infinitely more about the restaurant than I did. Since I was the newcomer in that industry, I took initiative in order to feel worthy of my position. I studied restaurant management diligently and worked as hard as I could. I never gave them any excuse to regret their confidence in me.

Eventually, I was named *second in command*, and therefore, I was in charge whenever the ashram leader was out of town. Our daily discipline consisted of rising at 3:00 a.m., taking ice-cold showers, and each of us convening for three and a half hours of yoga, meditation, and scriptural readings from the *Siri Guru Granth Sahib*, the Sikh religious writings.

I remained in Denver for one year before transferring to the ashram in Boston. In preparation for my upcoming move, I participated in a number of spiritual disciplines. These included extensive fasting and even a forty-day silence.

The fasts were very difficult for me, as it might be for most people. The initial three days of any fast were excruciatingly difficult. All that I thought about was eating, and my painful hunger pangs made it more difficult. However, by the fifth day, my body and mind came into submission, and it became more easy and effortless.

I had read in several biographies of famous yogis and swamis that undertaking a forty-day silence accentuated their spiritual progress. I thought, "If they can do it, so can I!" My forty-day silence was a welcomed experience. In this newest endeavor, I felt an unexplained peace that I had never known.

It was far more difficult to speak once my self-imposed silence ended. I even experienced headaches from talking to my coworkers and fellow pilgrims. It took nearly three days before re-acclimating to communicating my thoughts, desires, and expectations through speech.

I felt very proud of my success in both of these disciplines. The experiences even strengthened my motivation to control my spiritual progress through hard work and dedication.

* * * * *

My move to Boston made it more convenient to visit my family in New York. I was given similar managerial responsibilities as I did with running the Golden Temple Conscious Cookery. Later, I managed the Golden Temple Emporium.

The emporium sold Birkenstock sandals and other extremely comfortable New Age shoes, as well as Native American jewelry and pottery. I would travel to the Zuni, Hopi, and Navajo reservations, as well as various wholesalers in order to find new items to purchase for our store inventory. I was always accompanied by my closest friend in the ashram, Gurubachan, who was an extremely friendly and extroverted man.

Gurubachan was of Lebanese descent, who grew up in Columbus, Ohio. In addition, he and his family lived in Mexico for a number of years. Whenever my parents came to visit me, Gurubachan went out of his way to make them feel welcome by cooking Lebanese, Indian, and Mexican dishes. His warmth helped them to cope with my bizarre lifestyle, which included wearing all white clothes, a turban, and a long flowing beard of at least six inches in length.

I lived in the Boston ashram for nearly three years. There I studied and taught yoga, as well as practiced martial arts in Tiger Crane Kung Fu, Wing Chun Kung Fu, and Tae Kwan Do. After that time, I was asked to be the ashram head in Amherst, Massachusetts, but not before being matched with one of the women in the ashram, Alice. Despite our lack of familiarity or personal feelings toward each other, Alice and I were married in 1977. We never even had the opportunity to date each other, and certainly never had a chance to fall in love.

Once moving to Amherst, I began managing a shoe store which was owned by the director of the ashram in Boston. It was a very small store nestled between other stores on the main street not far from the campus of the University of Massachusetts. Our ashram only had Alice and me, plus one other couple.

During this time, my difficulties with asthma reached dangerous levels. In a year's time, I had to visit the local emergency room eighteen times for adrenaline injections. When I visited Norman in Chicago, I was hospitalized and placed on the critical care unit. The asthma attacks continued without any letup.

* * * * *

My marriage to Alice was fraught with strife. Since we had never dated, we hardly knew each other, and I had not developed even a modicum of romantic feelings toward her. This frustrated her immensely, since she longed for affection and romance.

To complicate our personal differences, Alice also came into the marriage with many of her own emotional challenges. To begin with, she and her mother shared an unhealthy symbiotic relationship. In addition, Alice had related to me that her father was a heavy social drinker, who had a number of extramarital affairs.

Several weeks after our wedding, I visited my parents in New York, and my mother shared a story that was both shocking and reprehensible. According to my mom, Alice's father had approached one of my aunts and propositioned her during our wedding celebration. While I was not there to witness it, I did not doubt the veracity of my mother's story. I shared this with Alice, and she did not seem surprised, much to my surprise. Alice's mistrust of men was the very reason she tried to control me.

While living in the ashram in Amherst, there were several events which laid bare Alice's emotional struggles. She had often accused me of being angry with her, which I consistently denied. With each rebuttal I gave her came more accusations and tears. This consistent cycle eventually created a tremendous sense of frustration and anger. This only served to affirm her original assumptions.

I became withdrawn and developed a sense of hopelessness. I thought, "What have I gotten myself into?"

There were several other instances when Alice accused me of not loving her. During some of them, she released an escalated torrent of spite and anger I had never seen before. On occasion, she would even scream in my face with a twisted, almost grotesque look. To top things off, she would cry uncontrollably and scream, "Why don't you hug me!"

I was often frightened by her displays and did not know how to respond. My emotions ran the gamut from fear, frustration, and anger to despondency and pity. Although my marriage was highly dysfunctional, my commitment to my marriage was unshakable. I freely admit that had I fallen in love with her and felt some attraction, I would have responded differently. At least I hope to think so. So, as our marriage continued on a downslide, I tried to make the best of my situation and was firmly ensconced in the spiritual lifestyle I had chosen. In fact, it gave me confidence and a sense of purpose to continue in my marriage. As I was approaching the age of thirty, we talked about starting a family.

* * * * *

When my daughter Cyndi was born on August, 1979, I gave a great deal of thought to my future. Remembering the test results that Maria had shared with me years before in Boston, I decided to get a master's degree in counseling psychology from Antioch University, School of Professional Psychology in Keene, New Hampshire. In the fall of 1979, I was accepted into the program and began taking classes.

I found this program to be as challenging as it was exciting. That was especially true since all of the teachers were therapists with private practices. The teachers' real-world experience gave me a great opportunity to learn about many unique cases.

While I learned a great deal about theory, the main thrust was to become a proficient therapist, and I put in a great deal of effort. We not only practiced therapy on each other, the program afforded me the opportunity of working through several unresolved emotional issues such as my poor relationship with my father as well as the trauma of losing Jay.

One day after class, one of my teachers pulled me aside and said, "Jeff, you are by far one of the best students who have ever come through this program, and I've been here since it began."

I was somewhat stunned. "Wow, really? Thank you for the words of encouragement, because I want nothing more than to be the best therapist I could be."

"Just keep up the good work. You will be very successful in this field."

Our conversation reminded me of one that I had with my teacher while attending the yeshiva. I had been committed to excellence in the field before that conversation; however, my commitment grew exponentially at that moment. I worked extremely hard and completed it in 1981.

Upon graduation, I was unable to find any employment in my field. In order to support my family, Alice and I began cleaning people's homes, and we did quite well. Although I felt a sense of accomplishment in helping to support my small family, I had a passion for doing psychotherapy.

Luckily, my counseling skills were being called upon by yoga students, as well as the members in our ashram, which eventually grew to more than twenty members. I did not earn any income from these endeavors. The primary benefit I received was that those informal counseling sessions gave me additional experience that I had not received during my two internships while earning my master's program.

Unfortunately, my asthma attacks were unrelenting in the cold New England winters, and it became apparent that I needed to move away. Not long after receiving my master's degree, I contacted the ashram's regional director and informed him that moving to Phoenix was crucial to my health.

The director helped to facilitate my move to the Phoenix ashram, and within two months, we arrived. While my health vastly improved in the dry desert climate, I did not have much success in finding work in my field. I finally found a position working in the Arizona State Hospital in the unit for the criminally insane.

I was not a therapist, as I had hoped, but rather a mental health worker. That basically meant that I assisted in crowd control and take-downs when patients acted on their paranoid delusions. I did manage to secure a part-time position as a clinical consultant at the 3HO Drug and Alcohol Abuse Program in Tucson, which was located several hours away.

After inspecting how their rehabilitation program was organized and operated, I found it to be very unprofessional. The program had been created by Yogi Bhajan, and its staff was severely lacking in clinical skills and training. In fact, many of their clinical notes were written on paper towels, which were placed in patient charts.

I instituted psychological testing upon entrance into the program, as well as when people graduated, so that we could have some ways to measure success. I also added individual and group therapy as new dimensions to the program, which proved to be vital to the patients' care. Within a year, I was offered a full-time position as the clinical director.

Alice, Cyndi, and I moved to Tucson and remained with the ashram for nearly five years. Our relationship was never easy, resulting in a stormy marriage. We argued constantly. Our marital discord was due to the fact that our union was founded on our shared religious beliefs and lifestyle commitment, instead of a loving relationship with each other.

Since Alice and I did not have the mutual love for each other, we lacked the desire to grow intimately on most levels. This lack of emotional cohesion made it nearly impossible to develop any sense of intimacy whatsoever. Since I had never fallen in love with Alice, I found it difficult to express my feelings intimately or romantically with her. Instead, I chose to relate to her as a co-parent, roommate, and spiritual partner. This is not to say that we never had fun together or shared intimate moments. However, it was obvious that she was frustrated at not feeling loved.

Alice's early childhood left her struggling with her identity, and her issues with rejection and criticism evoked anger and bitterness. In addition, she regularly voiced harsh criticism of my habits, traits, and ambitions. Nonetheless, we persisted in keeping our marriage intact.

In 1984, I began training in clinical hypnotherapy. I had the opportunity to study with some of the best trainers in the world. Part of my training included neuro-linguistic programming, which is a therapeutic approach that focuses on connections between communications, thought processes, and behavioral patterns.

My training in both hypnosis and neuro-linguistic programming allowed me to see how evident Yogi Bhajan's manipulations and psychopathology had been. I noticed that Yogi Bhajan often used manipulative strategies after one of his high-profile leaders had left.

He would publicly state, "There comes a time in everyone's spiritual practice that he or she feels more accomplished than me. Their egos cannot stand to stay under my direction, and they leave. This is called *Shakti Pad*. People that fall into this trap are destined to spend an eternity in hell for abandoning their guru!"

When I shared many of my observations with Alice, she became frightened that I might leave the ashram and our marriage. Alice's commitment to her Sikh faith strengthened. She even devoted a lot of time and effort to praying for my soul. As a devoted Sikh wife, Alice became concerned, if not frightened, for me and did her best to alter my perceptions of Yogi Bhajan and 3HO.

* * * * *

My daughter Rachel was born in February, 1984. Although her birth brought us great joy, Rachel's bilirubin count was very elevated due to a sluggish liver. Her complexion was extremely jaundiced, and her little body was yellow, red, and orange. She had to undergo phototherapy and was placed under a sunlamp every day for a week until her skin color changed to a healthy pink.

Rachel's neonatal health challenge brought great fear to me. I was deathly afraid that I would lose my little girl in the same way that I lost my baby brother, Jay. I cried and prayed throughout the week, but did it secretly so as not to frighten Cyndi and Alice. As I witnessed the bright colors fading, I felt tremendous relief and praised God for my baby girl's health.

As clinical director, I began witnessing many instances of patient abuse and systemic corruption. It became even more obvious as we developed our marketing plan to be presented to our funding entities. Yogi Bhajan met with the three program directors, as well as the ashram director and primary staff. He informed us that we should claim a success rate of 86 percent.

I was shocked and dumbfounded at his instructions. I knew the real results from my own research over the course of five years that I had worked there. In that entire time, only two people remained drug-free two years after graduating from the program.

Once the meeting was over, I requested a meeting with the ashram director and his wife, who was the executive director. I lodged a protest about the very misleading statistic. They were very upset with me and demanded that I relinquish my position.

"Who are you to question Yogi-ji!"

"How do you both live with the fact that he is lying and manipulating the truth? If you feel that the ends justify the means, then you are as much of a sociopath as he is!"

Upon leaving my position, I began working on my doctorate and developing a private practice. I realized that I had been living in a cult. It made me feel duped, disillusioned, and angry. Alice and I grew more distant, because she believed that my negative perceptions of Yogi Bhajan had taken root in the soil of professional arrogance.

Many women within the 3HO organization came forward accusing him of rape and sodomy. In fact, there was at least one lawsuit against him for allegedly raping and sodomizing an underaged girl. After speaking with several close friends who had left the organization, I made the decision to leave as quickly as possible with my family.

I had previously attempted to talk to Alice about leaving. However, she resisted, as do many people who are caught up in cult ideology. I was very fearful that I would have to leave without my two daughters. This time, my resolve to leave with my family intact was unmovable. I approached her about it after putting both of our children down for the night. Before beginning this difficult conversation, I carefully planned my strategy.

"Alice, I need to have a talk with you about our future."

Alice looked uneasy, not knowing where I was going with our conversation. "Okay. Is something wrong?" she asked.

"Let me ask you, do you trust Stephen and Jean-Paul?"

Both of the men and their wives were close friends and confidantes who held high positions within 3HO.

"Yes, why? Have you spoken with them?" Alice's voice took on an edgy, fearful tone. "Did you?"

I sat down beside her on the couch and looked into her eyes, searching for some clue as to how she might respond to my decision. "I did speak with them, and they both had information that you need to hear. The integrity of our family depends upon your open and honest ability to listen to what they told me."

Alice's breathing quickened as her heart rate increased. After sharing all of the information I had learned, as well as my observations of hypnotic and cognitive manipulation, Alice asked me what I thought we should do.

"It's very simple. We need to leave them and get back to living normal lives while I expand my private practice. Perhaps we should also consider relocating to another part of the country."

I was greatly relieved to learn that Alice was very open to my suggestions. However, she was concerned that the leaders might feel threatened by our exodus and try to physically harm us. I relayed to her that my plan was to call the local leaders and assure them that we had no axes to grind. I'd explain that we only want to live our lives in peace.

I called the very next day to the local leaders. They sounded nervous, insecure, and somewhat threatened by my decision. After all, I had very damaging evidence regarding the official effectiveness of the rehabilitation program.

Before leaving, I made the decision to seek therapy for my uncontrolled anger toward Yogi Bhajan. My rage was evident in my impatience with Alice, as well as with drivers on the road. Therapy helped to diminish my anger, although my therapist and I both recognized that it was not completely dealt with.

Chapter 14

Within a year, we moved to Coral Springs, Florida, to be close to my parents, as well as both of my sisters and their families. My parents sold their home in Staten Island for a large profit and decided to move to balmy South Florida. My sisters and their families soon followed. They all resided in the wealthy town of Boca Raton.

It was 1986, and my young daughters were now seven and two years old. The new move finally enabled them to develop relationships with my family. My marriage of eight years was not fulfilling, and relocating to Florida put even more strain and stress on it.

Alice informed me that she would not allow my parents to have unannounced visits. In addition, she was not willing to clean or straighten up whenever they were scheduled to visit. It was my job, since they were my parents, despite the fact that Alice did not work. It did not matter to her that I was busy working in a community mental health center, and developing a private practice, either.

While I agreed to her demands, my resentment and emotional distance grew further by the day. In fact, I prayed that our marriage would end. I did not have the courage to throw in the towel, because the thought of leaving my daughters was more than I could bear. So, my prayers changed. *God, please take me out of this marriage, because it feels like I am dying. Please have her meet another man so I don't have to be the one who breaks up this family.*

I recognized that I was not taking control over my life, but hopelessness filled my entire existence. Our relationship became so toxic and dependent that I felt trapped. I gave up my love for martial arts and relinquished a newfound love for playing the saxophone.

This was all in an effort to appease Alice, because she felt that I was not spending enough time with her. It was irrelevant that I only attended martial arts classes three times per week for a total of six hours. Every other moment was spent with my family. I was miserable, and because she had no life of her own apart from me, she was miserable as well. Neither did she wish to allow me any positive experiences apart from her.

Although I cared deeply for Alice, we continued to argue about finances. She was also very upset about my lack of emotional intimacy and affection. In spite of our many years together, I never did fall in love with her, and felt little attraction to her.

Alice's continued sense of rejection led to angry outbursts and crying fits. In addition, she exerted stronger control of our finances. Her responses only reinforced my feelings of being stuck in an unhealthy marriage.

I became even more isolated, depressed, and unresponsive. Within seven years after leaving the ashram world, I was completely miserable and emotionally lost. Finally, after several years of discord, I decided to leave our home for six weeks in 1992. However, my longing for my children brought me home.

Our marriage endured another year, until I was suffering from psychological and emotional anorexia. We sat with both of our children and explained the decision to divorce. While it was a unilateral decision, Alice considerately informed our children that it was a mutual decision. We cried and mourned as a family, and my children suffered greatly as a result.

Afterward, I left with several pieces of luggage to live with my sister. Rachel grabbed onto my ankles and cried, "Daddy, please don't go! Please, Daddy, don't leave!"

My heart broke due to the emotional damage and upheaval I was causing my beautiful seven-year-old daughter. I bent down to hold her against my chest.

She pleaded once again. "Daddy, please! Please, Daddy!"

"I am so sorry, Rachel. I will be back to see you tomorrow. I love you so much!" I hugged her tightly and then held on to Cyndi, who had placed her arms around my neck.

After packing my car, I drove around the block and sobbed uncontrollably. I was unable to see the road due to my tears and felt overcome with guilt from self-preoccupation. I was placing my needs for happiness and emotional survival before those of my children.

"God, will you please forgive me for being so selfish? Please, watch over my young girls. I pray that they won't hate me for my decision."

Like with many divorces, the emotional damage caused by our marital split affected both of our children. To make matters worse, a financial crisis soon overwhelmed me due to a lengthy, expensive, and extremely contentious divorce.

After living with my sister and her family for two months, I rented an apartment several blocks from my daughters. I saw them as often as I could. In addition to my financial issues, I also faced enormous emotional costs. Yet, the damage done to my children was far worse than anything I had to endure. To this day, my heart still breaks for the pain I inflicted upon my beautiful daughters.

* * * * *

As my marriage was ending, I became interested in Native American mysticism and shamanism. I read many books on these subjects and took a class on shamanism. I had become disinterested in meditation and yoga. Despite the fact that both helped to increase a relaxation response while reducing anxiety, I still felt uninspired and unfulfilled.

I thought, "There must be more. There must be a method to experience the profound presence of God." I hoped and prayed that this new theological practice and perspective would finally give me the peace I had longed and searched for since Jay's death.

I had been introduced to another therapist who had emigrated from Peru as a child. He had led many spiritual pilgrimages to Machu Picchu and other cities along the Inca Trail. I decided to meet with him to learn the details of his Incan tour, but not before co-teaching a shamanistic workshop with a good friend of mine. We had led several of these workshops and were advertising them in two national New Age magazines.

I made the decision to join the twelve other sojourners and had made all of the necessary preparations to leave. Unfortunately, the stress of my divorce triggered a major asthma attack, and I had to be hospitalized for six days. My physicians prescribed Prednisone, a powerful steroidal medication to reduce the inflammation in my bronchial tubes, and I left two days after my discharge.

We flew from Fort Lauderdale to Lima and then connected to a flight which landed in Cusco, Peru. Cusco was the capital of the Incan Empire and was declared a World Heritage Site by UNESCO. A tour bus met us at the airport and took us to our modest hotel located within the historic city. Upon getting settled, we all met for a small lunch and several cups of coca tea to help us adjust to the altitude change.

Alejandro had led many of these tours to Peru and was therefore very knowledgeable about the areas which would be of the highest interest. He was an intelligent man and used a great deal of New Age theology and techniques with his patients. In fact, a number of his patients were my fellow pilgrims on this journey.

My time in Peru was largely characterized by visiting most of the Incan spiritual ruins, as well as meeting local shamans who gave coca leaf readings. We spent a good amount of time at Pisac, which was created to protect the city of Cusco from invaders. We walked along the footpaths on the terraces located along steep hillsides which scaled high to the azure skies. Pisac also has a very colorful marketplace, and I wasted little time in purchasing several alpaca sweaters.

Another notable Inca ruin was located at Saksaywaman, a walled complex constructed from large polished dry stone walls. The boulders appeared to mesh perfectly without the use of mortar. The ruins struck me as being perfectly constructed, while pulled from a timeless calendar. It was easy to feel fairly insignificant in the face of such ancient mastery.

Our guide had us meet another local shaman who exuded personal power and spiritual strength. He met with each of us and prayed over us with his hands placed firmly upon our heads. As he prayed, I sensed a mystical presence around me. Afterward, he whispered something to Alejandro.

After spending two days exploring the city of Cusco, we travelled to meet a train which would take us to Machu Picchu. The steep and winding train ride was magnificent, and the vistas were unlike anything I had ever seen.

We spent two days in Machu Picchu, which is something I shall always remember. I marveled at the craftsmanship of this ancient civilization, as well as the spiritual connection they apparently had with the Creator. On the second day, Alejandro took me aside and shared the conversation he had with the shaman at Saksaywaman.

As he began talking, Alejandro opened his backpack and took out a thermos. "Jeff, this is Ayahuasca. Shamans dating back to the Incan Empire used this for healing and divinity purposes. The shaman at Saksaywaman told me that it would help you break through some sadness you carry, as well as help you have powerful spiritual breakthroughs. Are you interested?"

I took a few steps toward Alejandro and stared at the thermos. In my studies in shamanic practices, I had read a lot about Ayahuasca and how the Incan shamans had used it to allegedly control the weather. I was excited to try it. I hoped that it would be the spiritual experience I had been searching for. I was carrying a lot of grief and guilt for breaking up my family and yearned for some relief.

"When will we take it?" I asked him.

"After breakfast tomorrow, and then we can continue to visit the ruins up here." Alejandro smiled for my willingness to partake of this shamanic juice. "When it wears off, many of us plan on climbing Huayna Picchu."

After waking up and enjoying breakfast at our hotel, Alejandro doled out the Ayahuasca to several of us. After about an hour, the effects of the Ayauhuasca came on rather quickly and dramatically. Surges of energy circulated through my body, giving me a euphoria seldom experienced. Inanimate objects, such as rocks and plants, even seemed to communicate with me.

After walking through the ruins with others, I went off by myself in an effort to process this experience. I wanted to use introspection in order to look deeply into the direction my life seemed to be taking. Chills overtook me, and I began vomiting violently. I felt quite ill, but my introspection illuminated a truth that was very evident to me.

After traveling nearly three thousand miles to see the beautiful, ancient culture that I fully enjoyed, I finally understood that the most important thing to me was my relationship with my children. A great piece of my spiritual identity was woven into my soul as a father to my wonderful daughters. I longed to return home to comfort Cyndi and Rachel as I knew their lives had been radically altered by the demise of my marriage. Even the fever and diarrhea which came later that night could not detract from the joy and anticipation of seeing them.

While I would never suggest that any spiritual pilgrim try this hallucinogen, it made me acutely aware of how far away I was from any real sense of godliness. My immense thirst for true spiritual experiences had deluded me. I had become more interested in mystical experiences than in developing a relationship with my Creator. I had been discontented and disappointed in my ventures. Unfortunately, I was no further along in my quest to know God than when I began TM and yoga.

Chapter 15

My divorce took well over a year to be finalized, and my legal bills bloated to well over $40,000. During this time, I ventured into the world of dating. Although I initially thought dating would be an exciting and fun experience, nothing could be further from the truth. While I had met a few interesting and very attractive women in my new ventures, not one of them captured my interest until I met Miranda.

During a particularly slow day in my office in Coral Springs, Florida, I asked my sister and office manager, Lori, if she had any checks for me to deposit. Normally, this task was her responsibility; however, I was bored and restless. I decided to make the trip to the bank.

As I drove up, I was immediately taken by the bank teller's beauty. I could not identify her ethnicity, but was intrigued by her innocence and charm. Plus, she had the most exquisite and captivating eyes; their color was similar to photos I had seen of the Mediterranean Ocean. I was determined to get to know her. So much so that upon returning to the office, I asked Lori to create another deposit so that I could return to Miranda's line. When I got to her window, she had a look of surprise and confusion.

"Weren't you just here?"

"Yes, but you are so pretty that I just had to make another deposit and see you again." I was never a big flirt, but I wanted to get a date with her.

Miranda giggled, blushed, and smiled, but said nothing. As soon as I returned to my office, I called the bank and asked to speak with her. Unfortunately, she was busy, so I left her a message.

"This is Dr. Jeff Rifkin. Please tell Miranda that I would love to take her to dinner. Have her call me please."

"Thank you, Dr. Rifkin. I will be sure she gets your message." I left the woman my telephone number.

After not hearing from Miranda for several days, I made another deposit through her drive-through line. She recognized me and smiled.

"Hi," I said. "Did you get my message to call me?"

Miranda's brows narrowed. "No, I never got a message to call you."

I leaned closer to her. "I asked if you'd like to go to dinner."

"I'm sorry, but I'm married."

Now, it was my turn to blush. I imagined that everyone within a mile radius heard her turn me down for a date, in spite of her very legitimate reason for her refusal. I drove off as inconspicuously as I could, which was even more difficult with a new black Nissan 300ZX sports car.

The following week, I reviewed the two interactions we shared and sensed that her responses to me were inconsistent. While she said she was married, her nonverbal cues told me that she was inexplicably interested. I decided that I would place a sticky note on my next deposit and ask her to lunch instead. She accepted my invitation.

We met at a local restaurant, and she explained that she and her husband were considering ending their two-year marriage. During our lunch, we had an easy and smooth conversation. Afterward, we agreed to meet the following day at a mall.

We met again as planned, and each purchased Rollerblades and even talked about spending time skating together. Another topic we discussed was about when she and her husband would be parting ways. According to Miranda, their separation was an imminent and certain event.

Miranda began stopping by my apartment each day on her way home from the bank. We had spirited discussions and shared a lot of laughs. During one of our discussions, I learned that Miranda and I had a twenty-year age difference, which deeply concerned me. I looked quite young for my age, and I never suspected she was only twenty-four years old!

"Does it concern you that I am forty-four years old?" I asked.

"No, not really. I've dated guys my age, and I am tired of being a babysitter!"

We agreed to continue seeing each other and even shared several kisses. This went on for several weeks until Miranda told me that she and her husband were considering a last-ditch effort to save their marriage. As they began marriage counseling, we no longer saw each other, and I began dating another woman. Soon after that, Miranda contacted me and told me that she was leaving her marriage.

"I don't want to be away from you anymore. I want to be with you."

While I was overjoyed to hear her declaration, I was still concerned about our age difference. Miranda seemed emotionally immature and not very confident as an independent adult. The fact that she loved watching cartoons only reinforced my concerns. Yet, I loved her very much. Her only concern about our age difference was that she would be faced with being completely alone when I left this earth, since I was close to her parents' ages.

"Perhaps you should find someone closer to your age, Miranda. While I'm in love with you, I understand your concerns."

"I have thought about it, but I don't think I'm going to find anyone as wonderful as you are. Let's not worry about this now. I'd rather concentrate on our future, without having fears. Besides, I already love Cyndi and Rachel."

There was no denying that Miranda had already formed a loving and close relationship with my girls. In return, they loved her as well. Miranda moved in with me at the end of October 1992, but we waited more than a month to share any sexual intimacy. She also began working alongside Lori. She was well integrated into both my professional and personal lives.

Our life together consisted of working with each other every day, then going out for dinner and drinks each night. In fact, we never made love without having alcohol beforehand. I had never been a big fan of alcohol yet found myself imbibing on a regular basis.

On the other hand, Miranda was a Cajun, and her culture was very fond of alcohol. After meeting her parents in New Orleans several days before Mardi Gras, I gained more insight into the Cajun culture. They were already inebriated by the time we had lunch. The beer and hurricanes continued well into the night. Since they were warm and welcoming to me, I decided not to judge their excessive drinking and just accept and love them for who they were.

* * * * *

I struggled financially as my divorce took my car, home, and private practice as the result of the legal costs, as well as an extensive monthly alimony and child support. In spite of this, Miranda and I decided to get married, and we set our wedding date for wedding to be in March, 1993.

I asked my friend Richard to officiate, since he was an ordained minister. Richard was also a shamanic co-workshop leader. Together, we had led several workshops in our area and had developed a fairly close relationship.

Miranda decided that she wanted our marriage ceremony to be informal. Since it was her second marriage, she insisted upon it being a small ceremony, with very few people in attendance. While I didn't want to make this issue a point of contention, I did have a problem with it.

"I don't understand why you wouldn't want my parents and Lori's family to join us." My eyebrows began to knit as my head tilted toward my right shoulder. I felt confused.

"Look, I just want to have something short and sweet. Let's not make a big deal out of this. It's not like we've never been married before."

Cyndi and Rachel wore smiles from the time they entered Richard's girlfriend's home, until we all piled into my car to return to our apartment. Strangely, however, Miranda barely smiled and actually seemed bored by our rite of marriage. It was if she were anxiously thinking, "Let's get this over with."

I elected to remain silent about my perception, despite having a nagging concern about her motivation for marrying me. I chose to believe that her lack of joy and apparent boredom was because she felt that our ceremony was a mere formality.

Within months, Cyndi joined us due to a very stormy relationship with her mother, Alice. I was concerned about having a thirteen-year-old living with us since we were newly married. Fortunately, Miranda welcomed Cyndi with open arms. In fact, I could not have found a more perfect stepmom for my daughters. Rachel continued to stay with us on alternate weekends, as well as one night during the week. It did make things much easier on everyone, since both Rachel and Cyndi were extremely close to Miranda.

Miranda and I had many discussions about what our lives might be like if we were to have a child of our own. However, there were two big hurdles to clear if we would be able to conceive. The first obstacle was that Miranda had been told by her gynecologist that she would be unable to conceive as the result of having a tilted cervix and mild dysplasia. In fact, neither she nor her husband used any form of birth control during her previous marriage.

The second challenge was that I had undergone a vasectomy nine years earlier while married to Alice. When I met with my urologist to discuss reversing this procedure, he told me that there is only a 10 percent chance of success when someone has had a vasectomy for ten years. My urologist would also recruit the services of a surgeon, since a vasectomy reversal surgery would be tedious and relatively lengthy. I decided to undergo the surgery, as my love for Miranda demanded this sacrifice.

I appeared at the outpatient surgery center by the time their doors opened. After filling out the appropriate paperwork, I waited in the small waiting room until both physicians arrived. After exchanging smiles, my urologist looked around the room for Miranda.

"Where's your wife?"

"Oh, she's home."

He looked shocked and incredulous. "She's home! Who's going to drive home?"

"I can't drive myself?" I never thought I would need any assistance to get myself home.

My physician shifted his weight, and his eyebrows shot up in disbelief. "Are you kidding me? You're getting a nerve block which will make your legs totally wobbly. There's no way you'll be able to walk without help, let alone drive!"

"But I planned on working this afternoon," I replied.

Now, he was beyond shocked. He looked at me as though I were a psychiatric patient rather than a psychologist.

"You planned on working later! Holy crap, you need help!" At this point, he was chuckling at both my ignorance and driven personality.

"Give me your wife's phone number and I'll have my staff call her. Jeff, you'll be using an ice bag for the next few days. I highly doubt you'll want to listen to other people's problems."

The surgery went on for several hours, and my urologist was correct in his prognosis. I was extremely uncomfortable and in pain for the next three days. Despite the challenges we faced, within three months, Miranda and I were expecting our first child! I knew that God was never limited by human or earthly obstacles. Although I was extremely excited, I was not surprised by the supernatural outcome.

Chapter 16

The initial years of our marriage were very blissful, despite having to deal with the enormous stress due to my divorce aftermath. I could not even make enough money to keep us all afloat because my child support and alimony were so high. Miranda and I hit some very low points in our short marriage due to my financial burdens. At one point, I lost my new Nissan 300ZX and my private practice. I was even evicted from my apartment for failing to pay my rent. All of my money went to meet my obligations to Alice. I was frequently hauled into court under the threat of being put in jail because I was behind in my payments.

After being evicted, my sister Rosetta was kind enough to open her home to Miranda, Cyndi, and myself so that I could reconstitute my practice. We stayed with Rosetta, her husband, and their three children. In addition to providing a place to stay, they served meals for us every day and never asked for any money in return. We were so poor at that time that going out to dinner or lunch meant counting our nickels and dimes to see if we had enough money to buy some burritos or tacos at Taco Bell. As a man and sole provider for my family, I struggled with feeling like a complete failure; however, I innately knew that God would provide a way for us to get back on our feet.

I know that God was faithful in answering my prayers. After six months, we finally moved out to a townhome in Boca Raton, and my practice was once again starting to thrive. Although I had not accepted Christ as my Savior, God already knew exactly what I needed. He also knew what would occur when I attended Calvary Chapel on April 5, 1997.

On August 7, 1996, she graced our home. I picked out the name, London, for her.

I felt so incredibly blessed to have my third beautiful daughter with the woman I loved so deeply. The first few months were overwhelming and difficult for Miranda because she had some insecurity about being a new mother.

Cyndi and Rachel were so welcoming to their new sister. Their reaction not only brought increased joy but seemed to ease Miranda's anxieties. However, a pattern began to emerge that I had hoped was temporary. Unfortunately, it actually plagued us throughout the entirety of our marriage.

Miranda had no libido after London was born, which I attributed to hormonal changes. We never had physical intimacy more than twice a month for the next fifteen years, and there were times when we were only intimate once a month. As my sense of rejection mounted, so did my frustration. The more frustrated I became, the more pressure I placed on Miranda. As a result, she began to resent me.

Chapter 17

We had gotten some counseling from a husband and wife pastoral team from our church. They each implored Miranda to at least make an attempt to meet my needs, but no changes ever occurred in her attitude. I fully recognized that my reactions fostered Miranda's responses and vice versa. I also wish that I could have handled it better. Yet, as I look back, I honestly feel that I tried everything I could to foster a more amicable relationship with Miranda. That was especially true regarding this one issue, albeit a very important dynamic in any marriage.

While physical intimacy was not a priority for Miranda, on one of the seemingly rare times when we were intimate, she became pregnant with our second child. The due date was nearly two years after London's birth.

During this time, my mother was very ill, and I found myself weeping as I anticipated losing her. In an attempt to ease my aching heart, I would listen to worship music while driving to my office. On one of these occasions, the Holy Spirit revealed to me that He was blessing me with a son. I heard His quiet voice whispering, "Since you have embraced the Son, so shall a son be given unto you."

Months later, when Miranda and I went to her ob-gyn to have an ultrasound to determine the sex of our child, the technician told us, "It looks like a girl."

I was certain that she had to be wrong. "Please, look again and you'll see my son's penis."

Miranda looked quizzically at me as I had not shared what was revealed to me. The technician peered up and said in a patronizing tone, "Okay, but I'm pretty sure it's a little girl." Within moments, the technician confirmed my assertion. Soon after her doctor had met with us, we walked to our car. "How did you know? I felt embarrassed because I was afraid the tech thought you were arrogant."

I smiled at her and replied, "The Lord told me."

Miranda seemed very confused, but we both got excited about having a sibling for London. I felt overjoyed that my last child was a boy, especially since I had lost Jay and had always wondered if both Nancy and Alice had not had abortions, if one or both might have given birth to a boy. Knowing that God was in control of my life gave me peace about my past. Miranda and I spent many hours poring through baby name books, and we finally settled upon his name. Our son, Matthew was born in June, 1998, at 11:40 pm, just a mere 20 minutes from "Father's Day".

Soon after his arrival, Miranda and I had a discussion that opened my eyes to the cause of our problems. It was customary for us to set aside one day in the week as a date night in order to reconnect as friends and lovers, and not just parents. We usually went to dinner and/or a movie. Often, we would simply take walks along the beach or in Mizner Park, which is an upscale outdoor shopping center in Boca Raton, Florida.

During one such date night, after another several nights of rejection and resentment on both of our parts, Miranda and I opened up to each other as we walked. We discussed her previous relationship in Louisiana with someone whom she had been very much in love with yet had cheated on her several times. As a result, she decided to leave Louisiana and live with her aunt's family in Fort Myers, Florida.

It was my belief that Miranda did not trust herself and needed to create a good deal of physical and emotional distance so that she would not be tempted to take him back. I asked her if she was still in love with him. She told me that she wasn't since she could never trust him for being so unfaithful. It was a difficult conversation for me, especially since I had been feeling rejected and insecure for quite some time.

As we continued to talk more about Louisiana, Miranda suddenly blurted out, "The reason I married you was that I didn't want to go back to Louisiana."

I stopped dead in my tracks, not sure if I heard her correctly. She repeated her statement. It felt as though I were in an alternative reality or having a bad dream. My mind went numb and began to flit from every conversation and interaction we had experienced since we had been dating. I could not think clearly and was extremely quiet for the remainder of the evening, as was Miranda.

When I awoke the very next day, I tried my best to process what she had said the night before. It suddenly made sense to me. Prior to having children, whenever Miranda and I were intimate, we were inebriated or high on marijuana. Once we invited Jesus into our hearts, we both stopped smoking marijuana, yet we still drank before making love. I finally connected the dots. Without any substances, Miranda had no desire to be intimate with me. She had never fallen in love with me. Rather, she had married me for convenience, security, and possibly even some status.

After breakfast, we took both of our children for a walk around the park. I was extremely depressed since I could not see staying married to a woman who married me under false pretenses. She asked me why I was so silent. I looked at her and said that since she had married me for all the wrong reasons, I no longer wanted to stay married.

Miranda did not miss a step. She continued to walk and dismissed my statement by saying, "I do love you. We are a family now."

I said nothing but processed what it would be like to divorce for the second time. I was not keen on the idea of leaving two more children to deal with the aftermath of divorce. In an effort to move forward, I tried to forget about the conversation the night before and did my best to make our marriage work. To that end, I prayed daily for God to change my wife's heart and for her to fall in love with me.

In order to help God, as though He needed my help, I thought that getting in even better shape might help. I had already started working out daily, thinking that if I were more muscular, Miranda might be more attracted to me. After contemplating our discussion, I regularly exercised with a strongly renewed purpose. I even returned to martial arts school. Sadly enough, nothing changed her feelings toward me.

Another important thing I realized was that I had a very co-dependent marriage. As a result, I felt the change I really needed to make was to be more dependent and in love with Jesus than with Miranda. Although I was still very sexually and emotionally frustrated and starved, I was spiritually content. I continued to wake up at 5:00 a.m. daily and began my routine. After drinking a strong cup of coffee, I spent time in the Word and praised God. By 6:00 a.m., I was in the gym. Unfortunately, my workouts elevated my depression and anxiety.

April 1, 1997, was a typical balmy day in South Florida. I had barely walked in the door after work when my wife confronted me in the kitchen. Miranda began discussing our mutual friends Joe and Nina. I had great admiration for both of them, as they were people of tremendous integrity.

Joe was a physiatrist, who had referred many of his patients to me for pain counseling. We had quickly forged a friendship and frequently socialized with our wives and children. His quick wit and intellect caused me to develop a deep respect for him.

Unexpectedly, the conversation with Miranda took a turn that I was unprepared for.

"I spoke with Nina today. We both agreed that, for the sake of our children, we need God in our lives."

Miranda's proclamation was not in conflict with any of my beliefs. I already had a strong relationship with God since as far back as I could remember.

My wife was not done. "We need to teach London about the Bible. I also want us to go to church with them this Saturday night."

"What? A church?" I asked in absolute disbelief.

Miranda went on to clarify that it was a nondenominational church, as though that would give me comfort.

I replied in my best professional, arrogant New York voice, "Hello! I'm a Jew, remember! The fact that it is a nondenominational church has no relevance to me."

In response, Miranda stated a fact that I could not refute. "You've always loved Jesus."

I had shared my Jesus experience with Miranda early in our marriage, and her decision to use it as a motivation for attending church mitigated my fears. I don't know if I was more fearful of exposing myself to the strange and unknown world of Christianity or worried about turning away from Jesus once again.

Miranda saw the hesitation on my face and leapt at her chance to close the deal. "So, you'll go? You'll come to church with us?"

"Sure, why not? What's the worst that can happen? I don't think Moses will disown me!"

I chuckled and slowly ambled into the kitchen to get a cold glass of water. While I said nothing else, I felt anxiety circulating throughout my body.

That Saturday evening, Miranda and I took a long drive in our minivan to Joe and Nina's home in Boca Raton. The couple joined us, and we headed to Calvary Chapel in Fort Lauderdale. They encouraged me in my decision to attend church that evening.

As I parked our vehicle, Nina suddenly blurted out, "Jeff, you are so lucky! Jesus is like a brother to you because you are both Jewish. Joe and I are like distant cousins."

I looked back at Nina from my seat and pondered her remark. Fortunately, Nina had not only captured my attention, she eased my anxious mind.

"Jeff, are you aware that almost all of His apostles were Jewish?"

"Really?" I was somewhat astonished by this declaration.

"Tens of thousands of early disciples were *all* Jews! In fact, Christianity is the expansion of Judaism through the Jewish Messiah."

In an almost arrogant tone, I said, "Well, at least this is not some *born-again* church, where people are all in a trance with their arms waving in the air!"

Nina shot a worried glance at Joe. I knew that I was swimming in water too deep to survive. Taking a deep breath, I nervously turned the engine off. Everyone filed out of our minivan and headed toward the church doors. I lingered as my anxiety reached a crescendo.

Miranda turned and looked back at me. "Jeff, are you coming?"

Not in any great rush to enter a large church filled with Gentiles, I slowly descended from the driver's seat and walked across the parking lot to catch up with the others. Upon entering the church, I was amazed at how many people were waiting in line at the sanctuary doors for the best seats.

Miranda and Nina both said goodbye as they walked through the sea of people. They were on their way to the nursing mothers' room, where they could watch the service from televisions.

As I followed Joe to the center of the church, I imagined that I was the only Jew among the thousands of Gentiles in this large sanctuary. After we each found our seats, anxiety and discomfort began to rise up within me to an alarming level. Being in this church was so far out of my comfort zone. I had never been in a church before and had formed very strong opinions about people who were born-again Christians.

Whenever I viewed an evangelical service on television, the congregation seemed like mindless sheep casting their arms to a God that I did not comprehend. Now, as I sat in Calvary Chapel, I was now one of those people!

As the band came out and the musicians took their places alongside their instruments, Joe turned to me. "At the very least, I think you'll enjoy the music. It's amazing."

I nodded as the music began. With each praise and worship song, my anxiety eased. I thought to myself, "Wow, these songs are well done. Being here is not so bad."

After five songs, the band left the stage, and Pastor Bob Coy came out to preach. His sermon was from the book of Romans. While I had no previous context to help in my understanding, his teaching style made the sermon interesting. He also had a very humorous delivery for his message. Finally, the pastor gave what was referred as an *altar call* before the service came to a close.

"If you want to experience the peace that only Jesus can give you, now is the time to make that commitment. All that you need to do is stand where you are. I will lead you in a prayer that will, in essence, give you a new heart and a new life."

Without thinking, I jumped up out of my seat and began my own prayer. "Jesus, if you are real, I need *you*. I have been lost for many years, and my pain is beyond control."

I began repeating the prayer that Pastor Bob recited. Tears that had been held back for many years streamed from my eyes and soaked the collar of my shirt. Flashbacks of my early childhood traumas began rising from the depths of my mind. I had stored them away in order to keep my life and relationships manageable.

My most compelling memory of finding Jay's lifeless body in his crib slowly came to the surface. My chest began convulsing with each passing second. Unable to control the powerful emotions of loss and parental abandonment, I began sobbing softly.

I became very self-conscious at my open display of emotion, especially in full view of Joe, who had never witnessed my emotional and vulnerable side. My sobs turned into load moans that I could not stop. I covered my face with my hands, as if to find some place of solitude to hide my grief. As this memory began to dissipate, another painful memory took its place. One by one, each trauma appeared before me. Much of my extreme sadness was the result of having witnessed too much death at such a young and tender age. As my sobbing intensified, I remembered the spiteful arguments that my parents engaged in for most of my childhood.

I felt Joe's hand reach out to comfort and console me. Although I appreciated his tender gesture, that moment was set aside for the Lord and me. As I stood there in the service, I felt very dizzy from the Holy Spirit touching my soul. At that moment, He found a way into my heart. My body was immediately weakened, yet strengthened at the same time. A peace I had never known filled my entire body. The sensation was something I had never experienced in my life.

I looked at Joe, who seemed completely in shock. I didn't know what surprised him more, my sobbing, which seemed to come out of nowhere, or the fact that I had been *born again* the very first time I set foot in a church.

When Joe and I caught up with our wives, Miranda was stunned.

"What happened to you?" she asked.

"What do you mean?" I asked her.

Miranda looked confused as she elaborated, "You went into the sanctuary all freaked out. And now, you look … transformed!"

My lips began to quiver. "I accepted Jesus! He is now my Messiah!"

As I explained my impulsive decision to accept the invitation to receive salvation, my eyes filled with liquid joy. I could not stop talking about the elation that filled my entire mind and body as a result of accepting Jesus as my Lord and Savior. Miranda's facial expression changed from shock to disbelief.

As we walked outside and toward our van, it was obvious that Joe and Nina shared in my joy, yet Miranda appeared to be bothered by my nonstop chatter. When I was driving, she even cordially asked me to stop talking and concentrate on the road. I wondered why she seemed so upset.

Quickly and quietly, I began a silent prayer of thanks to God for leading me out of my dark world. It was amazing how His Spirit filled my world with light. I could not contain the joy I felt. I likened it to falling in love with the sweetest, most beautiful, most kind, and most intelligent woman in the world. The world took on a glow that I had never experienced before. I already knew that April 5, 1997, would be the most important day in my life, and a new beginning for the rest of my days.

I had heard that *nothing in life is free, except the grace of God*, and I was just beginning to get some small inkling of what that meant. I read from the Bible twice daily in order to learn more about God and Jesus. I ferociously thirsted for any jewel of understanding about my newly found faith. In an effort to discover any further insight into the goodness of God, I read every book I could get my hands on, attended adult education classes at Calvary Chapel, and listened to Christian music. During this time, Miranda openly expressed her displeasure at my zeal for Christ. She could not seem to join me in my desire to be more like Him.

* * * * *

It was during the first few months after my salvation experience on April 5, 1997, that my family and close friends began noticing that something was very different about me. It is said that when a

Jew comes to know Yeshua, the Jewish Messiah, it is the ultimate homecoming.

I played dumb when family members inquired about my newfound joy. When I tried that with my mother, who had previously had a quadruple heart bypass and was dealing with renal problems from polycystic kidney disease, it did not work. One day while visiting her and my dad, she cornered me in her small kitchen.

"What is going on with you?" she demanded.

"What do you mean, Mom?"

"Listen! I have known you all of your life, and I know when something is different in you. I have *never* seen you this happy. You seem content."

When I told my mom that I had become a born-again Christian, a *completed Jew*, she was initially stunned. That quickly turned into intense anger.

"You have turned your back on your family and millions of Jews who were slaughtered simply because they were Jews!"

Although I had anticipated such a response, it was my turn to be stunned. Her judgment and condemnation hurt me deeply. I explained that Christianity was nothing more than the second covenant and that Yeshua was the Messiah promised since the beginning of time.

I went on to educate my mother that Yeshua, all of His disciples, and many of the first multitude of followers were all Jewish. I then followed it up with the truth that Jesus came *for the Jew first* and then the gentiles and that the question in the first century was, should Gentiles be allowed to worship the Jewish messiah? My mom shifted her feet as she softened her face.

"All I really care about is that you are happy, my son."

"Mom, you know that I have practiced every spiritual discipline known to man. I have also done some pretty strange things in my search for God. The truth is that I have come full circle to worship the God of Abraham, Benjamin, and Jacob and Messiah Yeshua. I have never been so at peace and so hopeful about my life since inviting Yeshua into my heart."

My mom and I exchanged smiles and a loving hug. She hugged me to tightly that it was reminiscent of so many days from my early childhood.

Several weeks later, my mother was in DelRay Hospital after experiencing heart and kidney issues. She had several heart attacks and a quadruple bypass some years ago, and her heart function was very weak. That was her tenth hospitalization in that year alone. When I walked into her room, I found my sisters, their husbands, and several of my nieces there already. I bent over, kissed my mom on her cheek, and asked her how she felt.

"I'm fine," she quickly responded, looking at me with an intensity I had rarely seen. I knew that we were about to have a very serious conversation.

Motioning for to me to approach her bed, she desperately inquired, "Is it okay for me to pray to Jesus?"

I looked back at my family. Some of them shifted in their seats nervously, waiting for my response. Their twisted faces looked back at me with anticipation and concern. They had put up with my strange spiritual practices over the years, but I knew they weren't ready for any big changes in Mom's religious views.

I looked back at her and peered into her hazel eyes. "Mom, not only is it okay for you to pray to Jesus. When you get home, I will tell you who Jesus *really* is."

My mother did not say another word about the subject, and my family said very little to either me or my mother while I was there. The stillness in the room was unsettling. While nothing would give me greater pleasure than to share the good news of the gospel with my mother, I was keenly aware of how most Jews receive it.

Jewish people have a strong tendency of equating Jesus with all Gentiles. Therefore, many believe that Hitler, Stalin, and others who slaughtered millions of Jewish families were Christians. To say that I was shocked by my mother's desperate request is the biggest understatement I could imagine. I left the hospital room after saying goodbye to my mom and family, and then went home to pray.

After my young daughter London went to sleep for the night, I took out my Bible and sought the Lord's wisdom on how to witness to my mother. I realized that Mom would not live much longer and felt a huge burden for her salvation. I not only wanted her to secure a place in heaven but to also relieve her fear of dying.

I opened my Bible to the book of Matthew and began reading. In Matthew 19:26, Jesus was speaking to His apostles, all of whom were Jewish. He was discussing how difficult it was to enter the kingdom of heaven. His disciples were astonished, believing it was nearly impossible for anyone to get into heaven.

Jesus then responded, "With man this is impossible, but with God all things are possible." I pleaded with God to show me what to say to my mother so that she could be totally open to my words. The Lord provided me with the perceptive instructions I needed to accomplish my deepest wish. The relief I felt was very comforting.

It was only two days later when my mom called from her home asking me to come to see her. Her soft voice pleaded to me, "Please bring your Bible with you." Her request did not surprise me, for I knew Mom realized how quickly she could leave this world.

I quickly gathered up my Bible and notes I had written which were full of biblical references. Once again, I prayed that the Lord would guide my every word. My mother's salvation hung in the balance, yet I was reminded that redemption lies not in the words of men, but in the power of the Holy Spirit. I steadied and slowed my breath, as I left to witness to my mother. Upon entering my parents' condo in Century Village, a retirement community in Boca Raton, Florida, my mother ushered us into the den where we sat down. She did not wait for any pleasantries. "Did you bring your Bible?"

I smiled and showed her my Bible.

"Here it is, Mom. Are you ready to hear what God says about Jesus?" I sat down on her couch and began a series of questions that the Holy Spirit had led me to say. "Let me begin by first asking you, do you believe in God?"

My mother was indignant. "Of course, I do. Who do you think taught you about God when you were a child?"

"I know, Mom, but so many Jews are more into their religion and customs than their belief in God, who created them."

I asked my mother if the Old Testament was written by men or the Spirit of God. She did not hesitate to tell me that the Spirit of God wrote the Old Testament through the prophets that God had chosen.

"So, King David, Isaiah, Micah, Jeremiah, and others who wrote books contained in the Old Testament were actually written by the Ruach HaKodesh, the Holy Spirit?"

Mom nodded in response.

I quickly leafed through my Bible to Psalm 22. "Mom, let me show you what King David says in this Psalm: 'My God! My God! Why have you forsaken me? Why are you so far from helping me and far from the words of my groaning?'"

I looked up at her and asked, "Mom, where have you heard these words before?"

She hesitated and said, "Jesus said these words."

"What would you say if I told you that King David wrote this Psalm nine hundred years before Jesus was born?"

My mother's jaw dropped.

"During King David's time, there was no such thing as crucifixion!" I continued, "Jesus said, 'They pierced my hands and my feet; I can count all my bones. They look and stare at me. They divide my garments among them; and for my clothing they cast lots.'"

With an almost inaudible voice, my mom proclaimed that she had heard this story from several Christmas cards she had read in the past. My mother was now hungry for more.

I read Isaiah 7:14. "Therefore the Lord Himself will give you a sign. Behold, the virgin shall conceive and bear a Son and shall call him *Immanuel*, which means, *God is with us*."

I continued discussing other Old Testament prophesies and actually read eight of them as examples. Upon finishing, I explained, "There are over three hundred prophesies of the Messiah in the Old Testament. The statistical odds of one man fulfilling only eight of them are mindboggling."

"What do you mean?"

"The odds of Jesus fulfilling all eight prophesies I just read are 1 in 10 to the 17th power! If we go on and calculate the odds of him fulfilling forty-eight of the prophesies, it is 1 in 10 to the 157th power! Mathematicians agree that when we look at those statistical odds, there is a zero probability that it happened simply by chance. Mom, do you understand how astounding that is?"

"Mom, do you remember when we drove home from my college graduation and how long it took us to get through Texas?"

"Oh, my gosh! It seemed like eternity, and all your father did was sleep!"

"Right. It was as though he took the Greyhound bus home and left the driving to us!"

We roared with laughter just as we did when we drove through Texas so many years ago.

Mom took a deep breath and relaxed.

"Well, a well-known scientist stated that if we took millions of silver dollars, marked one with a red X, and then stacked them two feet deep throughout the entire state of Texas, the likelihood of someone picking out that marked silver dollar on his first attempt would be the same as one person fulfilling forty-eight of the three hundred prophesies of the Messiah." As a true understanding of that statistic hit me, goosebumps covered my body with a tingling sensation. My mom stood there silently as if trying to comprehend what I had said.

"Mom, did you know that it is said that the Messiah will come from King David's lineage?"

"Yes, of course, many Jews know that."

"Well, let me say this. Throughout the New Testament, Israelites referred to Jesus as 'Son of David.' The temple held all of the birth records where Jesus's genealogy was well known and documented. After the temple was destroyed, so were the records. If the Messiah has not been born yet, how will we Jews know that He would come from David's lineage?"

For several second, her only response was silence. Mom stared into my eyes, waiting for more.

I continued, "This must mean that the Messiah had to have been here before the temple was destroyed. Right?"

All my mother could utter was, "When are you going to church? Your dad and I will meet you there."

Chapter 18

My mom and dad met Miranda and I several days later as we attended the Saturday evening service at Calvary Chapel. Mom busied herself by trying to locate other Jews among the thousands of people in attendance. My father was a staunch Jew, although he had only stepped inside a synagogue once in the past fifteen years. He was extremely bored and agitated with the entire experience. Unlike my dad, Mom immediately volunteered to meet us again the following week.

As we made our way into our seats, there was an air of expectation that I could not identify. My initial reaction was that the congregation was so hungry for God, that this hunger filled every space in the large sanctuary. After the praise and worship music was over, the pastor began teaching from the book of Romans. Pastor Bob Coy talked about how God was not done with the Jewish people in His plans for salvation. He went on to teach that since the Gentiles had received the Jewish Messiah as their own, this was all part of God's plan to provoke Jews to feel jealous for what the Gentiles had received.

"Gentiles, do not be boastful of your relationship with Christ, for you were grafted into the Olive Tree, the Tree of Life that is Israel." He continued by quoting from Romans 11:26–29. "The delivered will come out of Zion. And He will turn away ungodliness from Jacob; for this is My covenant with them; when I take away their sins."

I shot a quick glance at my mother, who sat silently stoic.

Pastor Bob went on to add that the "gifts and calling of God are irrevocable." I whispered to my mom that in God's eyes, Jews will always be the apple of God's eyes. She gave me an almost indistinguishable smile. Citing a passage from Psalm 22, the pastor said that Jesus was not recognized as a handsome man with blue eyes and light hair, as Hollywood frequently portrays him. Jesus was an Israeli Jew with dark skin and curly black hair.

"In Psalm 22, the Messiah is described as 'a worm and no man; a reproach of men, and despised by the people. All those who see me, ridicule me. They shoot out the lip, they shake their head, saying, 'He trusted in the Lord; let him rescue him. Let him deliver him, since he delights in him.'"

Mom leaned over to my ear and said, "This sounds terrible. Why was he so hated?"

I gently touched her hand and shot her a soft, reassuring smile.

Wow! I thought. *Mom is starting to ask some very important questions.*

With a tremendous inspiration coming from his words, Pastor Bob went on to say, "The Hebrew word for "worm" is *tola'ath*. The crimson tola'ath, or worm, is found in Israel. When the female is prepared to produce offspring, she rigidly attaches herself to a tree and cannot be removed without tearing her body apart. When the offspring hatch, they feed upon the living body of their mother.

"This is the story of a painful sacrifice, much like the one Jesus suffered for all of us. When the young are able to survive apart from her, she dies. She leaves a scarlet dye staining not only on the tree, but the young as well."

It was my turn to be stunned by this revelation. I looked at my mother and whispered, "Can you see how this all fits in, given Jesus's sacrificial death?"

While I was so inspired by this additional knowledge and felt so doubly blessed to be a Jewish believer, my mom was dumbfounded. At the close of the service, Pastor Bob invited people to the altar to give their lives to Jesus. What followed next took me by complete surprise.

"My son, will you walk me to the altar?"

With tears streaming from my eyes, I got up from my chair and waited for Mom to follow. She took hold of my hand as we slowly walked toward the altar. Throngs of people rejoiced and applauded her decision.

As we stood at the altar, we were pushed together by many others anxious to give their lives to Jesus. Pastor Bob congratulated everyone for their decision and told each person at that altar, "Jesus loves you so much that He is exchanging your heart for His."

In typical fashion, Mom used her sardonic humor to decrease the anxiety she was experiencing in making such a monumental decision. She turned to me and said, "With my heart? They should all hate me for giving Jesus such a diseased piece of meat!"

I chuckled and put my arms around my mother. "I am so proud of you, and love you so much!"

The date my mom's name was written in the Lamb's Book of Life was September 14, 1997.

* * * * *

During the ensuing months, my mom had many questions. "If I am now a born-again Christian, does that mean I'm no longer Jewish?" Mom's struggle to determine the balance between her faith in Jesus and maintaining her Jewish identity was troubling to her.

I replied, "I've wondered about that very same thing. You don't have to give up being Jewish any more than any of the apostles did. They all continued to celebrate the feasts and viewed themselves as Jews, because Jesus did not come to establish a new religion. He came to usher in the New Covenant."

Mom seemed puzzled. "What do you mean by the New Covenant?"

"The Old Covenant was built around the Old Testament Mosaic law which was about being obedient to rituals and sacrifices. In the Book of Jeremiah, he predicted that there would be a time when God would make a new covenant with Israel. That time was made manifest when the Messiah came. Jesus came to fulfill the law of Moses, and through the Holy Spirit, we were no longer under the penalty of the laws of Moses. Believers could never earn their way to having a close relationship with God, so, Jesus became our sacrifice.

Through His atoning death, the free gift of salvation was given to all those who believed. Do you understand?"

Mom's confused look was somewhat softened, but she still had unanswered questions. "Then why are we called Christians if Jesus did not create a new religion."

I was eager to respond as my passion for being a Messianic Jew was very strong. "All of the early followers of Jesus were known as 'followers of the Way' since Jesus had proclaimed that He was *the way, the truth, and the life*. It was only later after many Gentiles became believers that the term *Christian* was created."

Mom asked, "Is declaring Jesus as my Savior even necessary, given the fact that I am a good person?"

"Mom, people often compare themselves to murderers, rapists, thieves, child molesters, and the dregs of society. We are to compare ourselves to Jesus and His holiness. When we do, we *all* fall short. Scripture tells us that even our greatest deeds are like filthy rags in the sight of God."

"Well, that means I don't have a chance in hell of ever making it to heaven! I feel even more lost than I was before I went to church with you." Her despondency was unmistakable as she put both hands over her face.

"Mom, the great news is that our faith and relationship with Jesus is all we need. Just work on developing that through prayer, reading your Bible, and having open discussions with Jesus."

I iterated that if she were comparing herself to thieves, murderers, rapists, and other criminals, she would be considered a good person, but scripture tells us that even our greatest deeds are like filthy rags in the sight of a holy God. Her salvation and ticket to heaven was not based on her good deeds but her faith in the Jewish Messiah. She found peace in that understanding. However, her health continued to worsen as her heart grew weaker by the day, and her kidneys were failing.

We also delved into other interesting discussions. Mom and I even talked about my baby brother's death.

"When Jay died, I know that was very hard on you. You were only four when you went through the trauma on your own. You really didn't have any support from Dad or me."

I recounted that I still remembered every detail of that fateful morning. My lips began to quiver as I finished sharing my memories. My mom looked at me and stretched her hand to place it upon mine to comfort me.

"My son, I am so sorry that you had to lose your brother when you were so young. That must have been extremely painful for you."

"This event changed the course of my life, Mom. It was the most traumatic event I had ever experienced, and what made it worse was that you and Dad never uttered a word about it to me. It was if we all went into a pact of avoidance and denial."

Mom's eyes welled up. "Jeffrey, I was afraid that if I talked about it with you, you would re-experience it all over again. I was secretly hoping that you would forget about Jay's death, since you were so young. Dad never wanted to talk about any difficult or painful matters, so I knew he would never bring it up. And, I was scared that if I talked about it, I would have a nervous breakdown."

I told my mother that when each of my children were born, I was so frightened that they would die.

Mom's eyes widened. "I had that very same fear when Lori and Rosetta were born!" She told me that although Jay's death was forty-seven years ago, she too had never gotten over her loss.

"About a year after Jay's death, I had taken you to go shopping in downtown Brooklyn. We were on a bus when I suddenly realized that we needed to get off of the bus, immediately. I said, 'Jeff, we need to go home. I need to feed Jay.' You looked at me and wasted no time to respond. 'Mom, Jay's dead.'"

My mother's world had been so convulsed by my brother's death that she probably had a psychotic break.

"I truly believe that Jay's death drove me to the point of having a nervous breakdown. I became severely depressed and my only way of dealing with my baby's death was to pour my life into you." She wiped eyes and her nose with a tissue, which she took from her pocket.

"How did dad deal with it, Mom? As far back as I can remember, he always seemed distant and removed from many difficult situations. He seemed so avoidant, as if by ignoring his problems, they would magically go away."

Mom shook her head, and her mouth became taut. "Your father always left me holding the bag. I had to deal with every difficult situation that we experienced. I felt more like the man in our relationship. I think the stress mounted to the point where I broke down. I couldn't accept the loss of my baby, and your dad lost himself in gambling. Each week, he would gamble away most of his paycheck. I focused on my bitterness, instead of my sadness and grief. You were my life, and he was the man I resented.

"I am so sorry that you had to cope with that tragedy on your own. Jeffrey, you were the most sensitive, compassionate child I have ever known, and not because you're my son. You were always special. You still are."

We both arose from our chairs and consoled each other. My mom clung to me with such fervor. I imagined that she was desperately trying to hold in the immense unresolved grief of her loss. I believe that she had probably blamed herself for Jay's death. It seemed that the combination of her loss, guilt, and lack of support from my dad accounted for her break with reality. As I held her in my arms, I silently grieved for my own loss of innocence. It had been a great burden to be her reality check at age of five.

Chapter 19

Several months later, I walked into my home to hear my phone ringing after a full day of seeing patients in my family therapy practice. As I looked at the caller ID, I recognized my family physician's number. Immediately, my heart began to pound with fear and trepidation. The only reason Dr. Katz would call me was to tell me the test results that I was apprehensive to hear about.

"Oh my God! This is not good," I exclaimed. I was increasingly overwhelmed by a sense of panic as each ring echoed in the hallway. It did not help that I was alone in the house since my wife was out running errands with my six-month-old daughter. With some measured hesitancy, I took a deep breath as I answered the phone.

"Hello?"

"Can I speak with Jeff Rifkin?"

"Hello, Dr. Katz. Have you gotten my test results back?" I gulped and held my breath as I waited for his response.

"Yes, I've received the results of your ultrasound, and it is conclusive. You have polycystic kidney disease."

My hands shook, and my knees buckled as I began to weep. I was barely able to respond through all of my sobbing. "Do you mean I'm going to die?"

"I need to refer you to a nephrologist for your follow-up care. My nurse will call you with the doctor's contact information tomorrow. Take care."

As the phone line went dead, my emotions were left completely numb. Dr. Katz' cold and dispassionate delivery of the ominous news stunned and confused me. I could barely comprehend what he had said to me. Loud repeating beeps emanated from the receiver, shaking me from my trance with a flood of harsh reality. While holding the phone limply in my hand, I sat on the edge of my bed and sobbed uncontrollably.

As I hung up the phone, my mind raced at an amazing speed. In spite of my training as a psychotherapist, I panicked. No matter what I tried, I could not grasp what was happening to me. After all, it had only been one week since Dr. Katz had referred me to Coral Springs Hospital for an ultrasound. It all seemed so surreal.

My mind drifted back to that day when I registered at the desk of the radiology department. An elderly woman noticed the Bible tucked between my elbow and my side as she checked me in. When I told her the reason for my ultrasound, she placed her gnarled hand upon my own and reassured me.

"You have nothing to worry or fear because God is with you!"

I stared into her eyes wanting her to see the evidence of my faith.

"Your faith in Jesus will break this family curse. It will end with you."

I smiled warmly as I found a seat and waited to be called. In spite of my situation, I was extremely confident that the ultrasound would not betray God's promises to me. I truly did not believe that I had been afflicted by polycystic kidney disease. I knew that I had devoted all of my adult life to healthy living.

For many years, I had exercised regularly and practiced several forms of martial arts. I had been a vegetarian, herbalist, and complete health nut since 1969. Inasmuch as I was a new believer, I did not fully comprehend that disease occurs even in those who know and love God. To my detriment, I mistakenly thought that I would be protected from illness, calamity, and all danger because I had been *saved*. I was so naive.

In the Bible, Jesus made one thing very clear to His disciples. He told them that those who followed Him and His ways would be tested with trials and tribulations that would strengthen their faith. Disease and death are the consequences to living in a fallen world.

My sense of entitlement and narcissistic beliefs surprised me. The conflict between reality and the thoughts going through my mind filled me with disbelief. Images of my impending funeral with the grief-ridden faces of my young widowed wife and three children haunted me.

I was accosted by memories of the awful fate that slowly destroyed my maternal grandfather and aunt. Both of them had suffered and died from this same genetic disease. Polycystic kidney disease creates a plethora of cysts in the kidneys and liver, which continue to grow and multiply. This causes the kidneys to become enlarged and eventually lose all function. Unfortunately, there is no cure. Eventually, I would have to attend the inevitable dialysis sessions, and at some point, death would ensue.

To top things off, my mother and younger sister had both been recently diagnosed with this unwanted disease. I began to sob as I thought of my impending death. I hit my head with my hands as anger overwhelmed my fear.

My anger toward God was relentless. I screamed aloud, "God, how can you do this to me! I gave my life to Jesus just two months ago, and you let *this* happen! Why? *Why!* I don't understand!"

Despite my intellectual understanding, I was confused and bewildered. Soaked with salty tears, I prayed and bargained with God. Many promises rolled off my tongue. I hoped against all hope that the diagnosis was somehow incorrect and that the radiologist had made a mistake. Before I could call Dr. Katz to demand another test, I collapsed on my bed, emotionally spent. As I rubbed my eyes harshly, I begged to wake up from this nightmare. If that wasn't possible, I wanted to alter my perception of the current situation, at least.

After calling out to God for healing and His assistance, I decided to retrieve my Bible from my nightstand. I needed God to show me His truths about how to effectively cope with this tragic news. I looked up words such as "anxiety," "healing," "contentment," and "joy," in my Bible's Concordance section. During my studies, I stumbled upon passages that were exactly what I needed and lacked.

In Philippians 4:6, it reads, "Do not be anxious about anything, but in everything, by prayer and petition, with thanksgiving, present your requests to God. And the peace of God, which transcends all understanding, will guard your hearts and minds in Christ Jesus."

Over and over, I read the passage as I tried to fully comprehend what it meant. I wanted to understand its application in my particular circumstances. Since I had been a psychologist for so many years, my professional understanding made it difficult to prevent being anxious.

I knew that anxiety is experienced by everyone at some time or another. To me, anxiety seemed like a *normal* response to feeling overwhelmed by difficult circumstances. Yet, God was directing me to "not be anxious about *anything*"! My mind began to race, once again. *What was that? I shouldn't be anxious about learning I have polycystic kidney disease. Really?*

I began praying out loud. "Father, I read that I should be anxious about nothing. Instead, you instructed me to pray for your help. *Please, God! Please, help me!* Lord, I thank you for giving me the greatest gift a man can receive—the gift of salvation. Father, I also thank you for giving me a new child, who is a total blessing! I also thank you for Miranda, as well as Cyndi and Rachel.

"Please take these anxious thoughts from me and replace them with faith. Dear God, may Your peace guard over my heart and mind, and shield them from doubt, fear, and panic. In Jesus's name, I pray. Amen."

I waited as if I were expecting an important phone call. I looked up at the ceiling in my bedroom, as well as at the door. "Perhaps Jesus will visit me again and lay His hands upon me and cure me," I thought.

Ten minutes had passed, and my breathing had slowed down to a manageable rate, and my mind was finally quiet. A pervasive peace came over me that was beyond my ability to comprehend. My anxious thoughts and panic were seemingly gone, replaced by a peace that to my logical mind made no sense whatsoever. I had just been told by my dispassionate family physician that I had inherited a genetic disease that could ultimately lead to my forthcoming demise.

My relationship with God was the very thing that I had been searching for since my early childhood. I had looked for it in different religions, cultures, and countries, but I had come full circle—back to my Jewish biblical roots. I was so thankful to have finally accepted Jesus's free gift of grace and to have Him dwelling inside me.

I shared everything with Miranda, who was obviously very frightened for my health, as well as the financial security of our family. As we both lay in bed that night, I searched for other passages that would give me strength, resolve, and increased faith.

In Isaiah 40:29–31, I read, "He gives strength to the weary and increases the power of the weak. Even youths grow tired and weary, and young men stumble and fall; but those who hope in the Lord will renew their strength. They will soar on wings like eagles. They will run and not grow weary. They will walk and not be faint."

I looked back over to Miranda, who was reading one of her favorite fashion magazines. "Miranda, listen to this!"

I re-read the passage. As I did, my lips quivered, and my voice cracked. Overcome by the promise of this passage, I excitedly remarked, "Isn't this awesome! This is God's promise to me!"

"Yes, it is awesome. Just keep on praying that God will heal you."

I smiled as I turned back to the passage and read it once again. Silently, I prayed, "Lord, there is nothing I can do but have hope in you. Please, give me your strength so that I don't falter and relinquish what little hope I have."

I allowed my prayer to take root in my mind and heart. Eventually, I peacefully drifted off to sleep. Despite my diagnosis, I had faith that God would find a way for me to be healed. After all, He created me. I had a sense that He would use me to expand His kingdom in whatever fashion He chose.

Chapter 20

Two months had passed after my mother accepted Christ into her heart, and her health began to decline with great rapidity. Although my mother found comfort in her newly found relationship with Jesus, nothing miraculous was taking place with regard her health. In fact, during one of her last hospitalizations, she was put on hemodialysis. She believed that indicated the end was near. Days before Gramps died, he was put on dialysis, too.

Mom fought long and hard with her doctors to avoid this difficult and arduous procedure. However, she finally gave in when the doctor explained that her damaged heart would fail unless her kidneys received help to reduce the fluid which had built up in her body. As the Passover was approaching, my mother sensed that her time on earth was drawing near.

"Jeff, I'd like you to lead the Seder at Lori's house this year. I think that this is going to be my last Passover, and I want it to be special."

I was sitting next to hear on the couch in her Florida room. The sun light glistened off the lake and streamed through the windows.

Holding my mom's hand, I asked, "Mom, are you sure that's what you want? If I lead the Seder, I will make it a Messianic Seder and will discuss the significance of Jesus." I squeezed her hand as I continued, "Besides, you can't possibly know that this will be your last Passover."

"Jeffrey, God is not going to keep me around much longer. My heart is getting worse, and my kidneys are starting to get worse, too. Please, do me a favor and lead the Seder."

My heart sank, because I knew my mom was right. Her health had been failing for the past year. The thought of losing her made me desperately sad.

"Okay, Mom, I will lead it. Just be sure to tell Lori that we will have a real Seder this year."

Every year that we had celebrated the Passover, we had avoided any religious reference during the ceremony. It had never been like the traditional Seder found in most Jewish homes worldwide. Our Seders consisted of eating traditional Passover foods such as matzo, matzo ball soup, chicken, potato kugel, some vegetables, as well as drinking wine. We never read from the Haggadah or recited any prayers. When food was served, there was no remembrance of the miracles performed during the exodus from Egypt. Instead of honoring the Seder as a celebration of freedom, my family viewed it as the opportunity to freely eat as much as they liked, without giving any thanks to God.

Weeks later, we all convened at Lori's house. My sister's family consisted of her husband, Peter, three daughters, her son-in-law, and young her granddaughter. Rosetta's family was there as well. We were also joined by several of Peter's nieces and nephews.

Although my mom and dad had experienced some form of the traditional Seder in their past, I was the only one present who had any real familiarity with it. Before beginning, I began talking about the biblical and historical meaning of the Seder and how it related to the sacrificial and atoning death of Jesus.

I began, "Welcome, my family, to our Passover Seder! Tonight, we'll do things a little differently. Before we share in this delicious Passover meal, I want to talk about how Jesus is so intrinsically related to the reason we are meeting together this evening."

"Let's just eat!" someone blurted out. Many others chimed in with mockery and laughter, but I was undaunted.

"Most of you know about the Last Supper, but I'm sure that you probably never realized that the Last Support was, in fact, the Passover Seder that Jesus shared with His Jewish disciples. In the New Testament, Jesus picked up the matzo and broke it. He said, 'This is my body, which is for you. Do this is remembrance of me.'"

There was more murmuring from many of my family members, yet I continued, "After supper, Jesus took the cup in the same way as I am doing, and said, 'This cup is the new covenant in my blood; do this, whenever you drink it, in remembrance of me.' For whenever you eat of this bread and drink of this cup, you proclaim the Lord's death until he comes."

I went on to say, "The cup of wine that Jesus offered up was the fourth cup used in the Seder, which is the Cup of Sorrows. Jesus knew that he would be used as the sacrificial Lamb of God for the atonement of all sins." I attempted to talk more about the significance of the blood on the doorposts, but by then, almost everyone began to serve themselves food. Excitement and chatter filled the room, making it impossible for me to continue.

I looked at Mom, who shook her head in disappointment and disgust. She looked at me and whispered, "Thank you, Jeffrey. I have much to learn. I can only hope that God keeps me around long enough."

As Mom's birthday approached on May 27, we had made plans to celebrate at her favorite restaurant on Saturday, May 30. She had prayed that God would keep her alive to celebrate with her family. Mom was very candid about her fear of not making it to her seventy-first birthday.

On the evening of Mom's birthday, I received a call from my sister Rosetta. She had been living with my parents to help out. Rosetta called to say that my family and I should visit my mom tonight. I was confused as we had all planned on going out to dinner a few nights later to celebrate.

She quickly cut me off and said, "Come over, Jeffrey. You better come over now!"

"Why? What's wrong?" I knew something wasn't good. "I'm on my way."

I quickly rounded up Miranda and my twenty-one-month-old daughter, London, and we all left within minutes. When we arrived, my mom was lying in her bed, complaining of extreme fatigue and weakness. She was also experiencing shortness of breath and some chest pains. As we spent precious time with her, we gave her what would turn out to be the last birthday card she would ever receive.

Mom motioned me to come closer as she struggled to breathe. "Jeffrey, I am dying. I just want you to know how proud I am of what you've become, and assure you that I love you so much!"

"Mom, you'll be fine. You're too tough of a lady to kill off. We will celebrate your birthday in a few days."

I did my best to assure her that everything would be all right, and began praying for her. I was in complete denial of how gravely ill my mother was. We spent about an hour with her and decided to leave in order to put London to sleep.

Before leaving, I told my mom that I would continue to pray and would stop by the next day. No sooner did we put London to bed when the phone rang. I ran downstairs to answer it and heard Rosetta screaming on the other end.

"She's dead! Oh my God! She's dead! Jeffrey, Mom's gone!"

After running upstairs to tell Miranda, I sprinted to my car. I drove all the way back to my mom's house, only to find it empty. My mind raced. I called Lori's home, and my niece informed me that my mom was taken to West Boca Hospital. My panic-stricken mind could not comprehend as to why my mother had been taken to the hospital by ambulance, unless she was not yet dead.

When I arrived at the emergency room, Dad and both of my sisters were there. Rosetta was pleading with the attending doctor to keep our mother alive. In front of all of us, he told her that my mother would not survive the massive heart attack she suffered. Her kidneys were failing, which made her prognosis very grim.

Still in shock, I looked in on my mom. Her belly was completely distended from the fluid that had already built up. The nurses pushed us away as she was defibrillated several times. Finally, they wheeled her into the intensive care unit.

Over the course of the next four days, she was defibrillated fourteen times. My family and I stayed at the hospital day and night. I always had my Bible with me.

The day before my mom passed, I walked into the ICU. My mom was in a semiconscious state, holding her arms held high to the heavens. I knew that she either saw Jesus and was praising Him, or she was crying out for help.

Right then, I knew that if I did anything good in my life, this was the defining moment. Leading my mom to the Lord was my act of love for the woman, who made me into the man I had become. My mom had told me from a very young age that I would become a doctor. She taught me how to love. Mom also showed me how to be a good husband who could gain the respect he needed from his wife.

Though I told her on a regular basis how much I loved and appreciated her, her reward would be found in heaven. I took great solace in knowing that I would be reunited with her when God called me home.

The next day, my dad, sisters, and I were summoned by her physician. He asked us how many times we were willing to have her defibrillated in order to delay the inevitable. My dad looked at us, and then turned to the doctor. "No more. Please, let my wife die in peace."

Within hours, we were called into her room to say our final goodbyes. I slowly walked into her room and found my way to a chair. As I scanned the room, my sisters and their children all gathered around her. My dad stood by the head of her bed.

Unwilling to face the reality of the situation, I did not want to look at my mom. I did not want to deal with the inevitability of her impending death. I turned toward her and began to experience tunnel vision.

We spent no more than twenty minutes with her. For that entire time in her room, she was the only person I saw. No one else seemed to exist outside of my tunnel vision.

I recalled that the sense of hearing was the last to go before death, so I strongly desired to speak to her. My face was covered with streaming tears as I spoke my final words to her. "Mom, thank you so much for being my mother." As I finished, I bawled uncontrollably.

Although my grief was immense, I felt so thankful that God had honored her prayers and kept her alive for her birthday. More so, that the celebration she expected on that night would not take place in a restaurant in Boca Raton, Florida. Instead, it would take place in a special room reserved in the Father's house. In the midst of my grief, I recognized that a miracle had taken place and was so grateful to God for making my mom's passing as painless as possible.

Chapter 21

My maternal grandfather was the first in our family to die from end-stage renal disease in 1967. While my mother taught me to love, my grandfather taught me how to love a wife. He was the most loving, affectionate, and doting husband I had ever seen, even to this day. He called my grandmother "my princess."

Despite his soft, loving nature, Ralph Goldberg was a tough, rugged man. Though he was short in stature and somewhat stout, he worked as a police officer in Brooklyn, New York. He was also very active in local politics.

Aunt Sylvie was diagnosed with kidney disease in 1989 and died on May 9, 1992. Our family was devastated, especially my mother, who was very close to her older sister. Although she had polycystic kidney disease progressing through the years, the pedestrian technology available at that time was not able to diagnose it.

When my aunt died, my mother became petrified that she too would have this deadly disease. One month after my aunt's death, my mother felt ill and went to the emergency room where testing was done. When the emergency room physician returned and told her that her problem was her polycystic kidney disease, she became hysterical. She screamed and cried so much that she had to be sedated in order to calm her down. Despite her knowledge of the disease, my mother did not follow dietary instructions, especially those limiting her sodium intake. Like her sister, my mom did not live long after her initial diagnosis.

My aunt had four children, two of whom have PKD. My cousin Alex had a successful kidney transplant several years ago. Of my mother's three children, my sister Lori and I have been diagnosed with PKD. Thus far, my oldest child, Cyndi has already been diagnosed with PKD.

My fear is that my other children might have inherited the gene from me as well. I can only pray that my other children will be spared. I also hope that by the time symptoms appear, there will be significant progress in treatment, and even a possible cure.

Not many people know about this disease. Organizations such as the PKD Foundation have educated the public about PKD, its symptoms and treatment. Thus far, there is no cure. It is estimated that 12.5 million people have been diagnosed with PKD.

According to the PKD foundation as cited on pkdcure.org, "Polycystic Kidney Disease (PKD) is a genetic disease. PKD damages the kidneys through cystic pressure to normal functional cells. This process may take decades, and PKD patients go into kidney failure by their late fifties, in most cases."

Polycystic kidney disease affects an estimated one in five hundred people, including newborns, children, and adults. These numbers are consistent, regardless of sex, age, race, or ethnic origin. It comes in two forms:

1. Autosomal dominant (ADPKD) is one of the most common life-threatening genetic diseases. It does not skip a generation. There is usually a family history of ADPKD. Parents with ADPKD have a 50 percent chance of passing the disease on to each of their children.
2. Autosomal recessive (ARPKD) is a relatively rare genetic disorder, occurring in approximately one in twenty thousand individuals. It affects boys and girls equally and often causes significant mortality in the first month of life.

PKD features numerous cysts in the kidneys. The cells lining the cysts escape monitoring by the immune system, and they can proliferate excessively. During the process of lining the cysts, liquid is secreted. As a result, the cysts multiply quickly and grow larger. With the swelling of these cysts, more and more functional kidney cells are affected.

The most serious result is cystic pressure to renal blood capillaries, for it leads to the constriction of blood supply in kidney, called ischemia. This speeds up the progression of kidney cell death. It is also common for other organs, including the liver, pancreas, and brain, to develop cysts, as well.

Since PKD is an inherited disorder, the dominant form of the disease (ADPKD) is passed from one generation to the next by the affected parent. An ADPKD parent has a 50 percent chance of passing the PKD mutation to each of his or her children at conception. In some families, all the children are affected; in other families, no one is.

The symptoms of PKD include:

- High blood pressure
- Chronic pain or heaviness in the back, sides, or abdomen
- Blood in the urine
- Urinary tract infection (UTI)
- Kidney stones

Kidneys serve many functions. Most people know that kidneys act as a filtration system, removing wastes such as urea and uric acid from the body, as well as producing urine, which is eliminated. It also maintains acid-base balance by reabsorbing bicarbonate from urine, and excretes hydrogen ions into the urine. Other functions include blood pressure regulation and hormone secretion.

When kidneys begin to fail, high blood pressure is typically the result, and hypertensive medications are used to not only control the high blood pressure but to also protect the kidneys from further damage. Fatigue, decreased libido, and poor sexual function result, as well.

If not treated, hypertension damages the kidneys, enlarges the heart, and can cause strokes. Chronic pain is one of the most common problems for people with PKD. The pain is usually in the back or sides, and occasionally in the abdomen. It can be intermittent and mild, requiring only occasional pain medicine, as allowed by the patient's doctor. In a small number of people, the pain can be constant and quite severe.

A normal kidney is the size of a human fist and weighs about a third of a pound. However, with the presence of PKD, cysts develop in both kidneys. When many cysts develop, the kidneys can increase in both size and weight, sometimes weighing many pounds each. There may be any number of cysts, and they may range in size, from a pinhead to the size of a grapefruit.

As of the publishing of this book, no cure has been developed for PKD. Patients diagnosed with PKD can only manage the symptoms through low-fat and low-sodium diets, along with drinking a great deal of water. If the patient's disease continues to progress, renal failure will ensue. The effects may result in treatment though dialysis, and even possible kidney transplantation.

* * * * *

When I was initially diagnosed, I became very angry. I avoided anything even remotely related to the disease. As a result, I would not participate in any talk or discussion of the disease. I truly believed that I would either be supernaturally healed or the disease would never worsen.

I finally had my initial consultation with my first nephrologist. He reassured me that, in spite of my disease, I could live into my eighties and die from something else. This well-meaning proclamation only strengthened my denial. "I have nothing to worry about," I told myself and went on my way.

Creatinine is a chemical waste product produced by muscle metabolism. An increased level of creatinine may accumulate in your blood and indicate renal function if your kidneys aren't functioning properly. Each year, my blood was drawn to determine my creatinine levels. My initial level was 1.1. Every year after that, I dreaded getting my blood drawn. It was not because I was frightened of needles. I was simply petrified to find out that my creatinine level had risen, which it did every year.

I was tempted to not return my physician's call whenever he would call after my yearly blood draw. Instead of responding right away, I would take time to pray and implore the Lord to heal me. No matter how often I prayed, my disease progressed further every year.

One would think that given my career as a marriage and family therapist, I would want to educate myself about PKD. Yet nothing could have been further from the truth. Whenever any of my afflicted cousins would discuss it with me, I would walk away or hang up the phone.

In 2008, my cousin Joyce and her family stayed with us for several days. The topic of PKD came up, and I began to weep. I explained that I felt that I had a ticking time bomb in my body and that I needed to stay alive for my young children. We talked about various clinical trials which were under way. She felt that medical progress would have been made to lengthen our lives by the time we went into renal failure. Once again, I retreated into my denial.

My father had always been an *avoider*, especially where finances were concerned. When bills would arrive in the mail that he could not pay, he simply dumped them in a drawer. He thought that if he didn't see them, he didn't owe the money. My attitude toward PKD was no different. Much like the growing pile of bills in the drawer, hiding from my disease did not change the fact that it worsened every year.

When I was originally diagnosed, I was immediately put on hypertensive medications because my blood pressure had already begun to rise. As my disease worsened, the other symptoms became more prevalent. Those symptoms not only affected me physically, they had a profound effect upon my marriage.

Chapter 22

When I was saved, Cyndi became very confused. My daughter had been initially raised in several ashrams and was strongly influenced by my focus on New Age teachings, practices, and theologies due to our very close relationship. When I began talking about Jesus and reading the Bible, she became a bit resentful, as if she felt like an outsider in our own home. Although Miranda rarely ever read the Bible, she, London, and I attended Calvary Chapel every Saturday evening. Then a series of events happened to Cyndi that changed her life forever.

Cyndi was in an auto accident. Fortunately, it was nothing serious, but it frightened her immensely. Two weeks later, she called me from the road and said that she had rear-ended another car. As a result, she had some neck and back pain. She also told me that while she was sitting on someone's stoop, an older woman gave her a glass of water and then said, "Jesus loves you!" Cyndi thought this was not only unusual but significant since it was the second time in only two weeks that someone had told her this.

Cyndi's neck and lower back pain were unrelenting even after receiving weeks of physical therapy. There was no structural damage to either her neck and back, yet the soft tissue was inflamed. In addition to giving her 5-HTP, an amino acid which I had used for muscular pain, we prayed for relief. It did not take very long for Cyndi to experience a reprieve from her pain.

After I knew she would be all right, I confirmed Cyndi's feelings concerning her spiritual welfare. I also told her that I thought God was trying to get her attention. My daughter agreed and planned to go with us to church the following week. She seemed to really enjoy the worship and teaching at Calvary Chapel and found that quite a number of her friends were in attendance as well.

Within several weeks, Cyndi quietly walked to the altar during an invitation at church. Without ever telling us about any intentions to do so, she opened her heart to receive Jesus that day. It felt wonderful that my household belonged to Jesus, in spite of my marital struggles.

While at church one evening, Cyndi shared some information with Miranda and I about a Messianic service that she had been attending on Saturday mornings. I had assumed that she was going to spend time with her friends when she would leave each Saturday. I had many questions that I wanted to ask her, but waited for our drive home to inquire about the congregation.

Cyndi articulated herself very succinctly. "Messianic synagogues are where Jewish Christians worship from a Jewish context. Many Gentiles are members of the congregations, as well."

She invited Miranda and me to join her on Saturday, but I politely declined since I felt very at home at Calvary Chapel. In fact, I had asked one of the associate pastors to mentor me, and he gladly accepted. After church one day, he spoke with me about being part of his advanced Bible college class on how to deliver sermons. I could not believe my good fortune! Our assignment was to create a five-minute sermon on any topic that we wished.

I wrote my sermon on the assumption that God answers all prayer. Since I was a Jewish believer, I cited many passages from the Old Testament and specifically referenced 2 Chronicles 7:14. Every classmate wrote their own critique on my message and performance. Two men actually wrote anti-Semitic remarks that indicated their belief that God was done with the Jews and the church had supplanted Israel as the *chosen people*. As I paid more attention to the content of Pastor Bob's messages, it was very apparent he was a dispensationalist.

In short, his belief was that the church replaced Israel as the *apple of God's eye* and no longer had the status of being the *chosen people*. This belief, which is commonly known as *replacement theology*, did not match up with what I had read in scripture, especially in the book of Romans. I also found the theology of Calvary Chapel to be disturbing and somewhat anti-Semitic.

Cyndi was faithful in attending the Messianic synagogue. On several occasions she graciously offered invitations to attend with her. The theology of Calvary Chapel, along with Cyndi's invitations, made me very curious about attending her Messianic synagogue. Several weeks later, I finally met with the Messianic rabbi over breakfast and made the decision to at least give the synagogue a try.

I asked Miranda to accompany me, to which she begrudgingly agreed. I was grateful for her willingness to participate in a Messianic Jewish service that focused on worshiping Christ. Being a Cajun from Southwest Louisiana, she had very little exposure to Judaism, except for what I had shared with her. She also felt very comfortable at the other church, Calvary Chapel, and could not understand or relate to my decision.

I had been so thankful to receive salvation while at Calvary Chapel in 1997. However, in 2001, I felt it was time for me to come full circle and return to my Jewish beginnings. Only this time, I did not reject Jesus's invitation to accept him as my Lord, redeemer, king, and hopefully, my healer.

Miranda and I felt very welcome there. It wasn't long before I was part of a group of men who delivered mini-teachings prior to the rabbi's preaching. Additionally, I played percussion on the worship team. After several years of attending, Miranda and I were invited to be on the leadership team.

Whenever a Christian healer was in town, I went to be healed of my PKD, fully believing that my healing was inevitable. On one occasion, we had a powerful *man of God* come to our synagogue to lead worship and minister to the congregation. While singing *in the Spirit*, the man announced, "God wants to heal a man who has sick kidneys!" The rabbi and I exchanged intense eye contact, and I raised my hands to the heavens to receive my healing.

In spite of my faith in God's miraculous power, my kidney function continued to worsen, which was as puzzling as it was unsettling. *Why won't God heal me?* That thought occupied my mind for so many restless nights, which eventually turned into years.

My marriage continued to falter. There were times when I would put my arm around her shoulders when we prayed, and she would shrug it off in front of others. When we were at home, I would move close to her, but she made it very clear that I was to stay on my side of the bed. Miranda wanted nothing to do with cuddling while we watched television together. Furthermore, she wanted to return to Calvary Chapel. I could not fault her for wanting to leave the synagogue.

At that time, Miranda was receiving counseling and discipleship with a very gifted woman in the congregation. They would meet on a weekly basis to work on spiritual issues, as well as marital ones. I never asked Miranda about the content of their discussions, nor did I notice any palpable changes in our relationship. I prayed that any spiritual growth she experienced might translate into changes that would bring us closer. My hope was that, through her spiritual counseling, my feelings of rejection, inadequacy, and resentment would be reduced.

The rabbi and his wife were incredibly controlling over the personal lives of the congregation. They would often admonish everyone for making decisions, such as the purchasing of a home, moving to a nearby town, or determining how they spent their money. There was one instance when I even contacted churches and synagogues in an effort to teach workshops and classes.

After I mentioned this to the rabbi, he looked hurt and angry as he asked, "Are you informing me or asking me?"

I responded by saying, "I didn't know that I needed your permission to further my career."

Without saying another word, he simply got up and left the room.

I found out that a synagogue was about to be planted in the area of Scottsdale, Arizona. I sent an e-mail via the synagogue's website regarding the possibility of speaking in a workshop to his congregation. The religious leader returned my e-mail, and we had traded phone numbers. We had many productive discussions about working together with the start-up.

Miranda and I prayed diligently about his proposal. Soon afterward, both of us had dreams confirming that this was definitely part of God's plan. We were in agreement that it was our duty to help in this righteous endeavor.

I was so excited about the opportunity that I spoke about it with our rabbi and his wife. However, instead of sharing in my joy about hearing from the Lord and getting more involved in ministry, they both became very upset. They resorted to using guilt and manipulation to keep us in their congregation. They even tried to push the idea that we were in *spiritual rebellion*.

We continued to pray about what we should do, but we still received confirmation to go forward with our plans. I decided that the best thing we could do was to meet the couple where they lived in San Antonio, Texas.

We spent three days in San Antonio with the couple. While there, we prayed, talked a great deal, and shared meals with them. I was told that he wanted me to head up the counseling ministry and be the second in command. That meant I would be preaching a good deal.

I was on cloud nine, because I loved teaching so much. While we were in San Antonio, I even led a workshop for many of the congregants there. I was pleased that the message I gave was well received.

Afterward, we flew out to vacation in Arizona. I was feeling so blessed that God would choose us to help spread His Word in the Phoenix area. As we drove around the city of Anthem, we found the most amazing community we had ever seen. What was truly unexpected was that we found a realtor who happened to be the sister of a girl I had gone to high school with in Brooklyn. We found a beautiful house and placed a bid that was quickly accepted, contingent upon our home in Florida selling.

We flew home to Coral Springs. Within days, we put our house on the market, and it sold in one day! How much more confirmation did we need to fully comprehend God's plans for our lives?

The most difficult task was to tell my dad of our relocation plans. We had always been very distant to each other. It took many years for our relationship to begin the healing process. Finally, during a Shabbat dinner on a Friday evening after my mother died, my dad and I repented for what we both had done to each other.

I wanted to talk to my dad before he retired to my living room to watch television and, eventually, fell asleep on my couch. I looked at him with tears in my eyes and uttered the words that I had needed to say for years. "Dad, I am so sorry for the disrespect I have shown you for so many years. My heart breaks for the way I mocked and made fun of you. Please, forgive me."

He thought I was kidding, until he saw the obvious and unforgettable look of true repentance. After studying me for a moment, he made his own confession. "I was always jealous of you."

I got up from my chair and invited my dad to do the same. Although we hugged tightly for only a few seconds, those moments were extremely cleansing for me. The miraculous change of heart I had was made possible because of inviting Jesus into my heart. When I did that, I gave Him permission to change me from the inside out.

Our relationship was never the same after that special Shabbat dinner. We met weekly for lunch. My dad was so proud that his son, the doctor, bought him lunch every week.

Before our move, I took my dad out to dinner with my family. I informed him that we would be moving to Arizona to help plant a Messianic synagogue. Upon hearing the news, my dad immediately hung his head sadly. My heart broke for him, as well as myself. That poignant moment, though painful for both of us, was a testament for what the Lord had done in our hearts and lives as father and son.

Before leaving on our journey to Arizona, we met with the rabbi and his wife in an effort to leave with their blessings. On some level, I believed that we were successful. We were able to discuss and rehash many issues. When we were ready to leave, they wished us a safe trip and invited us to stay in touch.

On the way home, I received a phone call from the woman who had been counseling Miranda. We had a falling out, too, since she believed that we needed to remain obedient to the government set up in the synagogue. She was not in favor of our departure. I told her I would call her later to discuss matters.

When I called back later on, we spoke about how much our relationship had meant to both of us. She discussed how loyal she had been to me. She said, "I counseled your wife and stuck by you, even when Miranda said how you repulsed her!"

It felt as though I was punched in my kidneys. The emotional pain was so deep and unrelenting that Miranda knew something was very wrong. I have never been the sort of person who can disguise strong emotions. Everyone knows when something is very wrong with me.

She urged me to tell her what was said to me, and when I did, she denied ever making that statement to her *counselor*. "I *never* said that! I told her I was repulsed by sex!"

In an effort to remain in close partnership with Miranda, I chose to believe her. I did not feel that it would benefit either of us to fight while preparing for our spiritual pilgrimage to the desert. We continued on our trip without further confrontation about the topic.

Before our move, I contacted the Marriage and Family Therapy Board in Arizona and explained that I was moving to their state and had been licensed for the past twenty years. They assured me that I would have no problem getting licensed. I would be grandfathered in, since there were no licensing requirements in the state at that time. I had all of my information from the Florida licensing board sent to Arizona in order to prepare in advance.

We loaded up our truck and began our 2,400-mile journey to the *promised land*. We made the trip without any incident, until we arrived in Tucson. After having lunch, we came out to the parking lot, which was completely filled with cars. Miranda screamed upon seeing that her brand-new Ford Expedition had a completely shattered window on the front passenger side. I ran to her vehicle and quickly noticed that both of our laptops, my new camera with many attachments, DVD player, and other possessions had been stolen.

My laptop had all of our banking information on it, and my camera had new shots I had taken of my father. I ran around the parking lot hoping to find the thieves. I was shaking with rage for being so violated.

After contacting my bank, we called the police department. An officer came to write up a report, as well as direct us to where we could get Miranda's window replaced. I could not help but think that our former rabbi was right and we were being punished for our rebellion. After praying for our family, my doubts changed rapidly as a peace overcame me.

"This is just a test, another trial that the Lord has allowed to toughen us for ministry. Let's not have the devil rob us of our joy!"

Despite my children's fears, we were in agreement and started the last leg of our journey. We arrived in our new home in Anthem in early September 2004. I was extremely excited for the blessings and opportunity of being able to be a part of a ministry. However, I felt very unsettled with my career. I had this nagging sense of dread regarding my application for licensure, which proved to be spot-on. I had not heard from the licensure board and did not believe that we would remain in Arizona for very long.

I finally received a letter denying my application, and it stated that my academic background did not meet their criteria for licensure. I appealed this decision, citing the fact that I had earned my degree in 1981 and had had a license in good standing from the State of Florida since 1986. After spending four months waiting and praying for my license, which I did not receive, I had to find a way to earn a living.

I applied for several positions, including a position with a large mental health organization called ValueOptions, and was granted an interview. I had finally landed a job making one-third of what I had earned in Florida and was quickly running through our savings from the sale of our house in Florida.

My experience with ValueOptions was both a challenge and a nightmare. I had been in private practice since 1986 and had no experience working within a large mental health system. Working in the unfamiliar city of Phoenix only made my challenge all the more grueling.

To make matters worse, my immediate supervisor was obviously threatened by my advanced education and my status as being internationally published. Every chance she got, she undermined my authority to the team I supervised. She routinely chastised me in full view of my team. She was not only an extremely poor manager but had mental health issues of her own.

After several months assisting our fledgling synagogue, Miranda and I decided to find another church. Our expectations turned out to be unrealistic as this couple's theology did not match ours. We felt it best to leave and attend another church in town.

We finally found a new church home, where I played bass guitar and percussion in our church. We also made many new friends. During this time, my stomach became distended, a sign that my kidneys and liver were swollen with cysts, yet I did not see a nephrologist during our time in Arizona.

We stayed in Anthem for two and a half years; however, we took a financial bath. When our home ballooned in value, we took a home equity line of credit and bought another home as an investment. Meanwhile, we had gone through all of our savings, which were in excess of $50,000, and were losing money every month we were there.

One day, while watching the HDTV channel on television, there was a contest to win a home in the Lake Lure area in North Carolina. It was a gorgeous home set in an idyllic setting in the mountains. In unison, all of the family said, "If we win this house, we're moving!"

I mentioned that perhaps we didn't need to win a high-odds contest in order to relocate to North Carolina. I immediately went online and looked up the address and telephone number of the Marriage and Family Therapy Board. I called them in the morning and informed them that I was currently licensed as an MFT in Florida and had been so since 1986. I was informed that the state had reciprocity with other states and all I needed to do was have the Florida board send them all of my information. I called the Florida board and began the process of seeking a North Carolina license.

Within one month, I received a letter from the North Carolina MFT Board. I was told that all I needed to do to obtain a license was to pass a national certification exam, which I was told was incredibly challenging. I spent each day deep in prayer, petitioning the Lord for His favor. I clearly heard the Lord tell me that I would get my license.

To be very honest, while I wanted and needed to move to a state where I can once again resume a private practice, at this point I did not trust the Lord. After all, he gave me every sign to move to Arizona to assist in creating a Jewish ministry. However, in the process, I had lost a great deal of money, which in all likelihood I would never regain.

I responded, "Lord, you know I need to move out of this desert, but I am scared to trust you. Besides, so many things have to happen in order for me to be able to move."

His response was to assure me that He would take care of all of the details. I must admit to having had this same conversation countless times, and each time, I received the same response.

I studied with intensity and resolve as I did not take passing this test for granted. On the day of the test, I took time to pray before going into the building, as well as before beginning the test. "Lord, guide my every response. I need to pass this test."

Within weeks, I learned that I did in fact pass the test, and my North Carolina license arrived in the mail the next month. The first thing we needed to do was to find a buyer or renter for our home. Next, we had to secure a temporary job in North Carolina so that I could be able to support my family until I could build a practice and qualify for a mortgage.

Just as the Lord had said he would, He took care of all the details. In late December 2005, we loaded up a truck, car carrier, and Miranda's Expedition and made our way to Huntersville, North Carolina. There, my sister Lori and her family were waiting for us. I could not believe how faithful God was and praised Him all the way to Huntersville. I was reminded of Jesus's words in John 20:29: "Blessed are those who have not seen and yet have believed."

I would like to say that Jesus was talking about a man such as me, but quite frankly, I was totally scared. I moved to Arizona based on my firm belief that it was part of His plans and purposes for my life. I had left behind my private practice, friends, and family and spent my way through $50,000.

Once again, I was moving my family for a job that paid me $20,000 less than what I earned in Phoenix. Once again, I had to place my faith in my Creator. I held on to my belief that while God cultivates faith through trials, ultimately His plans were not to harm me. Instead, they allowed me to grow more into the likeness of His Son. Faith is not only a gift, it is a choice. I chose to trust Him, and once again, I had my license to resume my practice as a marriage and family therapist.

Chapter 23

We drove the long distance to North Carolina without any problems or incidences. Finally, we arrived at my sister's house on New Year's Eve. We were saddened to leave our dream home in Anthem and the group of close friends we had made while living there; however, we were nonetheless excited about starting anew in Huntersville.

Our new home was but a few blocks from my sister's home, but we did not see it until the following day. At that moment, we were content to celebrate with my sister and her family and friends.

My new job was a nightmare for me. I was on call from Friday evening until midnight on Sunday. I was responsible for doing home visits to people who were experiencing mental health emergencies. Unfortunately, I had no prior knowledge of who the person was or what issues they were having. It made it very difficult because I never knew what to expect. This became even more frightening when I stopped to wonder if they were crackheads who were prone to violence and had weapons in their homes.

Within two weeks, I was very motivated to get my practice going, so I rented space from a local psychologist in nearby Davidson. After only two months, everything was going so well that I was able to quit my job and get back into private practice on a full-time basis. I felt on top of the world and thanked God daily for his provision.

Meanwhile, my kidney continued to worsen, and my stomach became more distended each year. Physical intimacy became even less frequent. To make matters even worse, I was even experiencing *erectile dysfunction*, probably from the combination of kidney failure and feeling rejected by Miranda.

Due to Miranda's apparent discomfort with sex, whenever she felt it was time to fulfill my needs, she used the code phrase, "Do you want to have a wine night?" We would often use wine as a method to relax and create an amorous mood. Miranda had admitted that she could not be intimate without being inebriated.

One night I approached her by using our code phrase, and for some reason, on this night she impulsively voiced a sentiment that cut deeply to my heart. "Let's get it over with!"

I refused to be treated as if having sex with me was some arduous chore. That made her feel guilty, and so she insisted that we follow through with my plan. The result was a loud and belligerent argument.

This pattern had repeated itself on a number of occasions, with similar results. There were times that I was just not up to arguing, so I swallowed my pride. I would agree to making love. Unfortunately, I could not perform, despite utilizing Viagra, Cialis, or Levitra.

We grew more and more distant, largely due to the complete lack of physical intimacy. We developed a pattern where we both began to feel very inadequate. Miranda often stated that she hated the way she looked. She was not happy about her body image, as she was about forty pounds overweight. In addition, her breasts had shrunk due to breastfeeding both of our children. Our marriage was a mess!

At one period in 2007, I was completely depressed and feeling very hopeless. I begged her to go to marriage counseling with me. Unlike most women who have to drag their husbands into marriage counseling, my wife refused to go with me, citing that she had *too much on her plate*. I was desperate to improve our relationship and pleaded with her on several additional occasions. Each time was met with the same response. "Absolutely not!"

* * * * *

While driving to Louisiana for Thanksgiving in 2008, I received a phone call from my family physician's office. "Dr. Rifkin, this is Sondra from Dr. Panuski's office. Do you have a moment?"

My heart began beating wildly. "Well, I'm on my way to Louisiana, so I don't have that much time. Is there something wrong?" I was told that my PSA test results had come back from the lab, and therefore, I needed to see a urologist as soon as possible. Before hanging up, the nurse said that she would set up an appointment with Dr. Polsky during his earliest opening after Thanksgiving.

I silently began to fret, recalling that my father had prostate cancer and had underwent the complete removal of his prostate gland. As a result of the surgery, it rendered him hopelessly impotent and incontinent. I did not tell anyone in my family because I did not want to burden them during this festive holiday. I also could not talk about my fears. I began to pray fervently and sought God's mercy and grace.

In Hebrews 4:16, scripture says, "Let us, therefore [because of what Christ did on the cross], come boldly to the throne of grace that we may obtain mercy and find grace to help in time of need." This was my time of need.

Suddenly, I heard a soft voice clearly say to me, "You will get the news that you didn't want to hear, but not the news you were afraid to hear." I found enough comfort in what I heard to quell the anxiety welling up within me.

I had a relatively fun time in Louisiana visiting with Miranda's family. However, the sixteen-hour ride home allowed me a tremendous amount of time to think about the reality of my situation. Once again, I began to worry about the health issues that I might have to face.

When we arrived home, I shared the news that I had to see a urologist and would more than likely need to be biopsied. While I thought I came across as being very worried, Miranda didn't seem ruffled or worried by my news. This might have been due to her perception of me as being calm, brave, and a man of deep faith. Miranda was a chronic worrier, and there were times I chose not to share my worries or concerns so I could shield her from them. I also did not want to process or absorb her anxiety. Although I tried not to show it, I was frightened since prostate cancer is the second leading cause of death of men, only behind lung cancer.

After I arrived at Dr. Polsky's office, he introduced himself and began his consultation. He discussed my elevated PSA score with me and asked about my parents' health history. When I mentioned my father's bout of prostate cancer, my doctor promptly did a rectal exam. He said that he felt a nodule, which definitely needed to be biopsied.

We scheduled the biopsy for the next week. He promised that his office would call me as soon as the biopsy results had returned. Out of professional courtesy, he gave me his cell phone number. He told me that I could contact him directly should I have any questions or problems.

Two weeks later, my cell phone rang, and Dr. Polsky's name appeared on my caller ID. Immediately, I thought, "Oh my God, this can't be good. He is personally calling me." I felt as though all of my energy had been drained from my body and soul. I answered my phone.

Dr. Polsky said, "Jeff, this is Dr. Polsky. You will want to sit down. I have your biopsy results."

Tears began trickling down my cheeks and onto my shirt.

"This is not the news you wanted to hear. But it's not the news you were afraid to hear."

My heart stopped. I grew impatient. "What?"

"Jeff, you have prostate cancer. However, if you were to have prostate cancer, this is the type you want."

He went on to explain that it was a nonaggressive type that was not life-threatening. I could even elect to have nothing done. I tried my best to explain that the Lord had told me the exact same thing, word for word. However, since he was not a believer, my sacred experience fell upon deaf ears.

I called Miranda. "Honey, I have good news! The biopsy came back, and I have a nonlethal form of prostate cancer."

Miranda was understandably confused. "Wait, you have prostate cancer and this is good news?"

Once I explained my entire conversation with Dr. Polsky, her confusion quickly turned into relief. Before ending our call, Miranda asked for clarification.

"By the sound of your voice, you are relieved. That must mean that you were worried, right?" she asked.

I confessed to her that I was indeed worried but that I did not want her to do so needlessly. "I was not going to share my concerns until I really knew there was something to worry about."

Miranda was satisfied with my explanation.

I met with Dr. Polsky to discuss treatment options. He presented several choices, including an expensive new therapy that my insurance would not cover. Another was to have an injection that would immediately bring my PSA down to zero but would permanently take away my libido. Finally, I could also have brachytherapy, where radiated seeds were implanted into my prostate gland.

I shared these options with Miranda, and she promptly thought that I should opt for the injection. She explained her reason for choosing it was that the injection would *get rid of the cancer completely*. I could not help but think that she had her own agenda for making that suggestion. In the end, I opted out of the injection and chose to have brachytherapy instead.

The surgery was scheduled for Monday, April 7. I had to report to Lake Norman Hospital at 5:30 a.m. My cousin Corky, who is two years older than me, volunteered to accompany me.

Since Miranda was not a morning person, she said that as long as Corky was going with me, she would stay home. While it would have been comforting to have her there with me, I had gotten used to her physical and emotional absence from my life.

It was a painful two-day recovery after the ordeal. However, instead of focusing on the pain, I felt grateful to just be alive and not maimed by intrusive surgery. I was given pain medication, as well as one to help reduce the size of my enlarged prostate.

After taking the prostate medication for several days, I was visiting with neighbors when I suddenly became very sweaty and dizzy. Without any warning, I passed out while sitting at their kitchen table. As everyone hovered over me, I was told that I had been unconscious for at least two minutes.

Despite my protests, the paramedics were called. My children were very frightened, especially when the ambulance arrived within minutes. My vitals were taken, and I was given fluids intravenously. They found that my blood pressure was 70/30, which was dangerously low. I was taken by ambulance to the local hospital, which was four miles away.

Miranda arrived at the emergency room. She called my sister Lori, who arrived shortly later. When I was discharged late that night, I was told that I had fainted from extreme dehydration. This occurred as a result of taking my medication without drinking enough fluids.

On the way home, Miranda informed me that she was extremely embarrassed that she had been asked if she were my daughter. I could not help but think how shallow and self-centered her concerns were. However, I was too tired to offer any response and just pretended to ignore what she said.

The next day, I reflected on the discussion we had about my hospital visit. It left me more depressed than I had ever been in my life, which worsened when Miranda dropped a bomb on me.

"If your kidney or prostate conditions worsen, I will not be able to take care of you. I will have to take the kids and move back to Louisiana."

To top it all off, she chose the most inappropriate time to tell me, which was while I was driving us home from the pharmacy after picking up several refills of my hypertensive medications.

I became very angry and shouted back at her, "You would leave me here to fend for myself?"

"I would have no choice. I don't want to take care of an elderly, sick husband. And I would have no way of supporting you and the kids."

I knew at that moment that I could never count on Miranda to be there for me, even in my greatest time of need. I know this sounds implausible, but on many levels, I had no one to blame but myself. Despite working on my co-dependency, I was still working harder on our marriage than Miranda was. She had been unable to handle any stress from the moment I met her. Instead of insisting that she carry her own load, I found it easier to handle most of the stress by myself.

Although it made me very strong, it caused me to feel completely alone in our relationship. In fact, I often felt that she was my third child in our home. By that time, I felt more alone than ever. I even began to plan on what I would do when the inevitable occurred, when my kidneys would eventually fail.

I pondered about moving to Japan, where Cyndi lived. I knew that she would never abandon me in my time of need. However, I did not want to be a burden on her and her husband, Benjamin. So, I began to plan my own suicide. I thought that the best way was to overdose on Xanax.

I had been taking Xanax in an effort to ease the severe muscle cramping I experienced nightly. I was told by my nephrologist that the muscle cramping was one of the symptoms associated with PKD, because my electrolytes were extremely out of balance.

* * * * *

During this same time, my son, Matthew, who at this time was twelve years old, had two visitations from the Holy Spirit while he was praying in his room. Since Matthew was a little boy, I had always prayed the Aaronic blessing over him.

The Aaronic blessing is found in Numbers 6:24. As I tucked him in nightly, we always finished with my hand placed upon the crown of his head as I recited this blessing upon him. I would recite it in Hebrew first. Then I would say it in English.

> Y'-va-re-ch'-cha A-do-nai v'-yish-m'-re-cha;
> ya-er A-do-nai pa-nav a-le-cha vi-chu-ne-ka;
> yi-sa A-do-nai pa-nav a-le-cha.
> v'ya-sem-l'-cha sha-lom.

The English translation:

> May the Lord bless you and keep you.
> May the Lord make his face to shine upon you,
> and be gracious unto you:
> And may the Lord lift up His countenance upon you,
> and give you His peace.

One morning, Matthew told me that he had a third visit from the Holy Spirit and sensed that it was time for him to be water baptized. As he told me of is experience, his eyes welled up. It was easy to see that he was deeply moved by his spiritual experiences. He then asked me to arrange his baptism at the church we were attending, Grace Covenant Church, where they perform water baptisms monthly. I was able to schedule Matthew's baptism for the following month.

Matthew has always had a tendency to be a little shy, so he asked if I would speak for him before his baptism. He would be experiencing a *mikvah*, which is the water baptism that was historically done in the Jordan River during Jesus's time on earth.

I was so honored to stand beside my son during this important time in his life. I treasure the memory of sharing his testimony and pronouncing my blessings upon him as a part of the ceremony. I did not know what I was going to say, yet I knew that it would include the Aaronic blessing, which had played such a prominent role in Matthew's spiritual growth. I knew I would not exclude it in this most important step of his life.

* * * * *

In August 2008, I received a call from Rosetta, who had moved into my dad's condo, along with her husband, Kevin. They were staying there in order to care for him. My dad was eighty-three years old at the time, and his health and his ability to care for himself were failing.

Rosetta told me that something very serious was occurring to him and that she was very concerned. He was unable to sit up straight without falling over and was unable to stand without falling. She had taken Dad to his family physician, who had performed a battery of tests. Unfortunately, the results were conclusive and did not convey any good news. All of my dad's organs were shutting down, and he would not live much longer.

After hearing the news, sadness and grief overtook me. I had difficulty functioning without sobbing. While my dad and I had never been close, the years since my mother's death had changed all of that.

Miranda was confused with my reaction to my father's imminent death. She commented, "I don't understand why you're so sad. It's not like you were ever really close to him."

I tried my best to explain that he was the only parent I had left. I received no comfort or understanding from her, whatsoever. Lori and I planned on driving to Florida after we heard that my dad had been placed in hospice care. The morning of the day we had planned on leaving, I was meeting with one of my pastors. As we were ready to go, I looked down at my phone when I received a call from Lori. Immediately I asked to be excused.

Lori was sobbing as she labored to share a painful message. "Jeff, Dad's gone. I just got the call from Rosetta. We need to leave immediately!"

I was stunned and began crying into my hands. My only thought was, *Dad, I love you.* When I felt composed enough to respond, the only words I could say was, "Lori, my heart is broken."

"I know. I know," was all that she could say.

We both cried.

When I returned to my meeting, I explained to the pastor the news that I had just received. He graciously offered me several tissues to wipe my eyes and nose.

"We will pray for you and your family, Jeff."

I drove to Lori's home, and we left immediately for Florida, but not before informing Miranda of my father's death. I felt some comfort when she said, "I'm sorry, Jeff. I can't imagine what it must be like to no longer have parents."

After driving for twelve hours, we arrived at my dad's condo in Boca Raton. All of the preparation for his funeral had already been made. Both of my sisters, their husbands, children, and grandchildren were present. They asked if I wanted to preside over the funeral service as I had done when Mom died; however, I declined.

While I was in prayer late that night, the Holy Spirit told me to have the rabbi read Psalm 90 as part of the service at the cemetery. I opened my Bible and began to read.

Lord, you have been our dwelling place in all generations. Before the mountains were brought forth, or ever you had formed the earth and the world. Even from everlasting to everlasting, you are God.

You turn man to destruction and say 'Return, O children of men.' For a thousand years in your sight are like yesterday when it is past. And like a watch in the night, you carry them away like a flood. They are like a sleep. In the morning, they are like grass which grows up. In the evening, it is cut down and withers.

For we have been consumed by your anger, and by your wrath we are terrified. You have set our iniquities before you, our secret sins in the light of your countenance.

For all our days have passed away in your wrath. We finish our years like a sigh. The days of our lives are 70 years; and if by reason of strength they are 80 years. Yet, their boast is only labor and sorrow; for it is soon cut off, and we fly away.

Who knows the power of your anger? For as the fear of you, so is your wrath. So, teach us to number our days, that we may gain a heart of wisdom. Return, O Lord! How long? And have compassion on your servants. Oh, satisfy us early with your mercy, that we may rejoice and be glad all our days!

Make us glad according to the days in which you have afflicted us. The years in which we have seen evil, let your work appear to your servants, and your glory to their children. And the beauty of the Lord, our God, be upon us. And establish the work of our hands for us. Yes, establish the work of our hands.

After reading the psalm written by Moses, I studied the meaning and intentions behind the words. I recognized that life is very short due to the fallen nature of man. I also realized that even if we are granted eighty years of life, those years will contain sorrow and labor.

God's anger at us is due to the way we squander the time allotted to us. We are admonished to fear our accountability to God for all of our actions in this life. Therefore, we are to seek the Lord for his direction for our lives that he might establish all of the plans and purposes he has for us.

This psalm affected me so deeply. I had been wasting my time worrying as I tried to get Miranda to love me. However, her actions were between her and God. I needed to use my time far more wisely. I also need to make God, my children, and the work he established for me as my top priorities.

When the limo arrived for us the following morning, my sisters and I tearfully entered and rode to the cemetery. As the rabbi met us at the limo, I quickly introduced myself as my father's son. He asked me if I had any requests, and I informed him that I would like him to read from Psalm 90.

"Most people want me to read Psalm 23. This is the first time anyone has ever asked me to read Psalm 90."

The day was already sweltering since it was 95 degrees with very high humidity. Everyone was sweating profusely as I smiled and took my seat along the graveside next to Lori. After greeting all of the mourners, the rabbi shared some stories about my father to everyone in attendance. He announced that I had requested the reading of Psalm 90 and began to read. Upon hearing his words, my sisters and I sobbed softly. It was so difficult to see our dad's casket next to my mom's grave site.

As the words penetrated my heart, something very odd, yet completely joyous happened. Suddenly, I felt a cool wind blow over my face and body. Considering the sweltering heat and humidity, that seemed extraordinary. In that moment, I sensed the presence of the Holy Spirit and began to praise the Lord with extreme gratitude and adoration. It was one of the most memorable events I have ever experienced.

The presence of my daughter Rachel at the funeral greatly added to my joy since I rarely saw her. I was greatly appreciative for the comfort she provided to me. Scripture says that *tears may endure for a night, but joy comes in the morning.* That inexplicable joy resonated throughout my body, soul, and spirit. It was a gift from God, the Creator of everything that has breath. I wanted to hold it for as long as I could. The night before I left, the Holy Spirit instructed me to share my experience with the congregation for Matthew's upcoming baptism.

As I left Florida, I was eager to see my family. I was so anxious to see London and Matthew. Upon arriving, I ran to hold them when Miranda and the kids met me at the baggage claim. In my grief, I had an overwhelming need to hold them and show them how much I love them.

It did not take long before Miranda began telling me about all that she had endured while I was in Florida. Although I understood how being a single parent can be very challenging, it was obvious that Miranda had no concern for my well-being. Her focus was entirely on the challenges she had faced while I was away and, therefore, provided absolutely no comfort for me.

Once again, I felt as though she was completely apathetic to my emotional needs. I reminded her that I had just buried my father, which started an argument with her. I mentioned how nice it would have been for her to comfort me, instead of asking that I empathize with her trials over the past four days. My words fell on deaf ears, and nothing changed her attitude toward me.

I was so sensitive to my perceptions and feelings of rejection that I resented Miranda and her needs. I retreated more from her, as I realized that I was not going to have my needs met. Instead of trying to fight with her about it anymore, I did my own thing.

In order to stay away from Miranda as much as possible, I took on additional patients. I even asked to teach more classes at Grace

Covenant Church. I was only able to fill a portion of the void in my heart as I spent more time with my kids.

* * * * *

When the Sunday of my son's baptism arrived, Matthew was very excited and nervous. He tends to worry a lot and needed reassurance that he wouldn't slip into the baptism pool. He also wanted to make sure that I knew exactly what I was going to say. Matthew felt much better after we spent time praying together. We were both ready.

My wife reminded me not to bore the congregation with my *story*, and admonished me to keep it short. When it was time for my son and me to make our way up to the pool overlooking the sanctuary, we were both excited, and I told him how proud I was of his decision.

He smiled and said, "Thanks, Dad."

As Matthew cautiously stepped into the pool of water, I told the congregation that it was Matthew's decision to be baptized. I related that it came as the result of his experiences of being visited by the Holy Spirit on three separate occasions. I also related the story of my dad's recent death.

In addition, I expressed how the Holy Spirit had led me to request Psalm 90 to be read at the funeral, as well as share it at my son's baptism, since both events relate to *death*. I told them that water baptism signifies joining Jesus in death, while coming out of the water represents his resurrection. I ended it by praying the Aaronic blessing over Matthew in both Hebrew and English.

Matthew was so proud of himself when he was submerged with Jesus in his watery grave. A smile spread across his face as he came up out of the water, refreshed and cleansed of his sins. Even today, he still talks about his finest moment.

Chapter 24

The following years were truly more of the same. Miranda and I both felt inadequate and rejected. In 2009, our situation was compounded when my kidney function was measured at 3.75. I was told that I would have to go on dialysis should it reach 5.0, which frightened me.

My belly continued to distend, and I aged significantly from the toxicity that ran through my body. Unlike my physical health, my practice was vibrant and strong. Although we did not lead an extravagant lifestyle, we were able to pay our bills and eat well.

In 2010, while my kidneys and marriage continued to fail, I approached Miranda and asked if we could at least be affectionate with each other. What was her response?

"I am not that needy," she told me.

I became insulted and enraged because she insinuated that wanting affection meant that I was emotionally needy. In an effort to find another way of coping with my empty, seemingly loveless marriage, I began to write my memoirs.

Miranda and I shared similar interests and enjoyed many years of fun and laughter. We both enjoyed vacationing, designing our homes, television, hiking, and much more. It was unfortunate that the last few years were extremely painful for both of us; more importantly, they were very painful to London and Matthew.

The biggest problem I faced was when she admitted that she had married me to avoid moving back to Louisiana. At that moment, I saw her in a very different light and felt used. Suddenly, the years of physical and emotional rejection began to pile up. I resented her so much that it became very evident.

I even joined Internet social media sites and made many female friends who shared my conservative political views. When I felt most alone, I would make a flirtatious remark to one or several of those women. To my surprise, many responded back. I realized that I was acting in ways which belied my faith. My guilt did trouble me, but I found ways to justify my actions.

One day, a woman contacted me, unexpectedly. She had read on my profile that I was a therapist and decided to ask me for help. We exchanged e-mails to discuss her situation further. I even asked her if she would like me to call her so that we could actually talk about them. After several conversations with her, she began to send me inappropriate messages.

Although I had never been unfaithful to Miranda on any level previously, I continued to correspond with her. Our discussions met my needs for female attention. Once again, I felt like an attractive man.

Social media can be very useful in today's world, yet it can also be very tempting and addictive. Given my personal and marital challenges, I found that it was so easy to exchange messages with someone I did not know. I felt it was safe and harmless since I was hiding behind the anonymity of my computer screen.

Within days, I found that I was addicted to this behavior. On several occasions, I told this woman that I could no longer engage in this behavior. She would stop as requested, but after a few days, she would resume in contacting me. I asked myself on many occasions why I did not block or "unfriend" her. The truth was that sin always feels good for a period of time. I was also very aware of the fact that since Miranda refused to attend marriage counseling so that we could repair our marriage, I was hoping to get caught. Either we were going to address my years of unhappiness, frustration, and rejection, or we would terminate our marriage.

Feelings of euphoria filled my mind and soul as I continued to be emotionally connected to her. I knew that my actions were wrong, yet I felt so hopeless in my marriage that I found it extremely difficult to give it up. I convinced myself that getting caught was far better than continuing with the marital status quo. However, my actions of self-indulgence and reckless behavior were stupid, immature, and destructive.

One day, my pastor asked to meet with me. He told me that he had received a letter from a man who stated that I was involved in an Internet relationship with his wife. My heart sank, and anxiety consumed me. I denied this allegation but sensed that my pastor knew that I was lying.

This Internet affair went on for two months, until I finally confessed my behavior to Miranda. To make matters far worse, the woman contacted Miranda and told her that she was in love with me. She even requested that Miranda let me go so that she could divorce her husband and marry me.

Miranda was furious at me, but I could not blame her for her response to my betrayal. She was completely out of control and threw a chair and books at me. Her rage continued for several months. There were many times when she screamed at me so violently that I prayed that God would take my life and end this horrible existence.

Very cruel words were said during this time. Unfortunately, sometimes we were even in earshot of our children. Our children suffered severely from our discord. Matthew became very angry and depressed. London developed an eating disorder, in which she would only eat the same foods at each meal and exercised a great deal. She lost weight despite eating large amounts of healthy food.

One day while getting ready to leave for the airport with our kids to visit with family in Louisiana, she told me that she was done. She wanted a divorce. I felt crushed, yet not surprised.

While giving her an obligatory hug at the gate, she whispered that she loved me. Tears of repentance streamed down my face. When she returned, she agreed to try to right our marriage.

It was during that time my kidneys became much worse. I attribute my decline to the extreme amount of stress that my body and mind were under. My creatinine levels jumped above 5.0. As a result, I was referred to another nephrologist who was connected to the kidney transplant team at Carolinas Medical Center in Charlotte. We talked about dialysis, but I made it very clear that I wanted to wait as long as possible, citing the fact that I "felt fine."

I had lied to my physician. At times, I was feeling fatigued, confused, and disoriented. My leg cramps became so painful that I would cry from the tortuous pain, which often broke blood vessels in my calves. We decided to delay dialysis. I began to attend several PKD support groups in the Charlotte area. To compound the situation, Miranda's rage and pain were unrelenting.

One day, my pastor requested that I join him for breakfast. Within minutes of sitting at the table with him, I tearfully confessed my transgressions to him. We talked at length, and he asked many probing questions about our marital relationship. I was straightforward and held nothing back. He suggested that Miranda and I meet with him in an effort to save our marriage.

While on our way to the meeting with our pastor, we virulently argued about whether we should divorce. In our meeting, our pastor made it very clear that what I had done was foolish and reckless. However, as he directed his eyes toward Miranda, he went on to say that he was aware that we had serious marital problems long before my Internet affair had occurred.

Miranda looked at him and responded with a confession of her own. It not only shocked our pastor, but it also confirmed what I had known for many, many years.

"I just wanted to be left alone!" she shouted.

The pastor leaned forward in his chair and, with a very puzzled look, said, "Is that what you think marriage is about? Being left alone?"

Miranda remained silent. My heart began beating so rapidly that I was forced to take a few breaths in order to quell the anxiety which consumed my mind and body. I felt incredibly uncomfortable with her lack of response and instinctively felt a need to interrupt the intolerable silence. I turned to Miranda and told her how much I truly loved her. In fact, I had never loved any other woman as deeply. I took her limp hands into my own and begged for her forgiveness. She quietly accepted, and we left the Pastor's office without any words spoken between us.

* * * *

Several weeks later, Miranda realized that our problems were not going to get resolved on their own, and asked me to find us a marriage counselor. We desperately needed assistance to help us resolve our crisis. I found a woman who had a stellar reputation. We met with her on several occasions.

The most difficult crux of her counseling was to get Miranda to realize that our problems began long before my Internet foray. It was especially true, given the fact that I had never before been unfaithful to her and was therefore not a womanizer.

Miranda finally admitted that she had been angry at me for years, in fact for the past thirteen years. When asked what I had done to merit her anger, she said that I wanted sex even when she did not. We worked on this issue only a few visits when Miranda decided after that "she does not understand what I am going through." Miranda dropped out of counseling; therefore, going alone was pointless.

During this period of difficulty, we had gone to Grace Covenant Church several times. I suggested that we see a Christian counselor who worked out of our church. Miranda went a few times, by herself. Fortunately, things were quieting down between us. I was very grateful for the truce. We actually shared some very nice moments where we held hands, hugged, and kissed. Miranda admitted to me that she was actually forcing herself to be affectionate with me, hoping that it would distract her from the feelings of betrayal and low self-esteem; however, it did little good.

The therapist asked to see me. I went twice and shared my pain and shame that I felt for not only betraying Miranda but also sinning against a holy God. I knew that scripture tells us that if we are quick to repent, God is quick to forgive. I needed to forgive myself; however, that was usually a long process and not a simple event.

Miranda felt so embarrassed by her talk with our pastor and felt so self-conscious that she began to attend our local church. I asked to join her so that we could worship together, and she agreed.

Within weeks, I approached the worship director, and asked if I could join the worship team as a percussionist. I had played on three other worship teams, and this band played Christian rock, which absolutely thrilled me. I was scheduled to play one or two times a month and quickly made friends with other members of the team.

A few weeks later, Miranda asked if I would be willing to join her at her next session so that we could begin marriage counseling. I jumped at the opportunity to hopefully repair our marriage. I even prayed day and night that God would give me the strength and power to forgive myself.

Before that period in our marriage, I had taken great pride in always being faithful to my wife. I had often judged other men for straying. I recognized that I was greatly humbled and considered myself no better than any other man. I was broken and clung to the feet of the cross, realizing that I truly brought absolutely nothing to any relationship, except Christ crucified in me.

During our conjoint session, the therapist acknowledged that Miranda's trust had been broken by my actions. She asked me if I had always trusted Miranda. I admitted that I hadn't since Miranda had confessed as to why she had married me. Whenever the therapist directed her questions to my wife, Miranda attempted to divert her focus away from her questions. Miranda's efforts only deepened the therapist's resolve to understand the truth of our situation.

Miranda was obviously very uncomfortable. Frequently, she would glance at me as if she wanted me to force the therapist to stop her line of questioning. I looked away and allowed her to struggle with the truth.

Suddenly, Miranda began screaming and rose from her chair, cussed at me, and told me she wanted a divorce. She stormed out of the office, slamming the therapist's door as she left. I sat in my chair, embarrassed, uncomfortable, yet feeling vindicated. The truth had been shared with another person.

Although I was not off the hook for my sinful behavior, the therapist told me that I should leave the marital home, given the state of my marital dysfunction and my declining health. I prayed for many weeks and cried out to God to help save my marriage. I did not want another divorce, as I knew what my divorce from Alice had done to Cyndi and Rachel.

Near the end of 2010, my PKD symptoms had intensified. The fatigue and nausea were debilitating, to the point that I could no longer play in the worship band. This was a very difficult decision for me to make, as I found it difficult to admit how truly ill I felt. It did not make it any easier of a decision since my participation in the band was one of the few joys I looked forward to at the time.

At this time, I was told by my nephrologist that I needed to start dialysis soon as my creatinine level was above 8. My avoidance and denial about my PKD had vanished, and I had decided that when I was to start dialysis, I would elect to do peritoneal dialysis (PD) so that I could perform dialysis at home. This necessitated an operation to have a catheter placed into my abdomen, and my nephrologist wanted me to have it before the year ended as she was fearful that I was about "to crash." I learned that PD was the closest thing to having a kidney, and I could cleanse my system of my toxicity while in the comfort of my home. I went through a great deal of testing both at Carolinas Medical Center and Baptist Hospital at Wake Forest University to qualify for the deceased kidney transplant list. Outside of having PKD, all of the physicians I had seen at both hospitals told me that I was a perfect candidate for kidney transplantation. Before the year ended, I came home from the hospital with a new appendage coming out of my abdomen, which at this point made me look as though I were about to give birth to triplets.

CHAPTER 25

Peritoneal dialysis was first used in the 1920s and is considered the most popular method of home dialysis. The other option for home dialysis is hemodialysis, which uses thick gauge needles to facilitate the dialysis process. I had to undergo a two-week training in which I would learn how to use the home automated cycler. It is computer operated and would be set up by my nurse according to my nephrologist's specific instructions.

I also learned how to properly sterilize my hands before touching my catheter, as well as how to use surgical masks during important segments of my dialysis process. I was also instructed in how to spot the signs of infection, which included a fever, nausea, pain, and/or irritation around the catheter site.

As mentioned earlier, the reason I chose PD instead of onsite dialysis three to four days a week was that it had fewer side effects. These included vomiting, cramping, and weight gain. On the positive side, PD had fewer dietary restrictions than hemodialysis, although I thought my restrictions were severe. It was also needle-free and I could do my PD in the comfort of my own home, largely while I slept.

I could not have any dairy products, except cream cheese, sour cream, and cottage cheese. I was allowed one slice of pizza every two weeks. I could not have any legumes, nuts, chocolate, or any food products which were high in potassium and phosphorus, including avocados. I was limited to thirty-two ounces of fluid each day. That included all fluids, such as coffee, soup, water, ice, ice pops, etc. I was always very thirsty.

Inasmuch as my dialysis was scheduled for nine hours every night of the week, I began my dialysis at 7:00 p.m. and would wake up each morning at 5:00 a.m. I would get two bags of dialysate. One was placed on the cycler and the other on a nightstand. Before starting my PD, I had to weigh myself and take my blood pressure and temperature. Then I would record each figure in a book.

PD uses the thin peritoneal membrane, where the catheter is surgically implanted. The dialysate that flows into the catheter pulls the wastes and extra fluid from the blood into the peritoneal cavity, where it remains for two hours. Afterward, the dialysate and wastes are drained from the catheter into my toilet through a thin tube attached to the cycler. This entire process was repeated and lasted for a total of nine hours.

The most amazing thing about this challenging time was that London and Matthew became my major support team. Since my diet was so limited, London took it upon herself to cook for me each and every night. She studied the dietary sheets that I had brought home from the dialysis center's nutritionist. She diligently made sure that every ingredient had low levels of potassium and phosphorus, as well as high levels of protein. Not only did she offer to cook for me, she did it joyfully, which made it very special to me.

Matthew would sit in my bed with me, offering to get me whatever I needed or wanted. There were many nights where Matthew and I would pray together. He would often voice his fear that I would die before receiving a transplant.

I felt so badly for him. I reassured him repeatedly, but he would often cite statistics that he found on the Internet. He had found that approximately one-third of people in end-stage renal disease had died before ever receiving a transplant. I reminded him that most of these people had severe health complications, such as heart disease, diabetes, and uncontrolled blood pressure. I had none of those complicating conditions. He would hug and kiss me and even tell me that I was his best friend. My heart would often melt at his devotion to his "amigo primero."

During my PD process, Miranda usually chose to stay in another room and watch television. While I could not understand her complete lack of involvement in my treatment, I chose not to say anything. I did not want to create more stress between us. Quite frankly, I felt that she should not have to be coaxed into spending time with me during this trying process.

One evening while undergoing my dialysis, I felt an outpouring of love and appreciation for the devotion shown to me by Matthew. I hugged him and told him that I would be alone in my room each and every night if it were not for his dedication to me.

Several minutes later, Matthew said he was going downstairs for water. Soon after, Miranda stormed through the door with a huge scowl on her face. I asked her what was wrong.

"I was *very* comfortable downstairs!"

Matthew walked in behind her and looked hurt and embarrassed. I quickly surmised that Matthew had obviously said something to his mom, which prompted her to come upstairs.

"You don't need to stay if you don't want to. I'm used to you not being up here with me!"

Miranda plopped herself down in a chair, while Matthew took his usual spot in the bed next to me. There were no words spoken between any of us for over thirty minutes, when Miranda finally broke the silence.

"I'm going downstairs."

She quickly left the room. Once she left, I turned to Matthew and thanked him for his efforts to have his mom keep me company. I also assured him that it wasn't his responsibility to have his mother join me.

Tears filled his eyes as he said, "I'm sorry, Dad."

I held him and told him, "I am so fortunate to have you as my son."

* * * * *

I had sublet space for my own therapist practice in a large medical office for well over three years. One day, while in the lunchroom, I had mentioned to some of the nurses that I was waiting to receive a kidney transplant when a compatible one became available.

One of the nurses came forward and told me that she wanted to be tested as a possible donor since her mother had died while waiting for a lung transplant. I was dumbfounded at her statement. Once again, I was hopeful of the possibility that I could resume a normal life.

Jenny went through all of the testing. However, since I have blood type B and she has type A, she was not a match. The only option open to me was to participate in the kidney exchange program. She would have the opportunity to donate a kidney to someone with whom she matched, and I would therefore be entitled to receive a suitable kidney from a donor with my correct blood type.

When I told Miranda about Jenny's generosity, she was excited; however, she then expressed a great amount of guilt over her decision to not be tested as a possible donor. Her reasoning was that since each of our children had a 50 percent chance of inheriting my PKD gene, she wanted to be able to donate a kidney to one of them, if needed.

I sensed that she was either afraid of going through the painful surgical process, or she had already thought more about divorce. I knew that if any of my children developed PKD, they wouldn't need a transplant until they were in their fifties or sixties. By that time, Miranda would no longer be alive or too old to be a kidney donor.

Realizing her recalcitrance at being tested, I chose to not say anything to her. I saw no benefit at making her feel more guilty or under pressure to be my donor. It was not an easy task since I was aware that she had blood type O, which happens to be the universal donor.

I also chose to believe that she did not want to donate because she feared the pain of the surgery and subsequent recovery. Yet my heart ached at her decision to not be tested. It only served as confirmation that my survival was not more important than her own physical comfort or inconvenience.

Each morning when I drove to work, my car became my prayer closet. I always started out by praising the Lord for allowing me to live yet another day. Daily, I would thank him for all the gifts, talents, and provisions he had given me. I prayed for all of my loved ones and friends. Finally, I would turn my attention to my own needs. I prayed with great fervor for God to find me a kidney so that I could continue to live and be a father to London and Matthew. I would also pray that Jenny and I would find suitable kidney patients as quickly as possible.

After five months of waiting, I received a call from the transplant center that a kidney was found for me and that I would be transplanted within two months. I was ecstatic at the news. Unfortunately, it quickly turned into a huge disappointment when I was told that something had come up with one of the other patients and the transplant had been called off. However, I was still confident that God would provide the kidney I needed.

During that time, Miranda and I decided to go through the process of either doing a short sale or a deed in lieu of foreclosure on our home as we could no longer afford to pay the huge mortgage payment. Since our children attended a Christian prep school forty-five minutes south of where we lived, we decided to vacate our home and rent a home near the school.

It was a beautiful home that was owned by another Christian family. We waited to make our final decision until after our family prayed together for His guidance. Our moving date was scheduled for June 1, 2011.

* * * * *

Prior to moving, I met with my transplant surgeon to prepare for surgery since I developed an inguinal hernia from the PD. I told him the good news about Jenny, and he informed me that the kidney exchange program only happens about 20 percent of the time. I felt very hopeless at hearing this news.

It was obvious to the surgeon, as he put his arm around me and encouraged me not to give up. He also told me that I would be off of PD for six weeks and would have to have hemodialysis four days a week. We scheduled the surgery to repair the hernia during the second week in June 2011.

On the morning of my surgery, Miranda dropped me off at the hospital and drove off to find a parking spot. I waited for her in the waiting room; however, before she showed up, I was ushered into the pre-op center. There, I met with the anesthesiologists and had all my vitals taken.

The surgeon came in to visit, and he talked about the surgery and how the recovery "hurts like heck." Finally, he asked where my wife was. I told him that she was parking the car. He looked puzzled, as I had already been there for more than forty-five minutes. The surgeon informed me that I could stay overnight to recover and he could arrange that for me, if I wanted to.

I suspected that he was concerned that I might not get the care I needed, inasmuch as my wife was not with me. I looked around the area, but Miranda was not anywhere in sight.

He marked the hernia with a large X and told me that surgery would occur in the next fifteen minutes. I was taken into the operating room, given sedation, and later awakened in the recovery area. Finally, I saw Miranda.

I was allowed to leave for home within one hour. For the pain, I was given a bottle of Hydrocodone. The doctor had been correct in his warning, because it really did "hurt like heck."

We said very little to each other on the drive home. Within days, I began my hemodialysis. It was very unpleasant, as it was always freezing in the dialysis center. Typically, I became very anxious while I sat back in my chair for four hours each time.

To make matters worse, since it was more difficult upon the body than PD, I often would experience excruciating leg cramps. This necessitated a nurse to massage and stretch out my legs. I tried my best to be patient, knowing I had to endure this form of treatment for the next six weeks. I had very few outlets to help me cope with the ordeal.

Finally, I stepped down from the worship team. Despite the level of illness I experienced each day, I never missed a day from work, unless I had an appointment with physicians and/or hospitals.

Inasmuch as I was on dialysis, my prayer life took on a greater sense of urgency. While uncontrolled sobbing and pleading with God occurred each time I prayed, I now begged him through the veil of my tears to find a kidney for me since I did not know how long I could emotionally and physically hold on.

One such morning after crying out to God, I heard His still voice say to me, "I will find you a kidney. There will be a miracle involved so that all will know that I, the Lord your God, did this for you."

It was the most comforting words I had ever heard. However, not knowing if my mind had created these uplifting words, I would sob and plead with God each morning. I heard the same consistent response each and every time. I was actually starting to believe that God would do this for me, because He is a loving God, who promises to shower us with his grace and mercy in our time of need.

One evening, I shared my conversations with the Lord to my family. Miranda looked skeptical, but to be fair, I think most people would be skeptical if I shared a conversation I had with God. Both of my children became excited, especially London.

She said, "Dad, I know God will find you a kidney soon. Don't ask me how I know. I just know."

* * * * *

Through the local chapter of PKD, I had met many other PKD patients whose daily struggles with PKD were as difficult as mine, if not more. I had met the wife of a physician who had relocated to the Mayo Clinic in Jacksonville, Florida, while he waited for both a kidney and liver transplant.

Several weeks later, I had heard that a compatible kidney and liver had been found for him. Many of us prayed for his complete recovery. We were overjoyed to learn that his transplants were successful.

I also knew another physician with PKD who frequently gave referrals. Upon hearing this, I sent him an e-mail and asked if he would be interested in meeting me. He was very appreciative and jumped at the opportunity.

When we met for lunch, we shared "war stories." He also told me that a story had been written in the community newspaper about his need for a kidney transplant. Many responded with a desire to help. He received a kidney from a living donor, after which he also recovered quickly to return to his practice.

I was so inspired by his story, I decided to contact the same newspaper, requesting that they write a similar article about my own plight. To my surprise, they agreed to do it. Once again, I felt very hopeful for a successful outcome. Perhaps this would be my miracle, the one that the Lord had promised me.

The journalist came to my office and asked me all about my struggle with PKD. He wanted to know how if affected my life, both personally and professionally. He also asked to explain my family's history with PKD, as well.

One day, when I was driving home from work, I received a call from my sister Lori, who seemed confused.

"I didn't know your blood type was AB?"

"What are you talking about! My blood type is B!"

Lori went on to tell me that my story had come out and the writer had written the wrong blood type. I was aghast with disbelief. Of all the things that needed to be correct, it was my blood type. Not only was it incorrect, but AB was the most rare blood type. I was determined to call the newspaper the following morning and plead that they redo the story the following week.

Upon reaching the editor, he apologized for the error. However, the best he could do was make a small correction notation in the newspaper the following week. Once again, I felt defeated and depressed.

I was so puzzled. I was very angry, disappointed, and disillusioned. I had two more weeks of hemodialysis and obviously drowning in self-pity.

"Lord, why are you allowing this to happen to me? Why is it that other people I know are successful in getting their transplants, but not me!"

* * * *

It was the beginning of August, and I was told by Miranda that she and Matthew were driving to Louisiana to visit with Miranda's family for three and a half weeks. London had chosen to stay home, which I greatly welcomed. Not only was she terrific company, but her cooking kept me emotionally and physically sustained.

The night before Miranda was to leave, she came into our room and said, "I feel like a fraud." She looked nervous and distraught. "I am not in love with you and I am not attracted to you. I have only stayed with you for the sake of our children and I am thinking of a divorce."

I struggled to find my sense of psychological equilibrium, as I felt I was in an altered, semiconscious state. I can't recall what I said, but I do remember walking away and getting into bed to rest. By then, Miranda and I had been sleeping in separate bedrooms for many weeks as my estrangement from her became unbearable for me.

The next morning as I was leaving for work, Miranda came out of her bedroom and gave me a sisterly hug goodbye. I spent the hourlong drive in prayer, petitioning the Lord to protect my children from the same emotional pain and scarring that Cyndi and Rachel had suffered. I also asked Him to help me cope with the death of my marriage. I was acutely aware of the rage which began welling up inside me.

When I returned that evening, my rage could no longer be contained. I called Miranda, who was still on the road, and began screaming obscenities at her.

"We just moved into our home and signed a two-year lease, and you wait to decide that you're no longer in love with me now! You have to be the most stupid woman I have ever met!"

She pleaded with me to "make our divorce civil for the sake of our children."

I would have none of it. All of the resentment that had been built up for years because of feeling rejected and abandoned was being unleashed. This time, however, I had no desire to control it.

I hung up the phone on her and did my best to have an enjoyable evening with London. She had lovingly prepared a delicious meal and was waiting for me at our dining room table.

The very next day, a peace came over me which I could not explain. I recognized that Miranda had finally found the courage to say a truth that I had already known for many years. Suddenly, I felt relieved that the years of rejection would come to a conclusion.

Upon arriving at my office, I immediately sent Miranda a text, informing her that I felt relieved that the pain of our marriage was finally coming to an end. I also told her that "I would rather be alone than feel completely alone in our marriage."

Later that day, she told me not to make a rash decision. She even texted to me, "Perhaps we should get counseling."

I could not believe what I was reading on my cellphone. There was no way I would ever agree to counseling after hearing her true feelings about me. This was especially true, since she had refused to join me in counseling when I needed her most. It did not help that she had stopped going to marriage counseling with previous attempts, without giving them much of a chance to benefit our relationship. I also wondered why she suddenly had a change of heart. I stood firmly on my decision to get on with my life, even though the quality of my life was so poor at the time.

Strong in my resolve, I faithfully went for hemodialysis, as difficult as it was to go through. It would not be long before I was ready to return to PD once again. When I considered that the kidney exchange program was not a viable option, plus waiting four more years for a deceased kidney while continuing dialysis did not seem like a lifestyle that I wanted to endure, I thought of another option.

One day, I had the idea of using social media sites to help me in my quest to find a living donor. I posted, "I am in dire need for a kidney transplant. Anyone with blood type B or blood type O is a potential donor. Please pray to see if you feel moved to save my life."

I received many responses, mostly from friends who would not qualify. To my surprise, some of my bandmates in my church band reposted it to their pages as well. A local politician also posted a blog about me on her own profile page. Suddenly, fourteen people of qualifying blood types came forward who were willing to be tested. This occurred on August 3, 2011.

I sent over donor packets to each person. On August 6, I mailed a donor packet to a good friend of our drummer, Chuck. Millie was a lady who lived in Raleigh, which is located nearly three hours from

Charlotte. After receiving her packet, she filled out the requisite paperwork and returned it to Carolinas Medical Center.

One day, in an effort to gain support, I decided to use social media to get in touch with several friends from my past. One particular old friend returned my invitation from a social media site. We exchanged several e-mails about where our lives had taken us and even spoke on the phone. One evening, while telling her about my need for a kidney transplant, she told me that she had received a word from the Lord.

"You will be transplanted around Thanksgiving." When she told me these words, she not only sounded sure of what she had declared, she was joyful, as though it was a "done deal."

A new sense of hopefulness began taking root in my mind and heart. I began pouring my heart out to God, weeping and pleading with Him to help me so that I would not leave my children fatherless. That night I found a Bible verse which directly spoke to the enormity of my despair. In Hebrews 4:16, it says, "So let us come boldly before God's throne of grace with confidence, so that we may receive mercy and find grace to help us in our time of need."

While my despair was at its highest level, I believed God's Word; because of Christ's redemptive death, not only do I have direct access to God, I could boldly go to Him in my time of need and openly receive His mercy and grace. There was no greater time than now. I cried out to Him, "Abba Father, I readily admit that I'm always in need of your mercy and grace, but have never needed them more than now. Please help me! Help me find a donor so that I can live out my life so as to not only love and help my children, I can also testify to Your great love. In Jesus's name, amen."

Chapter 26

Hebrews 11:1 says, "Now faith is sure of the things hoped for and certain of the things unseen." I began thanking God for the kidney I was about to receive even though a donor had not yet been found. Instead of feeling hopeless, I was now feeling elated, fully believing the words the Lord had told me some months ago. Instead of feeling resentment and bitterness, I was feeling joyful for my future, a future that God had promised to be healthy and more holy. Each and every morning while driving to work, I thanked God for being my Redeemer and my Provider. That was easy, given the fact that Miranda was fourteen hours and nine hundred miles away.

The proof of the absence of malice and vitriol would be evidenced once she returned. In the meantime, London and I shared a sense of warmth and closeness we had not had in quite some time. After dinner, we would spend our time watching many of the cooking shows on the Cooking Channel, such as *Iron Chef America*. We would share our thoughts on who we thought would win. We also enjoyed *Chopping Block*, *Good Eats*, and *The Barefoot Contessa*.

On the evenings I had hemodialysis, London and I would watch the same show, and we would talk on the phone for the entirety of the show, making my time there pass more quickly. I was so grateful for her desire and willingness to comfort and spend quality time with me.

When Miranda and Matthew finally returned, there was a palpable discomfort between us, largely because Miranda had appeared to have second thoughts about her decision. She told me of a conversation she had with her brother's wife regarding the text I had sent to her iterating my relief at no longer having to endure any more rejection. Apparently, she had not told her sister-in-law what she had told me the night before she left for Louisiana. Miranda related the conversation she had between them and stated that her sister-in-law said that "perhaps Jeff is not thinking clearly because of his kidney disease."

At that moment, the bitterness that I had believed to have been gone rose once again.

"Did you tell her that you told me that you were no longer in love with me and that you were no longer attracted to me!"

Miranda looked at me and told me that if we got divorced, it would be my decision. Now, I began screaming. "You have the nerve to shift the blame on to me? Any man in my position who has any shred of self-esteem and self-respect would never stay with a woman who uttered those words the night before she left for over three weeks! You *never* loved me, and to now blame me for our divorce is cowardly and unforgivable!"

Miranda simply stared at me and remained silent. I stormed out of the room and went upstairs to my bedroom. I had to lie down and pray for calmness; I could feel my heart pounding and my blood pressure climbing.

The following morning, I took Matthew to the local bagel shop as was our weekend routine; he and I had a difficult conversation. Matthew initiated our talk where he had told me that he and his mother talked about our impending divorce. I decided to not interrupt, but allowed him to vent his feelings. He went on to say that his mother told him that they would probably move to Louisiana should she and I divorce. I asked him how he felt about this potential move to Louisiana, especially since he and I were so close.

He said, "Dad, if we move, I don't want to leave you."

Having listened to children of all ages during my twenty-six-year career, I strongly sensed that he was not being totally forthright about his feelings.

"Matthew, if you move to Louisiana, I will visit you at least once a month." I saw Matthew breathe easier.

"Dad, I really love it there, but I would miss you."

I put my arm around him to comfort and reassure him. "Listen, son. If I wanted to, I could prevent you from moving, but because you want to move, I love you so much I won't stop you."

We both began weeping and holding on to each other. It was a tender but painful moment for both of us. On our way back from the bagel shop, we talked about how we would spend our time together in Louisiana. His sadness had slowly changed to excitement and relief.

Several days later, Miranda and I sat down to discuss our plans to separate. Inasmuch as I was the only wage earner in the family, we could not afford for me to find an apartment to rent. I had already spoken with my sister Lori and asked if I could live with her and her family until I could afford to move out, and shared my plans with Miranda.

We discussed a possible move-out date, but before we could proceed, I had to have an attorney draw up a non-abandonment agreement for both Miranda and me to sign so that my leaving would not constitute abandoning my wife and children. The attorney would not have it completed until September 10, and that became my move-out date.

One morning, while alone in the house, I was besieged with a crushing feeling in my chest that I had difficulty identifying. Suddenly, without any warning I began balling myself up in a fetal position and began crying as if I were a very young child. I became completely grief-stricken as I recalled all of the memories of abandonment I had experienced in my marriage. Due to the cultural scripting for being a male, and my desire to keep my marriage at any cost, I had stuffed many of these feelings throughout the years of my marriage. My tears were unrelenting, and I had never felt so vulnerable in all of the sixty-four years I had lived. As I recalled Miranda's words to me the night before leaving for Louisiana, my grief became intolerable. I realized at that moment that the rage I felt for her was a cover-up, a mask for the intense grief, betrayal, and abandonment I had experienced. My sobbing continued for well over thirty minutes, and when it finally ended, I felt purged. I got dressed and took a walk to the neighborhood park, just a few blocks away. There I sat with God and thanked him for exposing the source of my anger as well as the cleansing I now felt. I humbly stood before the throne of God and boldly asked Him for His mercy and grace.

"Please, heavenly Father, I ask you to help me to forgive Miranda for abandoning me during my greatest time of need. Lord, I know that I can never forgive her in my own power, but all things are possible with You. Forgive me, Father, for the mistakes and sins I have committed against You and Miranda. Lord, I need to let go and release my pain and anger, not only for my sake, but more so for the sake of my children. I thank you, Lord, in advance for the mercy and grace You are about to bestow unto me. In Jesus's name. Amen."

Chapter 27

My sister Lori, along with her husband and nineteen-year-old daughter lived but a few blocks from our old home in Huntersville. I moved in on a Friday, and Matthew helped me load and unload my car as it was our plan to spend the entire weekend together. Upon entering the home, I was greeted by Lori's eleven-year-old granddaughter, Taryn, who was not made aware of my marital breakup. She smiled at me.

"Hi, Uncle Jeff! Where are Aunt Miranda and London?"

"Aunt Miranda and I are getting a divorce, and I've moved in here with Grandma."

She quickly arose from her chair and put her arms around me.

"Don't worry, Uncle Jeff. We'll take care of you."

I was so moved by her love and assurance that in spite of the pain of leaving my family, I know that God had used my great-niece to deliver a message of love and assurance. I was so touched.

I held her head to my chest and simply uttered, "Thank you so much, Taryn."

While I was welcomed and given one of the guest bedrooms, Matthew refused to sleep in another bedroom and chose instead to sleep next to me. His love and devotion continued, and he voiced a concern that I might need something during the night while I was on dialysis. It was a difficult day for me, fraught with tremendous emotion as I hugged London and left.

Our plans were to spend time together each Sunday, yet that offered me little comfort as I would no longer experience the deep joy and pleasure of spending evenings and Saturdays together. I spent some time engaging in feeling sorry for myself, until Lori hugged me and told me how happy she was to be able to help me in my time of greatest need. I was deeply moved as I never took anyone's love for granted, even family members.

"Lori, I don't know how to thank you for being so kind and gracious."

She quickly hugged me. "Jeff, that's what family does for one another."

Matthew helped me set up my room so that my dialysis cycle would be easily accessible. We spent the rest of the day watching television, and every time I got up to go to another room, Matthew was right behind me.

My days went without much stress or drama. I went to work each day, despite feeling nauseous and somewhat disoriented, and came home to a hot dinner. My brother-in-law, Peter who was retired cooked each meal.

The nights were the most difficult as I fiercely longed for London and Matthew. While on dialysis, I would either call each of them or use Skype to see their faces and eagerly looked forward to the weekends when I would see them. Miranda would drive forty-five minutes each way to drop Matthew off at Lori's home, and we would always go out for dinner.

Like most teenage boys, Matthew's appetite was enormous, and he loved nothing more than going to a restaurant. We were together until Sunday afternoon, where I would meet London at the local mall near her home. Once there, Matthew would walk with Miranda, and London and I would window shop or spend valuable time in Barnes and Noble perusing through books. The fatigue that I experienced always limited my time with my daughter. Thirty minutes was my limit, and while I felt badly about making our visit so brief, London was always understanding about my impaired health. We hugged and kissed, and we all left, except that I drove off by myself in a completely different direction.

During one weekend when I shortened my Friday schedule, I drove to pick Matthew up to take him back to Lori's home. He seemed agitated, and when I questioned him, he told me that he felt fine, but it was obvious to me that something was bothering my son.

I probed a bit further, and he cried and yelled at me, "Hello, Dad! My parents are getting a divorce! Did you think I would be okay?"

I put my arms on his shoulder, which only made him even more angry and upset. "I'm in a no-win situation. If I move with Mom, I won't be with you and you're my best friend. If I stay with you, I will miss Mom!"

He was now cussing, and I made no attempts to correct his language. Instead, I allowed my son to get his anger and frustration out, even if I were the recipient of his rancor. He went on for almost five minutes with his head in his hands, and I wept with him. My heart was broken for my son's pain; he was feeling what most kids fear the most—the disintegration of their family. I kept my hand on his head and silently prayed for him. When his crying ceased, he looked up at me with his face taking on a repentant countenance.

"Dad, I am so sorry for getting angry at you and cussing at you."

"Son, I get it. I can feel how sad, angry, and frustrated you feel because the divorce is not something you wanted or feel you can control." Together, we wept again.

"Dad, I love you so much!"

While I fully appreciated the peace I had felt at Lori's home, I had difficulty accepting the fact that I was going through another divorce. I wondered if I would ever find a woman with whom I could fall in love. What helped me was the understanding that I would rather be alone than feel alone in a marriage. Though Miranda and I decided to have an amicable divorce, I did not think I could ever trust another woman with my heart. Finding another woman was far from my highest priority.

Chapter 28

On September 16, I received the following Facebook inbox message from Millie:

> New news! CMC received my blood and tested it with yours, and there was no adverse reaction when they mixed them, tested them, whatever it is that they do. So, I am on to the next step. Urine collection and more blood test. This time they are testing for function. I will be doing the next round of blood work on Monday. I am guessing we both should know something by October maybe. I don't really know what to expect.

I began to feel cautiously encouraged. After all, I experienced so much disappointment in my efforts to find a donor. Hebrews 11:1 stayed in front of my mind and deeply within my heart. Millie and I continued to stay in touch as she became my best, most promising lifeline to a new life.

I could not believe that a complete stranger would offer to donate a kidney to a man she had never met. I thanked God daily and asked that He bless Millie for her willingness to help me, regardless of the outcome of her testing.

Later that same day, I received another message from Millie:

> I felt very led to do this from the moment I saw your story from Chuck sharing it on Facebook. Several things reaffirmed that from your birthday being the same as my partner to our blood not

reactive adversely. I would hope that if the shoe was on my foot, someone would do the same for me.

Millie and I continued to stay in contact, and my children, along with Lori and her family, began to be excited about the promising possibility that Millie would be a match for me. I prayed with a fervor I had never known before, thanking God for the kidney I was about to receive, even though the testing was not complete. And I wept with each and every prayer, so thankful for what the Lord was doing for me and my children.

As this was occurring, my symptoms increased with each passing day. PKD produces anemia, which made me feel cold all of the time. My leg cramps would awaken me up to eight times each night, and I would often wake my brother-in-law from my moaning. The fatigue made me lumber as though I was an eighty-year-old man, and I had difficulty maintaining my weight from the constant nausea I felt.

Yet, I held on to the promise of God when he affirmed to me when He said, "I will find you a kidney, and there will be a miracle involved so that all will know that I, the Lord your God, did this for you."

Then on October 4, I received this message from Millie:

> I turned in my second 24-hour urine sample today, and had more blood drawn. So step 1 was the blood type verification. Then step 2 was the donor-recipient crossmatch. I just completed step 3 which was the preliminary blood and urine testing.
>
> Next will be the medical and surgical evaluations, tissue typing and diagnostic tests, then the surgery. I am guessing that even though our blood reacted fine together, there is still a slight possibility that our tissue still is not compatible. I am not really sure.

> My paperwork also says something about presentation and selection committee, but I am assuming that is when you are just doing the donation randomly and don't already have a donor in mind. I contacted my primary physician for a referral for a mammogram today as well. Hope you are doing well.

Millie told me that she felt very confident that we would be a match. To say I felt elated is an understatement. She added that she would like to meet me so that she could get to know the person who she might be giving her kidney to; I agreed to meet with her whenever it was convenient for her while she was in Charlotte to do more testing.

After answering Millie's question about how I was holding up, Millie said, "Well, hang in there. By the way the process has gone so far, I would expect that we have at least one month. I am going to make just one small request. That if the time comes too close to the weekend of November 19 that we wait until after that weekend. Unless of course it is a matter of life and death. Even over Thanksgiving is fine, but the weekend of the 19th will be my 40th birthday weekend. I hope that is not too selfish of me to ask. If it is next week or the next, well then, we go for it."

I could not believe what I was now hearing. The only request that Millie had was for us to have the transplant after her birthday on November 19! She hoped that she wasn't being too selfish by making this request. Really? My friend's word about getting transplanted at Thanksgiving might be coming to fruition, and I could not contain this unspeakable joy that was welling up in my heart.

We agreed to meet after my work day ended at 7:00 p.m. on Thursday, November 3. Millie had to come to Carolinas Medical Center for one final test, which according to the living donor coordinator was not a "make or break" test. The coordinator also assured me that Millie was a perfect match.

Millie and I agreed to meet at Brixx, a gourmet pizza restaurant in trendy Birkdale Village in Huntersville. I got there early and looked out for her face, which I had become very familiar with from Facebook. When she arrived with her partner, Elena, we all hugged. It wasn't long before we got a table and I shared my story of PKD. As all three of us shared stories about our lives, there was so much synchronicity between Elena and me. We shared the same birthday, had the same conservative political views, had the same blood type, and both of us were percussionists.

I looked at both women and could not contain my joy and appreciation for what was soon to take place. Elena smiled, and Millie told me how excited she was to help me, saying that she felt a calling to donate her kidney to me. I was speechless.

The only thing I could say was, "How can I possibly thank you?"

She flashed her pretty smile and gently touched my hand. "I am so happy to do this for you."

She once again brought up the surgery date and asked if I would agree to have my transplant two days before Thanksgiving. I felt compelled to tell her about how the Lord had spoken to me about my eventual transplant and what my friend had prophesied about the date of my transplant. Shivers ran up and down my entire body as I shared my journey with the Lord.

On November 7, Millie sent me another message. As I read it, I began to shake and weep at the same time.

> I did contact my living donor coordinator to follow up about doing the surgery on the Tuesday before Thanksgiving. She is supposed to call me as soon as she knows something. I am guessing no later than tomorrow. I really do believe it is a matter of when now, not if. Nothing they told me indicated otherwise. Yep, they said I was a perfect specimen. Everything where it is supposed to be just like a textbook. You will be getting my left kidney.

I read this message over and over in case I might have misread it in my excitement. I sent a copy of it to Lori and asked her how she interpreted it.

She wrote back, "You're asking me how I interpret this? You're getting her left kidney. She's a perfect match! How can you not see this?"

I thanked God repeatedly. "Lord, thank you for loving me so much. Thank you for allowing me to live!"

Tears gushed from my eyes with rapidity and force. It seemed as if the pain in my heart was quickly being relieved by a valve located within and behind my eyes. My entire face was drenched in tears, yet God was replacing my salty tears of pain with tears of joy and thankfulness.

I immediately called Miranda's home and shared the news with her, and she was excited for me. London got on the phone and squealed with appreciation as she repeatedly said, "Thank you, Lord!"

When I told Matthew that Millie was a perfect match, he had a very different perspective. "You mean, you'll be able to eat pizza again? Wow, Dad. I will have pizza waiting for you the moment you come out of surgery!"

I roared with laughter; he was not only humorous, he was correct. I could not wait to have pizza and all the other foods I could not enjoy for the past eleven months. The days leading up to my surgery were like a blur, although I shared my good news with the nurses and physicians whom I worked with and saw each day.

I also shared my news with my patients, knowing that I would be out of work for quite some time and had to cancel appointments which had already been scheduled. Scheduling was very challenging because my surgeon told me that I would probably be out of work for a minimum of six weeks. Inasmuch as I am in private practice, when I am not working, I am not earning any money, and I could not afford to miss any work, let alone six weeks. So I told my patients that I would return in three weeks and scheduled accordingly.

I received a call from Carolinas Medical Center and was told that I had to undergo preoperative tests the day before my scheduled surgery. On November 21, I awakened early enough to be at the hospital by 8:00 a.m. I quickly opened my laptop to my Facebook page and shared this with my family and friends:

> This time tomorrow morning, I will be prepping for surgery. I am fully confident that all will go well with me and Millie. "Now, faith is sure of the things hoped for and certain of the things unseen" (Hebrews 11:1).

I could not find a parking space near the hospital, so I had parked by the kidney transplant center and began walking. I was somewhat disoriented and stopped a physician and asked for directions. After telling me how to find my way to the main entrance, I could not help but tell her that I was getting a kidney transplant the very next day.

She looked at me and remarked, "God bless you!"

One of the things I appreciated most about living in North Carolina is that many people are believers, and I therefore felt very comfortable in sharing my faith and talking about God. Yet I found it somewhat odd that a physician would make such a bold declaration. I went through many tests. One of the last tests was an EKG and x-ray of my lungs, and I struck up a conversation with the EKG technician.

After talking about my kidney transplant, which would take place early the next day, she remarked, "Wow, the Lord must have some special plans for you 'cause He's giving you a second chance to live." We both began praising the Lord, and I felt so touched.

My last appointment was with Dr. Chuang, a kidney transplant physician who examined my kidneys and affirmed the fact that I was a perfect candidate for this transplant. He went on to say that he was part of a team of nephrologists who would do all of my follow-up checkups for however long I lived in North Carolina.

He then said, "I think the good Lord will protect you and your new kidney."

I said, "Dr. Chuang, you are the third person today who has affirmed this journey I am taking with God. I am choosing to assume that God is speaking through all of you."

He smiled and wished me good fortune. I drove back to Huntersville tired, but praised God during the entire drive home.

That night was filled with anticipation and preparation. London and Matthew called to inquire if I was nervous and to also let me know that they both had prayed fervently for a successful outcome. They inquired about how soon they could visit me while I was recuperating in the hospital, and I told them I would probably need a day to recover from the anesthesia and pain medications.

Miranda also wished me well and let me know that she would take the kids to the hospital as often as I wished, which I greatly appreciated. The rest of that day sped by until I found myself preparing for what I prayed would be my last dialysis treatment. Before hooking up to my cycler, I posted the following status to my social media site:

> Getting ready to do dialysis for the last time! Please pray that the surgeon's hands will be guided by the One who created the surgeon. Please keep Millie and her surgeon in prayer as well. Thank you all for your support, prayers and encouragement. See y'all on the other side of healthy!

As I the dialysate filled in to my peritoneal cavity, I began praying aloud, thanking God for the miracle He was about to perform, and was reminded of a scripture from Psalm 8:4, which reads, "What is man that You are mindful of him."

As tears began trickling down my face, I said, "Oh, Abba Father, thank you that You would even give me a thought! Thank You, God, for all that You are and all that You do for me. It is my prayer, oh, God, that all goes well tomorrow and that You would guide the hands of Dr. Casingal and all of the other doctors involved in my surgery. Please also keep Your hand upon Millie and her physicians and keep her strong and healthy. Abba, bless her tonight and every night for her willingness to sacrifice her kidney that I might live."

I set the alarm on my phone for 4:30 a.m., and while tussling in my bed for some time, slowly I drifted off to sleep.

Chapter 29

My phone alarm barely went off before my eyes opened. As my mind began adjusting to being awake, my impending transplant made my heart pound with delightful anticipation. I remembered several conversations with friends and family about whether I would be afraid to undergo such a dangerous surgery.

My response was quick and decisive. "I am not afraid of undergoing a kidney transplant because one of two things will occur. Either it will be successful and my life and health would be restored, or I will awaken in eternity and have Jesus waiting to welcome me! Therefore, I am far more afraid of *not* having a transplant."

I slowly began to unfetter myself from my dialysis cycle and found my way into the bathroom to shower. I heard Lori shuffling about as she prepared to shower and drive me to the hospital. Soon thereafter, we began our drive to Carolinas Medical Center in uptown Charlotte, and neither of us talked; we were both tired, and I spent most of my time in silent prayer.

Upon arriving at the hospital, we saw Millie and her partner, Elena, having already checked in. We hugged. I suddenly was overtaken with a profound sense of guilt. I could not believe that this woman, a person I had only met once before, was willing to undergo a dangerous and extremely painful procedure for me. I looked into her eyes, and while I did not say anything more than "Thank you," my heart was throbbing with gratitude and appreciation.

I sat down and turned my head in an effort to hide my convulsing abdomen and the sobs which emanated deep from within my soul. I was soon interrupted by a nurse who had called my name.

After checking in, I was soon led to a room with several beds, each separated by sliding curtains. As I was ushered into mine, I saw Millie and Elena directly across from me.

A nurse introduced herself and asked me several questions, such as "What is your name?" and "What kind of surgery will you be undergoing this morning?" As soon as she was satisfied that I was the right person, she placed a medical bracelet around my wrist and began taking my vitals. I was soon visited by the team of anesthesiologists who informed me of the different "cocktails" they would be serving me.

Miranda called and let me know that she and the kids had prayed for me and wished me well. I was very thankful for her thoughtful call and let her know how thankful I was. Other physicians began pouring in, including Dr. Casingal, who gave me more of an update on my impending surgery.

I was told that the surgery should take roughly four hours, and as soon as it is complete, I would be placed in intensive care for at least two days. After he left, Lori and I began joking with each other about receiving a woman's kidney.

"Lori, does this mean I will have to sit down to pee from now on?"

We laughed uncontrollably, not because it was such a humorous statement, but more out of nervousness and a bit of anxiety. Then, the curtains opened, and the anesthesiology team entered and administered Versed, a drug which would start to put me asleep. Within minutes, I experienced an onrush of euphoria and did not hesitate to let Lori know what I was experiencing.

I must have had a rather goofy look on my face, as unbeknownst to me, Lori took a picture of me with her cell phone, which she promptly posted on her Facebook page. Several days later, I saw the picture and was very embarrassed to say the least. I looked like a young Jack Nicholson in *The Shining*, only I had a blue surgical hat on, which only served to make me look even more ridiculous.

As my eyes began to close, the surgical nursing team came for me, and as they were wheeling me away, I let Lori know how much

I loved and appreciated her. This was the last moment I had remembered before awakening in the intensive care unit.

When I awoke, I looked up and saw Lori, and then I slowly scanned the large intensive care unit. Nurses seemed to be everywhere. No sooner did Lori ask how I was, a nurse came over to me and put her face close to mine and asked me how I felt. All I could do was nod my head, indicating that I felt "okay."

She told me that my surgery went well and that I was being given morphine and fluids intravenously. She went on to say that I had a catheter so that the staff could measure my urine output. I made a face of displeasure, and my nurse understood.

"The catheter will be in for several days. I know it is not the most comfortable experience, but it will help us know how well your kidney is working." The rest of that day was a blur as I must have slept for the remainder of the day and night.

I awoke at 2:00 a.m., fully awake and spent the rest of the night watching television. A nurse saw me and came to ask if I needed anything. She told me that my urine output had begun to pick up and that I was "peeing like a racehorse."

"Really, like a racehorse?"

I was excited and laughed wholeheartedly, and let her know that I was way too old to have a saddle thrown over my back. She chuckled and went on to tell me to not be alarmed when I noticed blood in my urine, which was to be expected.

The next day, I saw many posting from friends and family. Here are but a few of the most heartfelt prayers and words of encouragement:

> When you read this, my dear wonderful cuzzzin Jeeeeeffreeey, you'll have begun your new amazing journey called life. All prayers are with you and the unbelievable Millie. Love you lots. XOXOXOXO.
>
> Thinking of you, Dr. Rifkin!

> So thankful to hear surgery went well. Does anyone know if Jeff and Millie are well enough for visitors?
>
> Thank God they both made it through. Praying that they both have a fast recovery.
>
> Praying. Got nothing but love and prayers for you!
>
> I am praying for you tonight, Jeff.

Needless to say, I was so deeply touched by the tremendous outpouring of love and concern. I was a very fortunate and blessed man for many reasons.

Two days later, I celebrated Thanksgiving in my hospital room after Lori brought a home-cooked meal to me. As I partook in this meal, I considered how truly blessed I was to have been given another chance to live my life and to fulfill the plans and purposes which God had set forth for my life. I had never experienced the full meaning of Thanksgiving before my transplant. I certainly had so much to celebrate all of those years before. After all, being born and raised in the greatest nation in the world and having been given so many opportunities was more than enough reason to give thanks to the Living God.

As I ate, I pondered my life and wept. Despite my impending divorce and being separated from my beloved children, I nonetheless had so much to be thankful for. I remembered a song that I had sung so many times during my years at Calvary Chapel. "Enter His gates with Thanksgiving. Enter His courts with praise. Give thanks to Him and praise His Name." I sang these words while sobbing tears of joy in between bites of my savory Thanksgiving repast.

I knew that every Thanksgiving from this day forward would have as much significance as any other celebratory day, including birthdays, Christmas, Chanukah, Passover, and Easter. For me, this was the day the Lord fulfilled His promise and performed a miracle to bless me and every other person I had known or will ever come to know. At that moment, I rededicated my life to Him.

"Lord, Your Word says that our bodies should be as living sacrifices unto You. How much more should my body be as a living sacrifice? Show me, oh, God, how I should live out this new life so that You are glorified."

I heard the soft, quiet voice of the Holy Spirit, the same voice that promised me a kidney, say, "Preach and teach." I was being prompted to write this book and to teach it in churches around the country and world. I knew then that it would be entitled *Overwhelmed by the Grace of God*. Miranda, to her credit, had encouraged me to write a book for a number of years.

While I had written four screenplays, I never felt confident about writing a book. But when God, by His grace, did for me what I could not do for myself and found a way to save my life through a miracle, He birthed this book through Him. I finished my meal and was very eager and excited about the direction my life would soon take.

During the course of the next few days, I experienced a plethora of emotions. While I had thought I knew a good deal on kidney transplants, I nonetheless felt fearful that my body could reject my new kidney. I was informed by my physicians and nurses that I would be receiving all of my medications at 9:00 a.m. and 9:00 p.m.

One night, I did not receive my medications until nearly 10:00 a.m., and panic set in. I complained vehemently about the hospital possibly being liable for the loss of my kidney. As the days went on, I realized that I did not need to be obsessive about taking my medications exactly at the designated times. I also had gone through several days of total insomnia, which was more than likely due to Xanax withdrawal.

Ever since being on dialysis, the muscle spasms in my legs became more and more severe. My nephrologist prescribed Xanax to help my muscles relax and to also promote sleep. While in the hospital, I had not received Xanax since being admitted. After my third night of being unable to sleep, my attending physician prescribed Ambien.

I had an adverse reaction to this medication and had what I would describe as psychotic nightmares which made it impossible for me to sleep. I became overwhelmed with anxiety and despair. After speaking with a friend who was a physician as well as a kidney recipient, he recognized the source of my insomnia and subsequent emotional distress and suggested that I ask my physicians to prescribe Clonazepam to help me sleep. That night, I slept deeply and soundly, and when I awoke in the morning, I offered my praises and thanksgiving to God!

Friends and family visited me each day; my joy and newfound health were evident to everyone. Sharing my testimony of God's promise for a new kidney and how He used a stranger to fulfill His promise was impossible for me to not share. I shared this testimony with my nurses, technicians, physicians, and anyone else who came into my room. One day, my cell phone rang, and since I did not recognize the phone number on my caller ID, I assumed it was a patient of mine.

I answered, "Hello, this is Dr. Rifkin."

The voice on the other side of the phone was a new patient wanting to schedule an initial appointment. After explaining that I would be out of the office for the next three to four weeks, I asked if I could call her to schedule her appointment in several days.

One of my nurses, named Marianne, overheard my conversation and was curious about my profession.

"Did you say you were a doctor?"

"Yes, I am a licensed marriage and family therapist. My office is located within a large medical practice in Mooresville."

"So, you're a marriage counselor, a shrink, huh? I bet you've got some amazing stories!"

"Well, if you do my work for as long as I have, you'd have not only some amazing stories, you'd have some hilarious ones as well!"

Marianne's interest was captivated. "Do you have any that you can tell me? I could use a few laughs today."

I smiled, and as I did, Marianne saw that as a cue to move closer to my newly made hospital bed.

"Marianne, before I begin, I need to ask you, have you ever known any Jewish people?"

"Jewish people? Are you kidding me? I'm originally from Secaucus, New Jersey!"

"I'm only asking because you need to appreciate the Jewish culture to fully appreciate this story. I had a private practice in south Florida for twenty years and saw this Jewish family. The couple was in their fifties, and their son was twenty-six years old. They came to me because they were very concerned about their son, Seth, who seemed to have borderline mental retardation. He was a little slow."

"Okay," Marianne stated, not knowing where I was going with this story.

"We all met, and the parents discussed their concerns about Seth's decision-making abilities. Suddenly, the dad asks to ask Seth about his fiancée. This seemed like an odd request because Seth was sitting right there. I resisted."

"I don't blame you," Marianne said. "That seems weird."

"Dr. Rifkin, please ask him."

I nodded my head and relented.

"Seth, can you please tell me about your fiancée?"

Seth nodded his head and said, "I loved her a lot."

The father looked at me and requested that I ask Seth what she did for a living. Once again, I resisted, but soon gave in to the father's request.

"Okay, Seth. What did your fiancée do for a living?"

Without hesitating or blinking an eye, Seth said, "She was a street hooker—a crack whore."

"Oh my gosh! Are you kidding me? No way!"

I looked at the father, who sat forward in his chair and said, "Can you please ask my son why he broke up with her?"

"What!" Marianne screamed. She sat on my bed, stunned.

"Well, it was obvious why he broke up with her, right? Who wants to marry a crack whore?"

"Please, Dr. Rifkin, indulge me. Ask Seth why he broke up with her."

"Okay, Seth, why did you break off your engagement with your fiancée?"

"She wouldn't convert to Judaism!"

"Now, I am completely stunned, Marianne. I lean forward in my chair and ask Seth this question, 'Seth, how many men did your fiancée have sex with each day?'"

"Usually, about a dozen or so guys. It depended upon what they wanted."

I looked at Marianne and told her that I could not believe what I was hearing.

"What did you say to him, Dr. Rifkin?"

I looked at Seth and then his parents and then back to Seth. "Seth, are you telling me that your fiancée had sex with at least a dozen men each day and the only reason you broke off your engagement because she wasn't a Jew?"

"Yes," Seth said.

I looked at the dad, and all he did was shrug his shoulders while shooting both hands in the air, exasperated.

Marianne was hysterical and could not help herself from snorting. "What else did you say to him?"

"I said, 'Seth, you need a lot of help, my man!'"

At this point, Marianne could not stop laughing. I think she would have stayed with me, hoping I would tell her more stories, but my lunch tray was delivered to my bedside.

"You know the moral of this story? People tend to gravitate toward the familiar—familiar customs and religions even in spite of the possible consequences of doing so. This seems to be especially so with people who feel insecure or fearful about who they are. Plus, Jewish people put a high premium on marrying within our religion."

"Thank you. That made my day a lot brighter."

Marianne disappeared into the hallway as I began digging into my lunch.

On the fifth day, I was released from the hospital with three appointments for the following week with my team of transplant nephrologists. It felt so wonderful to return to Lori's home, but even more wonderful was knowing I would spend the weekend with Matthew at Lori's home.

I spent the entire weekend with Matthew, and he was such a protective son. He followed me from room to room, always asking if there was anything I needed. There was no doubt that each of my children had some modicum of fear about my transplant.

Since he had spent nearly every night with me for eight months before I moved out of our home, Matthew had taken on a caretaking role for me, and he needed to be assured that I was feeling okay. He asked me so many questions about my transplant.

"Does this cure you of polycystic kidney disease?"

"Will you ever have to go back on dialysis?"

"Will your medications stop your body from rejecting your new kidney?"

"Can you live with one kidney, Dad?"

I answered each of his questions and then addressed the more weighty fear.

"Matthew, are you afraid that I still might die?"

His eyes welling with tears and his lips quivering, he hesitatingly said, "Yes."

I pulled him close to me and reassured him that God did not bring me this far and have Millie sacrifice her kidney just to have me either go back on dialysis or die.

"Dad, I was so scared!"

Father and son wept together in a tight embrace.

"I love you so much, son!"

We continued to hug and sob together.

On Monday morning, my brother-in-law drove me to Charlotte to have my blood drawn and then meet with one of my transplant nephrologists. My nephrologist mentioned that my ankles and calves looked swollen, and he had therefore prescribed a diuretic to reduce the water weight and asked me to return in two days.

I mentioned that my lower back was aching, and we both assumed that the pain was the result of having been in bed for five days while in the hospital. I returned to Lori's home, and soon after taking the diuretic, I began urinating with great frequency.

By the following day, I felt very weak and in great pain. The pain was so severe that I could not move from the La-Z-Boy chair and had to have an ice pack at all times. I continued to take the pain medication prescribed to me.

Late that night, I noticed that I was running a slight fever and called the emergency number given to me by the physicians at Metrolina Nephrology. I was told that I needed to speak with my nephrologist as soon as I had arrived the next morning.

After looking at me and noticing that I was dehydrated, pale, and had an obvious infection, I was told that I needed to check back into Carolinas Medical Center immediately. Of course, my initial question was, "Is my body rejecting my new kidney?"

I was suddenly very anxious. My doctor told me that he believed that I had a urinary tract infection and that I had lost too much water and was anemic from losing so much blood during my surgery. I was immediately relieved, but was apparently still anxious.

"Don't worry. All of this is fairly typical with kidney transplants. You'll be fine in a few days."

As my tired body walked languidly back to the transplant floor of CMC, I was welcomed by the same nurses who took care of me several days before. I slowly found my way to my bed and was surrounded by two nurses who began taking my vitals.

They inquired why I needed to return, and I explained that my body was dehydrated and I obviously had a urinary tract infection. After they left, another nurse quickly entered and looked at my hospital bracelet around my wrist. She put an IV into my hand, and another nurse hung several bags on the pole—one was an antibiotic and the other was sucrose to hydrate me.

Later that day, I was transfused with blood. I needed three pints. I remained in the hospital for four days, and then returned home to Lori's house, feeling tired, but incredibly healthy!

Chapter 30

Upon discharge, I was informed by one of the physicians from Metrolina Nephrology that I would not be able to drive for four to six weeks and that I would probably be out of work for at least six weeks. I knew that inasmuch as I was in private practice, I would have to return to work earlier than scheduled.

Miranda and I agreed that she would continue to pay all of our bills. It was fortuitous that I had raised funds to cover many of my expenses through donations that friends and family had made through the National Foundation for Transplants.

I had used Facebook to get the word out for others to make tax-deductible donations to this organization, and these donations paid for our rent, utilities, and medical expenses not covered by my health insurance. I enjoyed most of my recuperative time at home, until I realized that I needed to return to work so that I would not fall more behind in my bills. So, after three weeks, I returned to my doctors and let them know that I had driven to the office pain-free and was ready to return to work. They agreed. The next day, I drove to work and was excited to see my patients and co-workers.

Walking through the doors of Lakeside Family Physicians seemed somewhat of a monumental event to me. Besides getting a hero's welcome from all of the nurses, office staff, and physicians, it seemed eerie to return to my office given the degree of sickness and debilitation I felt each day for the past eleven months. As I relaxed into my chair, I quietly gave thanks to my God, who had surely plucked me out of the grips of death and back to the ministry he had established for me. While I had been cautioned to make the initial several weeks a slow transition, I had intended to see as many patients as I could. But this was nearly Christmas, and my patients had either taken off to visit families in distant cities or spent discretionary money to purchase Christmas gifts. When I called many of my patients to inform them of my return, I also learned that a portion of them had found another therapist while I was home recuperating. So, despite my efforts to not heed my physicians' advice, my schedule was scanty nonetheless.

As I slowly built up my endurance, my schedule began to pick up. Once all of the physicians in Lakeside knew of my return, new referrals were coming in at a steady rate. By the end of January, I was back to a full caseload.

My immuno-suppressor medications, Myfordic and Prograf, prevent my body from rejecting my kidney by shutting down by immune system. This leaves me very prone to illness and cancer. One morning, while meeting with my physicians at Metrolina Nephrology, I learned that I had a latent virus in my system. The HPV virus originates from chickenpox and herpes. My physician predicted that sooner or later the virus would show itself and I would have to be treated for it. That day came sooner than I had anticipated. I became highly nauseous and ran a slight fever. My physician took me off Myfordic and called in a prescription for Valcyte. When I drove through Walgreen's to pick it up, I was told that my prescription insurance had capped and that I would have to pay out of pocket.

"Not a problem," I told my pharmacist. "How much is it?"

My pharmacist paused with discomfort. "It is a little expensive," she said while shifting her weight back and forth from one uncomfortable leg to the other.

"Okay, how much is it?" I asked while pulling out my debit card from my wallet.

"Ummm, it's three thousand dollars."

I chuckled out loud, wondering how much an "expensive" medication would cost me. "I'll come back tomorrow after I sell my car!"

The pharmacist stood there dumfounded, not knowing how to respond to my sarcastic humor. I drove off and called Metrolina as quickly as I could. I explained my financial predicament and inquired if they could give me enough samples to get me through. I took the samples for one month, yet needed to have more negative tests before I could stop taking the Valcyte. Metrolina spoke with the pharmacy at CMC, and they could supply Valcyte for only $150 for the month. In the meantime, I had been taking Prednisone in lieu of Myfordic. Prednisone not only creates bloating and weight gain, it can additionally wreak havoc on one's emotions. This was certainly true in my case. I have always been an even-tempered, patient person. Not so while on Prednisone. As was my habit, I spent time with God while in my car on my way to my office. One morning, while deep in prayer and praising God for His goodness and mercy, the traffic on I-77 suddenly came to an abrupt halt. Still praying aloud, I quickly looked in my rear-view mirror and saw a semi bearing down on me.

Suddenly, I screamed with all of my strength and will. The *F-bomb* flew out of my mouth without any forethought. (I couldn't possibly have thought and planned to yell that word out of my mouth beforehand, especially while I was immersed in prayer!) I began laughing loudly while continuing my conversation with God.

"Lord, I am sorry for cussing while in prayer. But you know it's the Prednisone."

My laughter could not be contained as I pondered how funny this would sound to others when I related this prayerful adventure. "Thank you, Father, that the semi had rolled onto the grass instead of killing me."

I tried to recover some sense of sobriety, and I managed to attain that goal, but not before arriving at my office. When I returned to Metrolina to have my labs done, I learned that I no longer needed Prednisone, however not before telling my nurse and physician about my foray on I-77. They joined me in gleeful laughter. Through her tears, my nurse said, "Dr. Rifkin, I am sure you are a fine therapist, but I think you missed your calling as a stand-up comic."

As the ensuing months rolled by, my creatinine levels continued to trend downward. My physicians are all very pleased about my health and progress and still feel very hopeful that my kidney will last me well into my eighties.

While London and Matthew live over eight hundred miles away, we stay connected through phone calls, Skype, and texting.

Matthew made the adjustment to living in southwest Louisiana. London struggles at times for lack of a social network. She had also asked if she would be able to spend next year with me so that she could graduate high school with her close friends. Obviously, no one knows what the future holds, yet I am certain that they and I will always be very close.

Despite my academic and career successes, I have treasured my role as a father more than any other in my life. I know that a father's relationship with his daughter will influence her decision when it comes time to choose a husband. She will often choose a man opposite her father's characteristics and character, or she will select a man who is very similar to her father.

That said, I had committed myself to being that father who will love, cherish, and reinforce his daughter's sense of self-worth. I had further recognized that only a father can teach his son how to be a man. To that end, I have instilled in Matthew the qualities and characteristics that make a man worthy of leadership in the community and in his home.

A mother's role is very different. Despite loving her son, she can never teach him how to be a man. She does in fact teach him how to love and, more specifically, how to love a woman. Respect, admiration, how to give and receive affection are qualities and behaviors imparted from mother to son.

I can only hope and pray that when it comes time for me to leave this earth, all of my children will confirm that I was a good and noble father to each of them. My commitment to each of them is unwavering, and I am blessed and enriched by and through their love.

Miranda and I have been quite fortunate in that our friendship has continued to flourish despite our impending divorce. At the outset of our divorce, we made a decision to remain friends despite feelings of betrayal and abandonment. She has called me on several occasions to talk about financial and career concerns, and I am only too happy to listen.

I believe that our shared commitment and ability to remain friends is not a rich blessing for our children, it is a testimony to the work that the Lord has done in each of us. We have both asked for forgiveness and have admitted a shared responsibility in the demise of our marriage.

I sensed that Miranda has come to grips with her own deficiencies as a wife and has readily admitted that she has had a lot of issues related to being self-centered and selfish. As I navigate my way through the world of being single at age sixty-five, I recognize that I thoroughly enjoy being single.

I have had a great deal of time to process my role in my failed marriage, and to that end, I know exactly what qualities I am looking for should I decide to date and seek out a potential wife. It is very important to me that any potential spouse be highly educated, intelligent, and financially self-sufficient.

At this stage of my life, I do not want to support anyone, and an independent woman with a career of her own will serve to garner my respect and admiration. I additionally need a woman who enjoys giving and receiving affection and possesses interests that align with my own. Time will tell if another marriage is in my destiny.

I pray each day that if I am to be married again one day, that God send that woman to me. Scripture says that He knows us better than we know ourselves inasmuch as He is our Creator. I don't trust in my own abilities to select a spouse. Not that any of my former spouses were not wonderful women. They were. They just were not right for me and me for them.

I do not want you, the reader, to misunderstand my feelings and characterization of Miranda. In sharing the events of the past nineteen years, my goal was to share the pain and troubles that I had gone through and to further illustrate the grace of God; for he has always been faithful to pour down his mercy and grace each and every day. It was not my intent to construct an image of her that is negative or demeaning. I believe that she is a giving, sensitive, and honest person.

Given the fact that Miranda married me out of convenience and not love, combined with the huge age difference, financial stress, co-dependency, and life-threatening illnesses, the foundation of our marriage did not endure. We initially tried to do our best to get along at least for the sake of our children. It wasn't long before my co-dependency reared itself whenever Miranda got into a financial mess, and I began to resent her tremendously. Yet, whenever I caved and helped her out, she stated that she told all of her friends that I was the best ex-husband ever!

While it sounded bizarrely humorous to me, the transparency of her thankfulness overrode my resentment. Regardless of how our marriage ended, we seemed to be equally committed to giving our children emotional security. I certainly wanted to be the dad who modeled behaviors similar to Jesus, and for that reason I had chosen to not tell my kids the back story of how and why our marriage suffered through the years. I wished that Miranda had chosen to not tell my children of my Facebook infidelity.

For that to occur, we need to repent of our sins and to forgive each other for the sins we committed against each other. My prayers for myself are no more than my prayers for Miranda. I want her to be whole and complete and to enjoy emotional, physical, and spiritual health all the days of her life. She deserves nothing less.

My prayers for you, the reader, are that you would be inspired by my story and it would serve to strengthen your faith. Additionally, if you or a member of your family is going through extremely trying times, this is an opportune time for you to seek God's face. Prayer is one of the most powerful ways to seek Him; it is vital that you remember that God owes you nothing.

In fact, if we all got what we truly deserved, we would live in a desolate world, divorced from the joys of knowing Him. Reading and being familiar with scripture will also serve to know His character and promises for those who love Him. I will share several scriptural verses which have inspired me with the hope that they can serve to inspire you as well.

In the Aramaic version of 2 Corinthians 1:3, it reads, "Blessed is God the Father of our Lord Yeshua the Messiah, the Father of mercy and the God of all comfort."

In Isaiah 53:4–5, we read, "Surely He has borne our griefs and carried our sorrows; yet we esteemed Him stricken, smitten by God and afflicted. But he was pierced for our transgressions; he was crushed for our iniquities; the punishment that brought us peace was upon Him, and by His wounds we are healed."

Jeremiah 29:11–12 says, "'For I know the plans I have for you,' declares the Lord, 'plans to prosper you and not to harm you, plans to give you hope and a future. Then you will call on me and come and pray to me, and I will listen to you. You will seek me and find me when you seek me with all your heart.'"

Lastly, In Hebrews 11:1, we read, "Now faith is the substance of things hoped for, the evidence of things not seen."

In *The Ragamuffin Gospel* by Brennan Manning, Manning relates a beautiful story that depicts the true relationship we need to have with our heavenly Father.

> A two-story house had caught on fire. The family, including a father, mother and several children, were on their way out of the inferno when the smallest boy became terrified. He tore away from his mother, and ran back upstairs. Suddenly, he appeared at a smoke-filled window crying like crazy.
>
> His father, outside, shouted: "Jump, son, jump! I'll catch you."
>
> The boy cried: "But Daddy, I can't see you."
>
> "I know," his father called, "I know. But I can see you."

This confidence in God's love and our desire to surrender ourselves into His safekeeping was a tremendous source of comfort to me. He wants us to trust Him with every fabric of our being.

In the midst of my despair, I prayed with all of my heart that God would find a suitable kidney donor for me. Not only did He find a suitable donor; He found an absolute perfect match! I believe that my faith and trust in God's character brought about this miracle. Not for one moment did I ever believe that God would rescue me from death because I was so wonderful and worthy of His help—far from the truth.

I fully recognized that I was no better than anyone else, and God did not give me preferential treatment because of my education, my intelligence, my standing as a father, or the fact that I had helped people throughout my career. He helped me because He chose to, for He is a loving and just God. Perhaps He has more work for me to do before He calls me home. Or, simply speaking, it might have not been my time to die. I do, however, know that He is always faithful, even when we are not.

It is very important to note that we cannot hope to expect that when we make our requests known to Him, that we will always get what we wished. He is the Creator of the heavens and the earth; He is not Santa Claus. Yet, we can be assured that when we make our requests known to him through prayer and petition, with thanksgiving, he will give us a peace that is incongruent with our circumstances.

Given our dire circumstances, there is no way we should be able to experience his peace. But God, who is sovereign over all of the earth, can do whatever He wishes. He can give us unmerited favor (grace), or He can choose to show us mercy even when we deserve punishment. I was incredibly fortunate to have received a large measure of grace … and I am still overwhelmed!

Sixteen years ago, soon after I gave my heart, my soul, and my life to Jesus, I was initially diagnosed with polycystic kidney disease. Not only was I devastated by this news, I became furious with God. I mistakenly believed that once I truly belonged to God, that he would protect me from illness and harm.

My spiritual naïveté not only confused me, it also disoriented my spiritual compass. I suddenly, without any warning, became dizzy, bewildered, and uncertain about my spiritual journey. Little did I know at that time that this upheaval was so necessary, even vital, to my growth as a believer in Yeshua the Messiah.

I had leaned upon my understanding and intellect for all of my life and had built up an enormous amount of egocentricity and pride. After all, not only did I have a direct experience of God before the age of five, I was also told I was a genius when I was in the fourth grade.

At that moment, I was in fear for my life without any safety net beneath me. I understood the role genetics played in the formation of illnesses, but I also knew that God had the ability to alter the course of illnesses and could even change a man's DNA. Why did He allow this to happen to me? My only recourse was to waive the white flag furiously and completely surrender my life to Christ.

Soon after God had sent me an angel whose name is Millie, I slowly began to realize why I had to go through this horrendous ordeal with kidney disease. All of us need to grasp the idea that God can do so much more for us once we live surrendered lives. Letting go of spiritual and intellectual pride sets the stage for God to mold us into the likeness of Jesus.

Until we commit to this process, we can believe that we don't need Him until, of course, we recognize our helplessness to save ourselves. Upon receiving Millie's kidney, I instantly knew that God also allowed my crushing bout with PKD to occur so that in the end, He would prove Himself to be faithful. He would be glorified in my healing. He would be glorified in the telling of my story.

Chapter 31

Since meeting Millie, I had wondered what would possess her to undergo such a painful operation and recovery. Besides feeling stunned at her generosity and immense compassion, I wanted to know who she was as a person and what some of her core beliefs were.

On the surface, Millie was so different than me. She was a southerner who in spite of being raised in the Baptist church was a lesbian. Despite our obvious differences, Millie and I cared deeply for others, especially those who needed our help.

I lived that out as a family therapist, intervening to assist my patients in bringing change into their lives so that emotional, psychological and relationship pain are reduced. Millie has been on a mission trip to Ghana and was so impacted by what she witnessed and experienced that she had strongly considered becoming a medical, foreign missionary.

Many people consider Facebook to be a scourge on our society and many, including myself have abused this social network. Millie was so impacted by my plight that Facebook became a blessing to both us. She had an opportunity to save another's life and I was blessed to be that person. Millie Bomar is an angel sent to me by God.

Millie's background included being raised in a Christian home by parents who have attended Baptist churches throughout their marriage which has extended beyond forty years. Millie became very involved in her church in Rock Hill, South Carolina. Though she sang in her church choir, like many young people she was involved in drinking and marijuana use. Without any warning, Millie suddenly knew that changes were necessary in order to grew deeper in her knowledge and experience of Christ.

"Something grabbed a hold of my heart and told me that I had to make a change in my life."

Millie then began making a much deeper commitment in her walk with the Lord. She increased her church attendance to twice on Sunday, Tuesdays for visitation, choir practice and three-year-old mission friends and Wednesdays for choir practice. She also began doing daily devotionals and eventually went on her mission trip to Ghana. Her life with God became closer and cozier.

Then, one day her life took a drastic turn. At the age of twenty-three, while still very active in her church, Millie had met 2 women who were obviously gay. She had never given her sexuality much thought prior to this chance meeting. Millie had always thought of herself as a tomboy and excelled in sports.

She had managed to keep herself sexually pure and largely focused upon her relationship with Christ and had this realization after spending time with these two women that her purity was rather easy inasmuch as she was never attracted to males. While many women with this same realization might feel liberated, Millie agonized for many months. She prayed with a zeal she had not known before.

"How could God do this to me?" she thought. "Hadn't I been faithful to Him? Why did He allow me to be a lesbian?" Her agony and despair became unmanageable. Depression set in as she prayed that God would change her sexual orientation, but no change had occurred.

One day, Millie got hold of her dad's .22-caliber revolver and jammed it into her mouth. As she pondered squeezing the trigger and bringing an end to her powerful emotional pain, she also wanted the fear of disappointing her parents and God to end. Then, God intervened. Suddenly, thoughts flooded her mind.

"How can I allow my parents to find my body with the back of my head blown off? Don't I love them too much to do this to them?"

The next thought was the deal breaker.

"How can you look Jesus in the face and say, 'I killed myself because I didn't trust You.'

Millie put her dad's gun down and decided to get professional help for her depression. Yet, her confession about being a lesbian, cost her all of her Christian friends. Millie was fearful of this probability, that she had beaten several of them to the punch and cut them out of her life.

While her parents told her that they will always love her, she felt judged by their declaration that her lifestyle was "sinful and wrong." Throughout the years, Millie's parents have not altered their perspective of her lifestyle and their love for her is as strong as ever.

While working with people with emotional and psychological disabilities, Millie had met Chuck, one of the drummers in our church band who had worked with her. Despite their friendship, they lost contact due to Millie's beliefs that they inhabited very different worlds. While she gave up on their friendship due to her fears of rejection from Christians, Chuck did not. Through Facebook, Chuck maintained contact with Millie and he had often sent her many messages and she responded.

On that fateful day when Chuck re-posted my cries for a kidney donor, Millie's empathy and sensitivity to people in need took over. Since she no longer is affiliated with Christianity or any other religion, she stated that she did not sense any calling from God to help me.

Millie explained her motivation to me.

"I was on Facebook and read Chuck's story about you. I was so saddened to learn that many of your family members had the same disease and therefore could not help you with a transplant. I was even more saddened to hear that your wife did not offer to be tested, even if she felt that she had good reasons not to.

"I wondered how alone and desperate you must have felt in your situation. I even wondered if you felt abandoned by God the way I felt all those years ago when I realized I was gay. I didn't want anyone to feel alone and abandoned. I felt deep down that I would be the one to help you, and if the stars aligned, I would do it.

"I felt extremely blessed to be as healthy as I am. I hadn't been to any doctor since I was twenty years old. I love beer, wine, food that is fried and partake in all of it quite often and there was absolutely nothing wrong with me except for my low vitamin D levels.

"After I learned that I was completely healthy, I was even more determined to help you. Elena, with whom I have been in a committed relationship since 2007, was aware of my willingness to give you my kidney. While having coffee together, I mentioned that you and she were 'birthday twins.' Though Elena appeared to be open to giving my kidney to a perfect stranger, I did not seem like a reality to her. When it became obvious that I was a perfect match for you, the reality of imminent danger hit her and hit her very hard. Elena loves me, and she was very scared to lose me should I die in the operating table or lose my remaining kidney through illness or injury down the road. Elena and I had also had many discussions about getting pregnant and starting our family.

"Giving you my kidney would also delay this process. We fought about my decision. I told her 'a promise is a promise and I will not break my promise to Jeff.' My parents were not supportive of my decision either. As the surgery date came closer, the stress levels between Elena, my parents and I became more and more pronounced. I decided that nothing was going to keep me from helping you."

Millie additionally felt that her guardian angels would pull her since they never failed her in the past.

"Since this was a noble cause, I knew they would be there for me and help me."

Millie had the good fortune of being able to take the time off she needed to fully recover without losing any of her salary. This seemed to confirm and answer many of her concerns.

"I had nothing to lose and everything to gain by helping you."

Millie also admitted to having another agenda.

"I wanted to prove to her father and other Christians that gays are not the evil-doers that many in the church and the media portray them to be. After all, how can someone with evil in their heart, be as loving and sacrificial to someone they had never met? I wanted to see the looks on the faces of nurses, doctors and other hospital employees when they see me accompanied by a woman, claim no religious affiliation and donate a kidney to a perfect stranger? I wanted to break the barriers regarding how gay people are seen while helping you when no one else was able to."

Millie is that kind of person who will always be there to help those who are willing to help themselves, but cannot. She is also a human being who is dedicated to always keeping her word even when the stakes are incredibly high. Even to the point of putting her life on the line.

"Jeff, I have no regrets about my decision and would do it all over again. I don't think about it much these days. I simply enjoy life and I am very happy that your children did not and will not lose their father to this disease while they are still so young. I am also saw happy that you no longer have to be hooked up to a dialysis machine to keep you alive and that you can eat, drink and enjoy every aspect of your life and live your life to its fullest. I wanted your grandchildren to know you like I never knew my dad's parents and I my hope for you is that you have a long and full life."

I have no doubts whatsoever regarding Millie's desire to help save me from a life of misery and eventual death. While it is also evident that she had additional reasons for wanting to donate her left kidney to me, I am not a gay male and therefore know nothing about the daily struggles she endures as a lesbian. I am very aware of what scriptures say about homosexuality. I also know that in the eyes of God, no sin is any better or worse than another. In fact, as we continue on in Romans, we read;

"And even as they did not like to retain God in their knowledge, God gave them over to a debased mind, to do those things which are not fitting; being filled with all unrighteousness, sexual immorality, wickedness, covetousness, maliciousness; full of envy, murder, strife, deceit, evil-mindedness; they are whisperers, backbiters, haters of God, violent, proud, boasters, inventors of evil things, disobedient to parents, undiscerning, untrustworthy, unloving, unforgiving, unmerciful…" (Romans 1:28–31).

In Luke 16:15, we read that Jesus had said to the Pharisees, who were lovers of money, the following: "You are those who justify yourselves before men, but God knows your hearts. For what is highly esteemed among men is an abomination in the sight of God."

There is a good amount of scriptures which talk about the activities and conditions of the heart which are considered to be an abomination to God.

I pray that you do not misunderstand my position on this matter. I am not endorsing homosexuality, nor am I trying to provide a justification for it. I am saying that it is not my job to sit in judgment of Millie or anyone else. Jesus, Himself admonished those who did. One of my favorite scriptures is in the book of Matthew where Jesus tells the people that many who expected to be in heaven upon their death will be told by to Him to "depart, for I knew you not" (Matthew 7:22).

My point is that there are many Christians who fully expect to enter the Kingdom of heaven who will be denied entry. There will be others who to the shock and dismay of others, will be invited to spend eternity with Jesus and their heavenly Father. As I stated, it is not my job, nor yours to judge others. I don't know about you, but I have enough difficulty keeping my own life in check without concerning myself with the sins of others.

It is important to note that the judgment of fellow Christians drove Millie out of the church and away from her faith. If her friends at church loved her as a sister in Christ, Millie's attitude toward her faith might very well be different. I have attended several churches where the prevailing attitude is to love visitors as well as congregants just as they are.

Followers of Jesus are all too often are seen as judgmental hypocrites, who are quick to criticize. Yet, scripture tells us that before we judge others, we are to make sure there is no sin in our lives. I wonder how many of us follow this biblical imperative. Jesus told us that he came to cure the lepers, heal the sick and bring hope for the sinners. The truth is, we are all lepers, sick and depraved sinners. He didn't just come to earth for a special segment of the human race. He came to bring salvation to *all of us*, because we are *all in need* of a Savior!

While homosexuality is not a sin I struggle with, there are others such as pride, envy, haughtiness, lust, unbelief and several others that I commit to prayer each and every day. Instead of judging Millie, I thank God each day for her for allowing herself to be used by God to save my life. I am extremely thankful to Him and Millie as well as those who love her dearly who eventually supported and respected her decision to donate her kidney.

Chapter 32

It is now December 25, 2012, and I have spent Christmas Eve alone in my apartment. On Christmas day I was invited to spend Christmas dinner with my closest cousin, Corky who lives only fifteen minutes away from me. While he is two years older than me, his birthday falls one day before mine. Consequently, until I went off to college, Corky and I always spent our birthdays together.

During my college years and the years beyond, regardless of where I lived, Corky and I would always call one another on our respective birthdays. As we both have aged, our time together seems so much more special and we typically spend Sundays watching sports and cutting up.

Both London and Matthew had called me to wish me a "Merry Christmas" and expressing how much they missed me especially during the holidays of Chanukah and Christmas.

London expressed her feelings in her Facebook posting on Christmas Eve:

> This Christmas is definitely a change from what I'm used to. Bitter sweet. I'm just thankful my family is happy and healthy even though it's different now. Miss you, Jeff Rifkin (Daddy).

I was deeply touched by London's declaration of love as well as her admission of mixed feelings. She enjoys living in Louisiana with Miranda's family, yet obviously misses me dearly. To say that I miss my kids is an understatement.

The following day, my Facebook posting was as follows:

> Merry Christmas to London Rifkin and Matthew Rifkin My heart is glad for the love that I feel for you and from you! May the Lord bless you and keep you. Today and forever.

Cyndi and I used Skype on a regular basis and I get to see and talk to my daughter, Hana who is two years old. Hana is a darling and had been talking with great fluidity. I have asked that she call me *saba*, which is Hebrew for "grandfather." When we Skyped several days ago, Hana, upon seeing me, gleefully greeted me with, "Hi, Saba. I love you, Saba!"

She squealed with laughter, apparently proud of her developmental progress. I've missed Cyndi, her husband, Benjamin and my granddaughter and cannot wait to see them when they visit next year. I am also hopeful that I will be able to travel to Tokyo and share time with them in their adopted country.

I moved from Lori's home to an apartment complex in Huntersville, North Carolina just minutes from the house where Miranda and I, along with our children lived. Whenever I drove around this pretty town, I could not help but be flooded with many memories, most of which are joyful and poignant. When I recalled the turmoil that Miranda and I were embroiled in, it was not uncommon for sadness to fill my heart, mind and spirit.

Despite the feelings of emotional and physical abandonment, despite my bitterness for having felt manipulated and used, I had been concerned for Sabrina and her ability to navigate her way through life. God has richly blessed me with a sensitivity, compassion and empathy for the hurts and pains of others. The fact that Miranda and I are no longer married, does not translate into having a hardened heart toward her. It does mean that my obligation to take care of her has ended and while I freely admit that while I have not missed my marriage, I do miss my family.

I have enjoyed living alone as the lack of attachment allows me to make independent decisions regarding important issues such as finances. I am a frugal person and I have refused to buy anything unless it was on sale. My frugality has afforded me larger savings despite paying a healthy portion of child support and alimony. Yet, while I have fully enjoyed living alone, I have frequently prayed that God would bring another woman into my life so that I can fall in love for the last time. I have had great clarity about the woman I have been looking for.

My main criterion is that she must be a woman of faith, a woman who is fully invested in growing in her knowledge of the Lord. I also desire for a woman to have a career of her own; while Miranda and I agreed that she would stay home and raise our children, she also hid behind our agreement in order to avoid facing her fears of inadequacy and independence.

At this point of my life, I want to have greater, if not full control over the money I earn. I recognize that while this desire is not unusual for divorced people, I know that it is a remnant of my marriage to Miranda.

I have dated and have met a few fine Christian women, some of whom were intelligent, caring, and financially independent. Like many busy professionals, I used online dating sites to meet people and the majority of women I met had personal issues that made it impossible for me to continue to see. Many lied about their age and a good number were looking for someone to provide financial support. While each of the women was unique, I had not met that special woman that God had handpicked for me. I have also been busy at working through issues of trust that will necessitate a slow and deliberate dating process.

In November of 2013, both Matthew and London had approached me about wanting to move back with me. London, being a highly intelligent, over-achieving young woman, was unable to attend high school in her local school for more than two days. She found the other kids to be intellectually vacant and very superficial. She therefore continued her studies through Grace Academy's on-line high school program. Yet, she missed her high school friends dearly.

We were making preparations for her move here until Matthew approached me with a far greater need. His grades had fallen drastically and his propensity for using crass language concerned me. Miranda worked long hours and London and Matthew have had no parental supervision whatsoever. Miranda and I have had several long and fruitful conversations about Matthew's needs and she broke down and wept, "Jeff, I have to work long hours and I don't have weekends off. Please know that I am doing my best to help Matthew and London. I feel so guilty. I hope that you aren't blaming me."

Nothing could have been further from the truth. I fully recognized and appreciated how difficult it was to stay on top of Matthew's scholastic needs, given her schedule.

"Miranda, there is no way this could be your fault. Regardless of anything else, I know the kind of mother you are and there is no way that any of this is your fault."

Miranda seemed relieved that I was not judging or condemning her. "Thank you for your understanding. I will miss Matthew so much! I can now imagine what you went through when we all moved to Louisiana."

"Yes, *and* I had to be apart from *both* of our children."

Her words moved me. Prior to this moment, I didn't think she had any idea or capacity to know what it was like for me to say "goodbye" to both of my children as they left North Carolina. We, along with Matthew's input made the decision for Matthew to move back with me and he arrived on January 9. I was ecstatic, although being a single parent to a teenage boy can be a daunting task. He appeared to be excited about raising his grades, getting back into church, doing nightly devotionals with me, and allowing me to help guide his life. Once again, the fact that Miranda and I were able to negotiate this process with no animosity or acrimony was a testament to the progress we have made and our desire to not hurt one another.

While Matthew adjusted to attending a new high school midyear and finding a girlfriend rather soon, he did not do as well as we all hoped and expected. He still experienced a great deal of anger for having to choose between living with his mother and me and blamed me solely for the break-up of our family. He often experienced, anger, depression and frustration, and refused my suggestions for counseling and/or medication.

In April, London moved back as well, and her move made it necessary for me to rent a three-bedroom home in Matthew's school district. Within days of her arrival, Matthew's discontent escalated, and it was not uncommon for London to chide him for his attitude to me.

Within a month of her arrival, Matthew informed me that he would be moving back to Louisiana upon completion of his school year. I took this news rather hard, and experienced depression for several months, but eventually made the emotional adjustment upon hearing how happy and content he was in Louisiana. Although I cannot be certain, I believe that London's arrival provoked a jealousy for my attention which quickened his desire to return to his mother.

My health has continued to be amazingly well. During my last visit with Dr. Chuang, he told me that my creatinine levels vary between 0.9 and 1.02. He went on to explain that he fully expects me to live a long life and that more than likely, my kidney will outlive me! I went from having to see my kidney doctors every three months to every six months! I still have blood draws once each month.

While I have thought of myself as being somewhat expert in the art of communications, I find it extremely difficult to express my deep love and gratitude for the love, mercy and grace that have been poured out upon me. When I attempt to do so, I am reminded of a song, "Thank You, Jesus," written and performed by Terry Clark. The opening verse and chorus are as follows:

> When I think about and remember how
> There was no way out and You rescued me
> There's no reason why
> You loved me then and You love me now
> Least, no reason I can see.
> Thank You Jesus
> For the grace that You have given us
> We could never repay
> But from my heart I'd like to say
> That I thank You.

Chapter 33

Since London's arrival our lives have changed dramatically. She has continued her on-line schooling through Grace Academy and has maintained a 4.03 GPA! Miranda and I are extremely proud of her performance, but even more proud of her maturity and commitment to excellence. When she originally came here, her plans were to finish high school and then seek a scholarship to University of North Carolina Charlotte where she would pursue a degree in English and specializing in teaching English as a second language. She openly desired to move to Tokyo, where she would reside with Cyndi and her family and pursue work in the Japanese school system.

Her plans dramatically changed. She decided that she would move back to Tokyo sometime in early December 2013 and enrolled in a one-year program to learn how to speak fluent Japanese, London's research found a few accredited American colleges that offer teaching and linguistic programs and it is her plan to pursue her college degrees in Tokyo. While I was extremely proud and excited for her opportunities, I was saddened as well. I prayed that my health and finances would be sufficient for me to visit both of my daughters and Hana as soon as possible.

Miranda had been in a committed relationship since January 2013 and married prior to London's departure to Japan. I was happy for her, though the news of her impending nuptials re-opened the wounds of rejection by her. We spoke on a few occasions and shared my blessings for her new life with her. She admitted that while she felt a need to tell me that she had fallen in love, her concerns that I might never have anyone in my life along with her probable guilt of ending our marriage made it difficult to say anything to me.

My prayer life remained very strong. God had shown me that I spent too much of my time worrying about not having enough financial resources. Most divorced men can certainly relate to this, especially when one is paying a healthy amount of child support and alimony. Yet, when my account swells from the blessings of having a full schedule of patients, instead of experiencing joy and serenity, I spent tremendous amounts of time and energy worrying about how to maintain what I had! Either way, I did not experience contentment and/or peace and cried out to God for help. He led me to Philippians 4:11–13: "I am not saying this because I am in need, for I have learned to be content whatever the circumstances. I know what it is to be in need, and I know what it is to have plenty. I have learned the secret of being content in any and every situation, whether well fed or hungry, whether living in plenty or in want. I can do all things through Christ who strengthens me."

This scripture brought deep conviction to my soul. My worry and discontent belied my faith as fear can always be overcome by faith in God. I also believed that every human being experiences fears; they often lurk beneath the surface of our awareness or they can overwhelm us.

My most debilitating fear is the fear of poverty, which stems from the poverty of my early childhood. Regardless of its etiology, I desperately needed God to change me from the inside out. Instead of praying for success and prosperity, which would only keep me addicted to my pattern of fear, I began praying for contentment.

"Lord, thank you for all that you do and all that you are in my life. Father, you have blessed me more than I have deserved and instead of resting in your blessings, the fear of losing what you've given me has cheapened your gifts and blessings. Lord, I now pray and plead with You to help me find contentment in every and all situations; whether my bank account is full or whether it is lacking. Bless me with contentment.

Lord, also help me to find contentment in my desire to fall in love for the last time. Father, I have put myself on dating sites and while I have met many women, I have not found the woman you have hand-picked for me. So, I now ask that you bless me with contentment regardless of my relationship status.

I do not know if you would have me remain single for the rest of my days, Lord; or if you have not yet brought her into my life. Abba, pour out contentment upon me and within me. Help me to be at peace regardless of where I find myself in this season of my life. I ask these things in the precious name of Jesus. Baruch HaShem. Amen."

I prayed this prayer each morning on my way to my office as well as before retiring for the night. Usually, change is not an event, but a process.

In time, I began experiencing fulfillment, peace and satisfaction on a more consistent basis and in turn, became more generous with my money. There were times when fear would show up and I took this as a prompting for prayer; Fear and anxiety had a new context-it was an invitation to spend time with my Creator and seek His equanimity and joy!

Chapter 34

I had been on Match.com for two months and while I met interesting women, none had captivated me. I decided that God's plan did not include falling in love again. Then, something miraculous occurred. After deciding to no longer continue my subscription to Match, I was prompted to renew my membership and immediately saw someone's profile and photo that captured my attention. I sent her a short note and was very pleasantly surprised that she had responded that very day. We had traded emails for a few days and I asked if she had any interest in talking with me on the telephone. While this request might seem innocuous to most, those who have been on dating sites can easily recognize the caution that one needs to use so as to not appear to be a stalker. There is a fine balance that one needs to find when it comes to taking the next step from sharing emails to chatting on the phone. Many want to take their time in getting to know you and others do not want to waste time by "being pen-pals." Shar agreed and we exchanged cell numbers. We spoke that evening for several hours and learned that both of us had previous health crises. Shar had two previous bouts with cancer and I shared my story of PKD and my subsequent kidney transplant. We also learned that we lived no more than one mile from each other and I jokingly said, "I was hoping for someone a bit closer. So, this could be a deal breaker." Shar found this statement to be uproariously funny; in fact, she thought my humor was one of my best attributes. After several phone calls, I asked if she were interested in meeting and she seemed as excited to do so. We began exchanging texts and I soon allowed my heart to once again be hopeful and excited. Shar expressed a great deal of anticipation about meeting me and it was as if she sensed that something very special might happen between us. She and I met on Wednesday, November 11, 2015, and our time together was far more exhilarating than I had expected. As we talked non-stop over a bottled of Malbec, there was a moment in time that I had never experienced before. As I looked into her eyes, time stood still. I found myself becoming lost in her beautiful aqua colored eyes. As she returned my gaze, our souls seemed to have touched and embraced like long-lost lovers. Our shared soul embrace was totally unfamiliar. "What just happened?" Shar asked. "I feel like you looked deep within my soul." "Yes, I think we just connected on a soul level and I don't know about you, but I feel mesmerized by what just occurred." Looking once again into her eyes, we shared soft kisses that made my cold and protective heart thaw with anticipation and longing. I instinctively knew that God was orchestrating this burgeoning relationship and began praising him in silence as we held hands while walking to our respective cars. Shar had already made plans with her good friends for Saturday night and asked if we could see each other Friday evening and early Saturday before meeting up with her friends. Our dates were light-hearted yet very romantic. We also made plans to attend Shar's church, which for me, served to be so significant; to have found a woman who is as tenacious in her faith as me and with whom I connected with on every level imaginable was miraculous. As we worshipped, Shar's hand found mine and as I my eyes found hers, we shared a smile. Shar's eyes twinkled with a love I had not personally received before. We pressed our foreheads together for several seconds and before we joined the congregation in worship, I looked deeply into her eyes. "I love you, Shar" I whispered. Shar squeezed my hand tightly and returned my proclamation of love. We both were cognizant that what we shared was far beyond special and we began seeing each other every day and while we both processed intermittent feelings of fear and cautiousness, we trusted in the Lord. One morning, I awoke from a what I believe was a prescient dream. In it, Shar and I were walking atop several bodies of water. As we did, I could see notable biblical scenes on the shoreline which changed whenever we moved from one body of water to another. At the end of the dream, I noticed a portal that several people were walking through which I sensed was a gateway to a deeper, more profound relationship with God. I awoke just as my alarm sounded. I arose from bed and made coffee. As the coffee brewed, I began texting the content of my dream to Shar. Before I had a chance to hit "Send" I received a text from Shar. In the text, Shar had told me that a week before we had made contact with each other, she was on a walk, crying about a family crisis, She had prayed that God would send her a man with whom she could share her life. Like me, Shar has been previously married and has had her share of heartache and emotional pain. As she did, "Bless the Broken Road," a song by Rascal Flatts played on her phone. This morning, as she walked, the very song played. Here is the first verse, along with the chorus:

> I set out on a narrow way many years ago
> Hoping I would find true love along the broken road
> But I got lost a time or two
> Wiped my brow and kept pushing through
> I couldn't see how every sign pointed straight to you.
>
> Chorus
> Every long lost dream led me to where you are
> Others broke my heart they were the Northern stars
> Pointing me on my way into your loving arms
> This much I know is true
> That God blessed the broken road
> That led me straight to you.

As she listened to this song, Shar heard God's still voice. "Jeff is the one you've asked for." As I read this, tears of joy and thankfulness filled my eyes. I hit "Send." Shar and I marveled at the synchronicity which the Creator of the heavens and earth could only provide. He was answering and confirming our prayers. We took each day as it came and while we perceived that God might be leading us into marriage, we did our best to live in the here and now lest our fears of rejection and heartbreak take root. We met each weekday morning for coffee, breakfast, prayer, and reading a devotional before our workday begins. At the end of each work day, we reunited at her house and spent most of our time talking, praying, watching some of our favorite television shows, and a lot of cuddling. It was not uncommon for us to spontaneously pray for our families and one another; our prayer time was vital to our relationship and our gratitude for bringing us together was never omitted or taken for granted. We looked forward to marveling and experiencing how God was knitting us and our families together.

We spent Thanksgiving with Shar's friend, Karen and her family and before we knew it, Christmas approached. During this entire time, I kept London informed about my relationship with Shar. London seemed so genuinely happy for me and invited both of us to a family sale at American Eagle, where she worked part-time. We drove ninety minutes to Greensboro and picked London up at her dorm room. After purchasing a few items, we drove London back to school and we left to return home. While driving, I received a text from London letting me know how much she liked Shar. I believe she already sensed how in love we were and wanted to support us. Getting her approval meant a great deal to me. No one with children wants to be caught in the middle of divided loyalties and love between their children and significant other, Thankfully, this was not the case.

Shar's mother, Adrienne came to North Carolina from Daytona Beach, Florida and we were often joined by Sabrina and Noah, Shar's daughter and grandson. Our Christmas together was so memorable; I joined Shar at The Cove's Toy Store, a yearly event which assisted the poor in our community in buying Christmas presents for their children. I counted my participation as a blessing and had so much respect and admiration for Shar's desire to help those in need. During lulls in our responsibilities, we found each other's eyes and we stole a kiss when no one was looking in our direction. The love we openly shared gave Shar's family some insight into how deeply we had fallen in love. One evening, while Shar was busy in the kitchen, Adrienne looked at me and stated, "I can see how good you are for Shar. She seems so happy!" To say I was elated at Adrienne's observation and assumed blessing upon our relationship was an understatement. "I am very much in love with your daughter," I confessed. Adrienne smiled and nodded her head. "That's wonderful."

When New Year's Eve arrived, Sabrina, Noah, Adrienne, Shar, and me spent the evening together. As midnight approached, I found myself becoming anxious. I realized that in my marriage to Miranda, New Year's Eve was another event when I felt alone and rejected. A peck on the lips accompanied the obligatory, "Happy New Year!" and as we counted the seconds down on the ball in Times Square, I was extremely uncomfortable until that moment when we found ourselves in the year 2016. Suddenly, Shar put her hands around my neck and kissed me while whispering, "I love you so much!" I began weeping. I was so grateful to God for having such an amazing woman who resonated so strongly with me; finally having a woman who spun in the same orbital path as me made me feel known and acknowledged on the deepest levels of my personhood, and I loved her more than I thought was humanly possible.

Our relationship blossomed with each passing day. We were blessed with excellent communication skills and found it effortless to spend our time together. Shar and I enjoyed the same activities such as exercise, football, museums, live shows, and live music. Going to church was the highlight of our week and relished the time of worship and prayer. As Valentine's Day slowly approached, I gave a great deal of thought to what I wanted to buy the most special person in my life. Most importantly, I wanted to propose and ask Shar to be my wife. Never had I ever been so certain of God's plan for my life and wanted nothing more than to walk through life with her. My nervousness turned to glee when she responded with a resounding "Yes!"

"Wow, we are engaged," we said and the very next day we went to one of the more upscale jewelry stores and Shar and I selected a beautiful engagement ring. I quickly called London and Matthew and shared this profound and wonderful news; they were overjoyed! We set our wedding date for September 17 and created a list of responsibilities each of us would be do. That night, we celebrated our engagement by going to one of our favorite wine bars which offered live music. It was there that we heard, One Paper Crane and quickly asked if this duo would perform the music at our wedding. They quickly agreed, and our to-do list suddenly became one item shorter. Before long, we had hired a photographer and florist and had one of the pastors at The Cove to agree to marry us, but not before meeting with us on a regular basis in order to get to know us and our walk with Jesus. Shar asked Sabrina and London to be her Bridesmaids and I called Matthew to inquire how he felt about being my Best Man. Shar's daughter as well as London and Matthew were excited and honored to stand with and by us on this memorable day. Cyndi, who lives in Tokyo with her family, was sadly unable to make the trip. Although we invited Rachel, she chose to not respond to our invitation. In fact, Rachel made a decision to not have a relationship with me years ago. The rupture in our relationship has been so strong much so, that she did not allow me to walk her down the aisle when she married in 2011. I remain very sad about the loss of my relationship with her, despite Rachel telling me I was a wonderful father. It is so difficult to accept this reality, yet what choice do I have? I will continue to pray for both of us, yet at the age of 71, I am running out of runway.

The grace that God has extended to me throughout my life has for some reason not found its way to my relationship with Rachel. I chose to concentrate on the blessings of my union with Shar and not upon my everlasting sadness about Rachel.

We've been married for four months, and while life presents many challenges and stress, it also provides countless opportunities to provide mutual comfort and prayer. God continues to grow, shape, and mold us into truer Jesus followers by softening our hearts and praying for friends and family who are hurting and frightened, I have always been a very sensitive person, yet my sensitivity has heightened to the point that whenever I inadvertently hurt Shar, I openly weep. I say this not to boast about my spiritual growth, but to more so convey the depth of God's love for me. I want to be more like Jesus and the closer I approach His likeness, the more I weep for hurting anyone, especially those whom I love most. It is my continued prayer that when I talk and interact with others, that they will witness the love and mind of Jesus flowing through me. Many years ago, I would have welcomed death as a cure for my trauma and innermost emotional torture; I now pray that God will grant me many healthy years to share with the love of my life.

As Christmas and New Years of 2016 slowly approached, we had made a decision to travel across the world to visit with Cyndi, Benjamin, and my beautiful grandchildren. Shar came up with the most wonderful idea-to bring both London and Matthew with us so that I could spend the holidays with three of my children. To say I was elated, would be a huge understatement. We made our way to Tokyo and enjoyed a trip of a lifetime. Cyndi and Shar formed such a quick bond that even Cyndi had remarked to Shar, "I can't believe how close I feel and how much love I feel for you in less than ten days!" Our families were being knitted together even more! The next day, we were all sitting around Cyndi's small home, when London sat down beside me on the small couch, put her head on my shoulder and told me how happy she was that I had Shar. "I love her so much, Dad."

As I have continued to work through old co-dependent patterns, I find myself having the capacity to love without an agenda of needing love and adoration in return. Instead, Jesus has taught me to love without conditions or strings attached. Sacrificial love has given me the blessings of not only loving, I care so much for Shar and am actively invested in helping her in all endeavors of our shared lives. Our love is everything I dreamed possible and I can unequivocally admit that my deeply troubled childhood set the stage for unhealthy relationships; and as God heals me from my trauma, my relationship with Shar is free from childlike expectations. I would add that no one has ever loved me with the loyalty, ferocity, affection, and a shared spiritual hunger than Shar. Our relationship, free from criticism and condemnation affords me the room to fully express myself with all of my silliness, romantic gestures, affection, spiritual leadership, and intellectual questioning. It brings me back and serves as a reminder of how I am overwhelmed by the grace of God.

Epilogue

While my transplanted kidney is doing marvelously well, it is estimated that 8% of people stricken with Polycystic Kidney Disease will also develop Polycystic Liver Disease. I was unfortunately in that population and my belly made me look as though I was about to give birth any moment. The pain of all of those cysts in my liver was crippling. I felt as though I had swallowed a bowling ball and often had no appetite or when I did manage to eat, I experienced early satiety; my stomach became full very quickly.

After much research, I decided to seek a hospital that had a stellar liver transplant program in case I qualified for a transplant. My research led me to Emory University Hospital in Atlanta and I began seeing a liver transplant specialist in 2014, and would travel there each year for an updated evaluation. In 2017, while at my desk early in the morning, I felt very dizzy and had passed out and fell onto the floor. When I had awakened, I was unable to use my right arm and probably spent 15 minutes trying to get myself to my feet. After seeing one patient, I went to the rest room only to find blood pouring out of my body filling the toilet bowl. I was frantic and immediately called Shar who took me to our local hospital where the doctors determine that I had variceal bleeding from my esophagus. I needed many blood transfusions and had a banding procedure to stop the variceal bleed in my throat. I was unable to return to work for 2 weeks and my wife and I were very frightened about future bleeds. Two months later while in our beach house, I awoke in the middle of the night to use the bathroom and began vomiting a massive amount of blood while filling the toilet bowl with blood as well. I awakened Shar and instead of going to a local hospital for fear that they would not be equipped or proficient to help with this unique problem, I decided to have Shar drive 4 hours to the hospital that treated me before. When we arrived, in front of the hospital, Shar ran inside screaming for assistance. When a nurse came out with a wheel chair, I fell into it as I had fainted from the loss of blood. The nurse was joined by two men in Hazmat suits. I was admitted and after being in a room for not more than thirty minutes, I passed out once more as my bleeding had not stopped. As the nurses were scrambling, I heard one of them say, "We need to get him to Intensive Care because we are losing him!" I was given 8 transfusions and had lost two-thirds of my blood. My attending Gastroenterologist called Radiology and I had undergone a dangerous procedure, called TIPS where the doctor had shot a shunt into my liver by way of my throat. Before having this procedure, the Radiologist told me that this should help until I get a liver transplant. Shar, one of my physicians, and several nurses all prayed for me as did I. The TIPS worked, and I was out of work for nearly a month.

I sent a message to my liver transplant doctor at Emory University Hospital, informing him of what I had gone through in the past few months. We scheduled another visit and we determined it was time to consider a liver transplant. He then scheduled two days of testing before I could be listed as a candidate for a liver transplant. As it turned out, besides the obvious liver disease, my breathing had been compromised due to my gigantic liver pressing on the bottom of my right lung. The last appointment was with a liver transplant doctor who told me that given my age and the massive size of my liver that he would be terrified to operate on me since there was a strong likelihood that I would never survive the operation. Both Shar and I became extremely depressed as my future looked very bleak. How could God have put me together with a woman I had dreamed of meeting and marrying since I was a young child? Furthermore, I distinctly heard the Holy Spirit tell me that I would be getting a new liver. I was so confused. Did I conjure up this conversation with the Holy Spirit in order to quell my fears? My confusion led me to email a message to my liver doctor explaining the horrid conversation with the surgeon. Within an hour, I received a response stating that the head liver surgeon, Dr. Magliocca wanted to see me after reviewing all of my tests and images. I made the trek to Atlanta and he and his assistant both assured me that they felt completely confident that they could successfully transplant me. I felt elated and after being told that they would apply for exception points since my MELD score was quite low. The higher the MELD score, the higher one moves up on the transplant list. I was then informed that if I did receive the exception points, it would take 3-9 months before getting a suitable liver.

On August 15, 2018, I learned that the exception points were granted and I was then officially listed for a liver transplant. After praising God for paving the way for another transplant, I began thinking about the ensuing months of waiting. Then, the unthinkable happened. Four days later, while we watched church on the Internet, I received a startling phone call. I was told that the hospital had a liver for me and I had to drive immediately as the transplant was scheduled for the very next day! I could not believe what I was hearing and began asking clarifying questions to make sure I heard correctly. I looked at Shar who seemed bewildered if not in shock. Then we realized that God did this for us! After all, who gets a liver transplant less than a week from being on the waiting list? We took turns showering, packed suitcases and made the trip to Atlanta. Shar made a quick phone call to the Mason House, where transplant patients and their families could stay at reduced rates and told them we needed a two bedroom apartment upon discharge from the hospital. It was the protocol to remain in Atlanta for a total of 6-8 weeks as I was required to have blood work done twice weekly and meet with a transplant surgeon weekly once I was discharged. The nearly nine hour surgery went without any complications and after being discharged, I had an appointment with Dr. Magliocca after spending the weekend at the Mason House. He took one look at me, took my blood pressure, checked my pulse and told me he was re-admitting me as I was winded after taking only several steps. As it turned out, I had developed pneumonia from a common cold. My immune system was much compromised from taking large amounts of immuno-suppressant medications. I spent five days in the hospital and then returned to the Mason House, my home away from home.

Shar was scheduled to see her Oncologist to begin Immunotherapy and she was in a great deal of conflict. "How do I leave you for probably a month while you recover" she asked. I reassured her that I would be fine, especially since she hired her nephew to stay and care for me. She reluctantly made her way back to our home in the Charlotte area, where she also had the huge responsibility of caring for our grandchildren. We had custody of an eight year old and an eighteen month old since Shar's daughter was unable to care for them. I felt lonely for her and I felt helpless to assist her and this was a huge motivator for me to get strong enough to be able to return home. I had a Physical and Occupational therapist and had to work on building up my endurance and weight as I was a mere 123 pounds when I had left the hospital. Although it was somewhat shocking to weigh that little, it made sense when I was told that my liver had weighed 20 pounds! I therefore walked as much as I could while not exhausting myself. Having 33 staples in my abdomen made it challenging to care for my hygiene but managed to shower every other day since the act of showering was difficult and tiring. Shar and I spoke each morning and Skyped each night. We both struggled with longing to be together; her cancer treatment was foremost in my mind and my recovery occupied her thoughts as well. On October 2nd, Shar's good friend, Barbara drove to Atlanta and took me home. Our reunion was one of the happiest moments in a very long time as Shar and I had never spent so much time apart from one another. She was outside and she ran into my arms. We embraced and kissed for several minutes. It felt so wonderful to feel and experience her deep love for me. Our grandson ran to me as well and I was the recipient of a big hug! After a little while, we drove to pick up our young toddler from daycare. When I walked into her classroom, she shrieked with delight, screamed "Papa!" and ran as fast as she could to my open arms.

As our marriage continued to flourish, both Shar and I were tested with severe health issues. Lynch Syndrome produced two cancers within the past two years. In 2017, I had accompanied her to Cleveland Clinic where she had 9 hours of surgery and had to undergo chemotherapy which wreaked havoc upon her body. The

Lord had heard our prayers and she was cancer free until 2018 when another cancer appeared. She is currently receiving immunotherapy and will be on this regimen for an unknown amount of time to not only eat up this latest tumor; it can be preventative as well. We have additionally read that a vaccine for Lynch Syndrome is being considered in an effort to boost the immune system to no longer produce cancer. While it appears that her course of immunotherapy is successful in dissolving the cancer, the side effects of bone pain and neuropathy in her hands and feet are troublesome to say the least. Yet, our faith is strong despite moments of fear where the mind creates thoughts and pictures of the worst case scenarios. It is a battleground that we fight together.

As Shar and I recuperate from our health crises, we have returned to our respective jobs and are considering retirement. It is extremely difficult for her to do her job to the level she and her superiors are accustomed to while remaining on immunotherapy for an indefinite period of time. When we take into account the pain and fatigue she experiences daily and being the primary caretaker for the grandchildren, they are demanding tasks which enervate her to the point of feeling overwhelmed.

I plan on retiring as soon as London finishes her last semester at college where she will graduate with a degree in Interior Architecture. Since I am the only parent supporting her, I need to continue to work. It has taken me a good deal of time and prayer to let go of my resentment of Sabrina for not contributing for our daughter's college experience and daily living expenses. I've learned long ago that it is a daunting task to get someone to change their beliefs and assumptions; Sabrina has stated that I should pay for all of London's college expenses because "If we were still together, you'd be paying it anyway." I tried explaining that when our kids were young and she home schooled them, I never intended for her to stay at home once our kids because adults. Plus, she decided to leave our marriage because she did not want to take care of a sick man. My explanation fell upon deaf ears and after arguing about it, we no longer have any conversations whatsoever. So, rather than stay angry, I've decided to focus upon what is good and wonderful in my life. I remain very close with Cyndi, London, and Matthew and still mourn the loss of my relationship with Rachel. I am embarking upon a career as a portrait photographer. I have loved portrait photography for decades and fully seeing God's blessings and grace in my life, I want to live out the rest of my life bringing beauty and art into my life as well as to those who want the same for themselves and/or family members.

My life has been an exciting if not difficult ride at times. It is my prayer that God will have me around long enough to pay his loving kindness forward to my children and grandchildren. I am so in love with Shar that I want both of us to be around for many more years as we seek after him and love others as he has loved us. One of my prayers is for God to love Shar through me and for that to occur, I need to let go of all resentment and bitterness and become the man he intended me to be. I pray to become that man.

Jeremiah 17:7-8

But blessed is the one who trusts in the Lord, whose confidence is in Him. They will be like a tree planted by the water that sends out its roots by the stream. It does not fear when heat comes; its leaves are always green. It has no worries in a year of drought and never fails to bear fruit.

Toolboxes

I have created a workbook which will help you, the reader, have a method of internalizing and processing my story. Each workbook chapter will have what I hope to be deeper truths about my experiences as well as associated scriptural verses and questions for you to answer. It is my prayer that you will utilize this format to learn more about yourself and how God has been there through each and every one of your trials and difficulties. While this book is "my story," I am not unique. During our lifetimes, we will have to endure health, relationship, and spiritual crises. How we choose to cope and deal with each crisis, often defines our identities; and our decisions and the choices we make have the power to determine the course and trajectory of our lives. We will either be crushed by emotional, physical and psychological pain or we will find growth in them. The outcomes are largely determined by several factors. Maintaining a sense of hope and believing that positive change can occur is imperative. Without hope, we will be besieged by despair and depression. In Romans 5:3–5, scripture says, "Not only so, we also glory in our sufferings, because we know that suffering produces perseverance; perseverance, character; and character, hope. And hope does not put us to shame, because God's love has been poured out into our hearts through the Holy Spirit, who has been given to us."

I am not suggesting that everyone should be able to rejoice and find glory in their sufferings without any difficulty whatsoever. That would belie our identities as human beings. I do not for a moment believe we can stand firm in this belief without the faith and the power of Almighty God. Nor am I stating that we won't go through times of faith crises. There were times when I prayed and then asked the Lord if he were real. "Am I praying into vapors, or can You hear me!"

Yet, I prevailed in my cries for help. God will make us increasingly aware of our inadequacies to alter and control many parts of our lives in order to increase our dependency upon Him. My back was also pressed against the wall and I had nowhere else to turn. When we sense that God has abandoned us when we need Him the most, our prayers and praise must prevail. Our prayers will ultimately bear the fruits of hope and faith.

Another factor which can create growth through and in spite of our crises is the opportunity of not having to bear our burdens alone. Talking with supportive family members, counselors, friends, and clergy will afford you the tremendous gift of not having to walk through theses crises alone; it will additionally give you the opportunity of getting the necessary feedback to check your beliefs and assumptions regarding your issues. The feedback can serve as a reality check and can often interrupt your patterns of negative and fruitless thinking. Thoughts can have very strong power, not only upon our emotions; they can directly influence the course of our lives. For instance, if I believe that my health problems are hopeless, the hopelessness can shut down our immune system, thereby rendering it ineffective and useless. This is turn will decrease our body's ability to repair itself and thus confirm our despair.

I will also add that we need to accept our vulnerabilities as well as our strengths. The ability to admit that we feel hopeless, afraid and alone can often be transformed and transmuted when we admit our failings and weaknesses, Scripture says that we when we are weak we are made strong by the power of Christ.

It is my prayer that you will read and participate in the Toolbox sections and as a result, you will personalize and therefore find growth through them.

Workbook Question 1
Finding Meaning in Loss

For my thoughts are higher than your thoughts,
neither are your ways my ways.
—Isaiah 55:8

What man can live and not see death, or save
himself from the power of the grave.
—Psalm 89:48

While it is an indisputable fact that each of us will experience the loss of friends and family and face the inevitability of our own demise, how we respond and react to our losses, will determine the degree of joy that we experience throughout our lives. Most people will agree that the passing of loved ones diminishes and robs us of happiness and peace. Yet, when we develop a close relationship with God, it is entirely possible for joy and contentment to reside within our hearts and minds. How is this possible? The Apostle Paul has modeled how to be content in any and all circumstances when his dependency upon Christ was so complete that he could find peace even when he was jailed, starved, and whipped. When we come before Christ fully trusting in Him for all things, we can find joy despite our human hearts being broken by the death of a loved one. As I sat beside my dying mother, my thoughts swirled and knew that this was the moment I feared most. It was inconceivable to believe that I would no longer have the hilarity we frequently shared. Those priceless times when our conversations had so much depth as we wrestled with the paradoxes which dotted everyone's life. My mother taught me how to love. Who will finish this incomplete task? How will I manage to deal with the complexities of living in a world that was so messy and gray, when I craved the certainty that a black and white world might offer? I thought of the Apostle Peter, who when asked by Jesus if he wanted to run for his life, responded, "To whom shall I go? You have words of eternal life." My only response was to draw myself closer to Him and I clung to Him, lest I died from fear and despondency.

Questions

1. During our lifetime, we will lose many loved ones. When you suffered a heart-breaking loss, how did you respond? Did your loss separate you from God or did it draw you closer? Please explain.

2. When you have lost a loved one, did you seek out others to share in your loss and allow yourself to be comforted? If not, why?

3. Many of us create assumptions as to why "God took my loved one from me." In addition, many people die because of poor decisions and habits which put their health and lives at risk. Since we know that whatever is born is destined to die, can you accept the loss of someone you love without attributing the loss as being part of God's plan for your life?

4. Since God's ways and thoughts are higher than ours, while we cannot know why loved ones die when they do, God will use our loss to grow you more into the likeness of Jesus. Can you describe when this has occurred to you?

5. When someone you love dies, it is not uncommon for us to have some measure of regrets. Do you have any regrets? If so, what regrets to you have?

6. What do you need to let go of your regrets? Have you decided to forgive yourself for your decisions and shortcomings?

7. How do you find meaning in life given the loss of a loved one? Do you give up or do you continue seeking God's plan for your life? Please explain.

8. When a loved one dies, can you give yourself permission to live a full life? If not, why? If yes, please talk about in what ways do you live out a full life?

9. A common belief is that when a loved one dies, he or she must have been special for God to take him. I believe that this is not a spiritually healthy belief because we live in a world that is frail and imperfect and tragedies naturally occur. Have you found comfort in believing that you lost loved one was special and was therefore taken by God?

10. How can your loss help another person who has had a similar loss? Please explain.

11. Can you live with and accept the fact that there may not be a satisfactory explanation for the loss of your loved one? Please tell me how.

12. I have found that there are times when, because of difficult circumstances I have questioned God's existence. I have also learned to give myself permission to question many things I have learned about God. Have you ever felt guilty because you questioned God's existence or His goodness when your loved one died because "that's not what a good Christian should do?" If so, please explain how you worked through that challenging time.

Workbook Question 2
Dealing with Early Childhood Trauma

Come to me, all who labor and are heavy burden, and I will give you rest. Take my yoke upon you, and learn from me, for I am gentle and lowly in heart, and you will find rest for your souls. For my yoke is easy, and my burden is light.
—Matthew 11:28–30

I sought the Lord, and He answered me and delivered me from all of my fears.
—Psalm 34:4

"But whoever listens to me will dwell secure and be at ease, without dread of disaster."
—Proverbs 1:33

"For the mountains may depart and the hills be removed, but my steadfast love shall not depart from you, and my covenant of peace shall not be removed", says the Lord, who has compassion for you.
—Isaiah 54:10

Many adults have sought counseling and psychotherapy for early childhood traumas. Many of these people experience depression, attachment difficulties, irritability, abandonment fears, and flashbacks. When I found Jay's lifeless body, I developed an insatiable desire to understand the mind and heart of God while also creating a dissociative, dreamlike state. This dissociate state was also accompanied by a mild, yet constant depression as well as social anxiety. I was fearful of being the center of attention when I was in the company of people I hardly knew. My self-esteem was very low, which when looking back should not have surprised me, given my father's ever-present criticisms of everything I did. I often entertained, daydreaming where I was the star athlete and most popular boy with the girls. These fantasies helped me cope with my profound loss. Yet, my relationship with God flourished despite the fact that God and religion were mentioned only during the Jewish High Holy Days and the other feasts. I fully realize that there might be many other therapists who would argue that my experiences with God were nothing more than another expression of my dissociative states I entered each night. However, I when I had completely stopped these wish-fulfillment fantasies, my experiences with God continued, as they do to this day. I had additionally received therapy for my trauma and I while there are still remnants of grief (I don't think anyone ever fully resolves intense loss), I have learned to fully accept my loss. Life must always go on, despite our losses, pain, and grief. My belief in Jesus and his resurrection brings me enormous hope that Jay and I will be reunited in heaven; and God demonstrates His love for me daily in very palpable, unmistakable ways. For that, I am eternally grateful.

Questions

1. Have you experienced childhood trauma? If so, please recount the painful experience(s).

2. How has the trauma manifested in your adult life? Do you and your spouse, significant other, and family others recognize that your difficulties can be traced to the trauma of your childhood?

3. What steps have you taken to heal and resolve the issues that have caused you emotional, psychological, and relational pain?

4. Are you besieged by painful memories, and if so, what have you done to find relief?

5. Many people have a sense of helplessness regarding their traumatic childhood. How have you sought God's healing hands so that you can find freedom from your past and fully enter into a less burdened life?

6. When these wounds have been healed, how do you envision your life changing? Please describe how your career, relationships, emotions, beliefs, perspectives, and walk with the Lord will be affected.

JEFFREY M. RIFKIN

Workbook Question 3
Finding and Nurturing a Lasting Love

Because Your steadfast love is better than life,
My lips shall praise You.
—Psalms 63:3

I have been crucified with Christ. It is no longer I who live, but Christ who lives in me. And the life I now live in the flesh, I live by faith in the Son of God, who loved me and gave Himself for me.
—Galatians 2:20

Love is patient, love is kind. It does not envy, it does not boast, it is not proud. It does not dishonor others, it is not self-seeking, it is not easily angered, it keeps no record of wrongs. Love does not delight in evil but rejoices with the truth. It always protects, always trusts, always hopes, always perseveres. Love never fails.
—1 Corinthians 13:4–8

Though One may be overpowered, two can defend themselves. A cord of three strands is not easily broken.
—Ecclesiastes 4:12

After two failed marriages and an apparent inability to find true, lasting love since my divorce from Miranda, I had firmly believed that I was incapable of ever loving again. My heart was scarred from the deep emotional cuts from my marriage and divorce, and while I experienced peace and contentment in being alone, my heart longed for the joy and elation I had dreamt of for most if not all of my adult life. I was adamant about not settling for someone who God had not sent for me. One day, I found a bible verse which read, "Unless the Lord builds the house, the workers labor in vain" (Psalm 127:1). Realizing that all of my choices in women were based on my criteria borne from a broken childhood, I simply asked God to handpick a woman for me. Self-reliance had not worked for me and I could no longer trust my judgment where women were concerned. Furthermore, if it was God's will that I live out my life without having found a true, lasting love, with His help I knew I could be content. Besides, the love that God had deposited in me on the day of my salvation was very active, especially since my life-saving kidney transplant. The love for my children, sisters, nieces, nephews, my grandchildren, friends, and strangers has given me deep emotional satisfaction.

While I continued to trust, praise, and seek God's will for my life, my most fervent prayer was to love others as Jesus did. After all, what good would come from God sending a perfect woman for me, if I could not love her unconditionally? Looking back upon my marriages and other relationships both prior and subsequent to marriage, my behaviors were very co-dependent—I loved in order to receive love. While I was for the most part, patient and kind, I did keep a record of how I felt short-changed in not receiving as much as I had given. Additionally, the love that I had given to other women was ultimately about me, for it is impossible to have co-dependent love without being consumed with one's needs. In short, I needed to change; my prayer life prior to meeting Shar took on a cry for God's help in re-shaping and remolding me into more of a Godly man, a man who can give love to others without any expectations of them being in debt to me. This way of loving was not only foreign to me, it gave me even greater freedom to love as I was no longer consumed by my needs to receive love from others. While God created palpable changes in me, the path to becoming Christ-like is never truly complete while one is still alive. He does promise however, that He will continue this endeavor until the day of Christ Jesus-that is until we join Him in heaven or when we witness the return of the Messiah.

When I was blessed to have met Shar, I was now faced with what my responsibilities were to keep our love alive and growing. I knew this- God had to be the center of our relationship. We both sensed the need to attend church regularly, participate in daily devotionals, and making our prayer life a primary activity in our burgeoning, budding relationship. We discussed the Five Love Languages, a book that speaks about the ways in which we know we are loved by our significant other or spouse. I soon learned that Shar greatly appreciated when I helped her with cleaning and stacking dishes and glassware into her dishwasher. This small act let her know that I did not take her efforts to cook a meal for us for granted, and she therefore felt loved. Knowing how these acts of service impact her, I often let her dog, Sam outside for a walk and will also massage her shoulders and neck which are both areas where she holds stress. She, in turn demonstrates a lot of physical affection and engages in meaningful conversation with me knowing that both of these areas are vital to my sense of feeling loved. In other words, we are very intentional about giving love to one another, lest our relationship withers and becomes mundane. I believe that when God is the cornerstone of a relationship, while we are not immune from difficulties and trials, He wants us to experience an extraordinary amount of joy. When we freely love, we can then encounter a love far greater than we knew possible. Joy becomes the manifestation of this extraordinary love whether it's for our significant other and/or the rest of humanity. When both intentionally love each other this way, the relationship has enough room for others to see God in the midst of this love.

If you wish to create and maintain a strong loving relationship, you must recognize that love cannot be sustained by selfish acts. Love always demands sacrifice; this is the model Jesus gave to us. Sacrifice can never co-exist with self-absorption for when we truly love, giving must be the natural response. This is a vital way to ensure durability in a relationship. We should always bring our desires and questions regarding a love relationship to the Lord so that the relationship is guided and led by God's will, while knowing that God has given us free choice. I have counseled so many couples over the years who either did not fervently pray for God's guidance or assumed that God was blessing the relationship based on feelings and emotional impressions. Often, we create God in our image, thereby attributing our desires for love to Him. I have found one litmus test to be extremely beneficial—if a relationship leads us away from God, this is a good indicator that this relationship does not contain His will or His blessings. Conversely, if the relationship draws each partner into a greater love for God, then we have the freedom to have God love our partner through us. God can love far more powerfully and consistently than we.

One important dynamic to pay close attention to is the expression of our needs. So many couples find their way into therapy because they fail to ask for what they want. Instead, they assume that their spouse or partner should know what their needs are. When questioned about this strategy, many have stated, "My spouse should know what I need or want" or "I want him/her to anticipate my needs." Unless we make our requests known in an explicit fashion, how can we expect our spouses to know what it is that we want or need? I often talk about this in therapy and I am no longer surprised how entrenched this dynamic is in many marriages. Unless these communications occur, couples often argue or suffer in silence feeling unloved and not understood. It amazes me how quickly a couple can repair their marriage when they make their requests known to one another. This therapeutic strategy is similar to what the Apostle Matthew says, "You have not because you ask not" (Matthew 4:2). While this passage speaks self-reliance and not asking God to meet our needs, the application works in marriages as well.

Despite loving unconditionally, disagreements and arguments are bound to take place in every relationship. Striving to avoid conflicts at all costs will cause us to be inauthentic and co-dependent. What then shall we do when disagreements, hurt feelings, and resentments occur? Without writing a comprehensive book on this subject, the following suggestions will serve as the Rules of Engagement. Instead of blaming your partner for how you feel, it is much more efficacious to make "I" statements. "I" statements tell your partner how his or her actions have affected you. An example would be as follows: "When you didn't clean up your mess as you promised, I felt as though you take me for granted. What I need from you is to keep your word when you make promises." As you can see, there was no name-calling or verbal attacks, which often create defensiveness and hurt/angry feelings. Instead, a direct comment which relates feelings to behaviors is utilized.

When we communicate disappointments, hurt, or anger, it is not uncommon for the partner to make defensive statements such as "You do the same thing!" or "Do you know how many times I clean up after you?" Another example is that when the husband returns from work to find a sink-full of dishes. He relates his upset, and the wife promptly states, "Well, I'm sick and tired of having to pick up your dirty clothes from the floor!" If both partners engage in this style of communication, it often turns into vicious cycle where neither accepts responsibility for their behaviors but instead, blames the other for past transgressions. If your partner makes an "I" statement to you with respect to something you did or did not do which annoyed or bothered them, deal with that issue without bringing up a complaint that you have. If you have an issue, process that with your spouse once you have settled the matter at hand.

No relationship is perfect. We are all broken people, subject to sin, selfishness, keeping a record of our partner's imperfections, and having issues related to intimacy. Yet, because of the indwelling of Christ, we can change in profound ways. Give freely to those you love without any agendas for when sacrifice and giving define your relationship, your love can flourish in ways that perpetuate your love.

Questions

1. God does not want us to keep a record of wrongdoings that our spouses or significant others commit. Yet, we often do this for all of the wrong reasons. One being the need to be loved. When have you loved someone so much, that you overlooked their obvious deficiencies as a way to substantiate your feelings for them? Please describe your actions when you participated in this dysfunction.

2. There are times when confronting an important issue is vital to resolving issues. However, there are times when it is more important to overlook the frailties of our spouse. How do you know when you should discuss an issue and when it is better to overlook it and move on?

3. What dynamics are present within yourself and/or your relationship which stop you from confronting important issues that you have with the person you love?

4. Godly love demands that you love your spouse without any hidden agendas or conditions. How have you either been able to accomplish this or have failed at accomplishing this?

5. Maintaining healthy boundaries are important to any relationship. Failure to do so eventually breeds contempt and resentment. What does healthy boundaries look like to you and your spouse?

6. How have you struggled or accomplished being able to love unconditionally while also maintaining appropriate boundaries so that your needs are also met?

7. Name some areas of your life where you forego your needs not because your love for your spouse is sacrificial and unselfish, but more so because your expectation is that you will be loved for your sacrifice?

8. Giving to your spouse with the expectation of receiving often puts us in the role of martyr, especially if we don't voice our needs and expectations. If you or your spouse is actively engaged in this dynamic, how does this impact your relationship?

9. What specific needs or wants do you historically choose to not share with your spouse?

10. Have you been able to identify why you might find it difficult to directly state your needs to your spouse? Do you have fears that if you did make your needs and wants known that you feel rebuffed or rejected?

Workbook Question 4
Christians and Divorce

Have you not read that he who created them from the beginning made them male and female, and said, "Therefore a man shall leave his father and his mother and hold fast to his wife, and the two shall become one flesh"? So they are no longer two but one flesh. What therefore God has joined together, let not man separate.
—Matthew 19:4–6

And I say to you: whoever divorces his wife, except for sexual immorality, and marries another, commits adultery.
—Matthew 19:9

For the man who does not love his wife but divorces her, says the Lord, the God of Israel, covers his garment with violence, says the Lord of hosts. So guard yourselves in your spirit, and do not be faithless.
—Malachi 2:16

It is very obvious that when God created mankind, He intended for a man and woman who have entered into the covenant of marriage, to remain together for the remainder of their lives. However, when sin entered the world, there was made a provision to break this covenant when sexual immorality occurred. When we look at the divorce rates among people who do not consider themselves Christians and compare it to the rate of divorce among those who are, there is little disparity between these figures. There is little doubt that Christians divorce only because of adultery; many cite marital problems such as communication breakdowns, physical and/or emotional abuse, substance abuse, growing apart, having little commonality, no longer being in love, anger issues, over involvement with careers, lack of sexual and emotional intimacy, extreme differences in parenting philosophy, mental health problems, pornography addiction, and extramarital affairs.

The question that most Christians should be asking is, why is it that our divorce rates are equal to those of non-believers when we have the power of the Holy Spirit dwelling inside of each of us? The answer to this question is multifaceted. Firstly, despite our faith, we are broken human beings who frequently limp through life. Our limps are caused by early childhood wounds, fear and anxiety, depression and hopelessness, addictions and other maladies that make us fractured "jars of clay." It is only our faith in Christ that keeps us from being crushed and destroyed. If this last statement is true, why then are we subject to broken relationships and splintered families? I believe that if couples embraced the teachings of Jesus and truly became His disciples, the divorce rate would descend and diminish. What then should we say to the woman who is routinely physically and emotionally abused and tortured? Or the wife whose husband would rather absorb himself in pornography rather than show her any love and attention? Or the man whose wife is an alcoholic and refuses to throw herself into a treatment program in order to save herself and her family? What does one say to anyone whose spouse has extramarital affairs and despite their promises to remain faithful, continue nonetheless? I always wonder whether God would have couples whose marriages are extremely dysfunctional and painful, remain in this marriage "until death do them part"? While God's original plan for marriage was intended to meet our need for companionship especially as it reflects His relationship with us, what is a couple to do when their relationship has devolved into a tangled ball of emotional pain, hurt, and betrayal?

This chapter is not intended to give you ample reasons to divorce your spouse despite the pain and suffering you might be experiencing. Every person should subject their decision to divorce to fervent and continued prayer, remembering that God loves both of you equally. It is my experience as a marriage counselor that most people select their partner from a place of brokenness and expect that he or she will give us what we need to feel whole and complete. Only God has this power. Additionally, many choose their partner, believing that they can change whatever deficiencies or habits they have and demonstrate. I remind unmarried people that the person they are engaged to will be the same person they will call their husband or wife. If one enters into the marital covenant believing that their partner will become someone they are not, the relationship will bring a great deal of frustration, resentment, and unhappiness. When infidelity or abuse of any kind takes place, true repentance and contrition must be present. Unless the offending spouse is truly sorry for the pain they've caused, it is likely to occur again. You might be thinking, "How can he possibly know this?" Over the course of my career, I have listened to many spouses voice their apologies not because they were truly sorry for the pain and betrayal they've created. They were sorrier that others know of their abuse or sorry they were caught in their duplicitous lies than the emotional damage they've done. This often leads to a continuation of the pattern unless the offending spouse is open to professional and/or pastoral assistance.

Lastly, if couples were to devote their lives to being more like Jesus, marriages can flourish and love can abound. Instead of believing that we deserve a good marital partner, ask God to help you become that person for your spouse. Furthermore, if each partner were to take their relationship with Jesus to be vital to their life, their discipleship can transform them into being far more than their past. Jesus has the power to help us love as He loves. That said, when there is no hope for changing the trajectory of marriage due to many factors, one should always subject their decisions to prayer and much introspection, remembering that in most instances, both partners have contributed to the demise of the marriage.

Questions

1. Many Christians have heard the message that unless a spouse has been unfaithful, there is no valid reason for divorce. Is this true for you? If not, what other circumstances would provoke you to consider divorce?

2. What changes do you need to make so that your marriage is more solid?

3. Do you feel that since "God hates divorce" you will be sinning if you have either gotten divorced or considering divorce due to any form of abuse, addiction, incompatibility, frequent or unrelenting arguments, or growing apart?

4. If so, what do you believe God would have you do if you have already tried marriage counseling, pastoral counseling, etc.?

5. If you have been divorced, do people in your church treat you differently than those who remain married? If so, what motivates others to treat you the way they do?

6. When we get divorced, we often need time to process our sense of failure, guilt, mistrust, or resentment before we consider dating. What issues do you feel you need to work on so that you don't bring these problems into a new relationship?

7. Divorce is often experienced as a death. It is the end of the hopes and dreams that you and your spouse formed when you first married. How has your grief manifested and how do you/have you coped with the grief associated with divorce?

8. If you have been divorced, do you have any doubts or mistrust regarding your ability to pick a good mate? If so, how will you know when you've met the right person for you?

9. What qualities or characteristics are most important to you when considering dating and remarrying?

JEFFREY M. RIFKIN

Workbook Question 5
Dealing with Personal Failure

But he said to me, "My grace is sufficient for you, for my power is made perfect in weakness." Therefore I will boast all the more gladly of my weaknesses, so that the power of Christ may rest upon me. For the sake of Christ, then, I am content with weaknesses, insults, hardships, persecutions, and calamities. For when I am weak, then I am strong.
—2 Corinthians 12:9–10

My flesh and my heart may fail, but God is the strength of my heart and my portion forever.
—Psalm 73:26

If we confess our sins, he is faithful and just to forgive us our sins and to cleanse us from all unrighteousness.
—1 John 1:9

Whoever conceals his transgressions will not prosper, but he who confesses and forsakes them will obtain mercy.
—Proverbs 28:13

But God shows his love for us in that while we were still sinners, Christ died for us.
—Romans 5:8

Failure is very much like death and taxes, it is unavoidable. In fact, many educators, businesspeople, workshop leaders, and athletes have opined on how failure is always experienced within success; failure often drives and motivates people to work harder and smarter to achieve success. The failure I am speaking of in this workbook chapter is more of a personal nature. While I have had two failed marriages that have caused pain and suffering to my children as well as my ex-wives and myself, I am more concerned about my failure in violating my moral code. How does one who is deeply committed to his walk with Jesus, knowingly involve himself in a lascivious online relationship? Earlier, I admitted that my decision was purely borne from rejection and extreme frustration and I had hoped to be caught in order to force Miranda into marital counseling or divorce. Regardless of my motives, what I did was not only sinful; it led me into deep depression as I was unable to reconcile this reckless decision with the pain and suffering it brought to my children.

While my love for each of my children was constant and unrelenting, when the truth came out, London and Matthew's perception of me was greatly altered. Instead of the loving, caring, and fully participating father they believed me to be, I was now a man who cheated on their mother. Inasmuch as Miranda had no filter and therefore yelled and screamed at me in earshot of my children, they knew all that I had done. While I explained to them that what I did was inexcusable, I wanted them to know that I had never kissed or touched another woman during my marriage to their mother. This seemed to ameliorate some of their huge disappointment in me; yet, their pain persisted as our family unit broke apart. I could have explained to them why I chose to act so selfishly, but had sense enough to realize I would do more damage by offering up my reason for my actions. Sharing my frustrations about the lack of intimacy in the past fifteen years was of course, totally inappropriate. My perception of myself had also been altered by my infidelity. As explained earlier, I took great pride in knowing that I would *never* be unfaithful on any level. I now recognized that I was no different from the many men I had judged, and this knowledge brought me to my knees. I was a broken man, left to deal with possibly facing death with no wife or children to comfort me. At this lowly point in my life, my moral failure left me with no other place to go than to the cross where my sins would be cleansed by my confession and repentance. I had often heard from the pulpits of many churches that God strengthens us when we are weak. These echoing words began to take root with my heart and mind. I finally realized what that truly meant—weakness and frailty are as part of the human condition as is the need for food, oxygen, and sleep and when we let go of self-sufficiency as a means of coping and getting through life, God's strength, grace, and mercy carry us beyond our personal failures.

So how should anyone who has made decisions which bring about personal failures respond? Firstly, it is vital to admit that you are not any more special than anyone else. Regardless of our position in church and in society, we all fall short of the glory of God. Therefore, we are prone to moral failures simply because of our sinful nature. It is equally as important to remember that if we've not strayed from our walk with Jesus, it is not cause to boast. Instead we should thank Him for our faith and steadfast commitment lest we think we are better than others. Secondly, we need to confess our sins so that God will forgive us from all unrighteousness. I knew an elderly gentleman who was highly displeased in his five-year marriage and had planned on having an affair while his wife sat at home. He purchased wine and filled his prescription for Viagra. His plan was very thought-out until he decided to share it with me. He anticipated that I would be very encouraging and instead questioned him why he would be so casual about committing adultery. He replied with, "No problem; I'll just repent tomorrow." I could not believe what I was hearing because plan of repentance was not true repentance.

Premeditated repentance is not truly being sorry for one's transgressions. It's a cavalier scheme to justify one's sins before they are acted upon. Please understand that I am not condemning this man for what he did for after all, my sin was no better or worse than his. I was truly lost during my online escapade and did not realize how broken I was until after the fact. I accepted that I betrayed my wife's trust and to this day, I feel sorrowful about the pain and the cost of my transgressions. True repentance drives us closer to God with the knowledge that we bring nothing to the table, except Christ crucified in us. Repentance should bring about a deep sorrow for sinning against others and God. It literally means to "change one's mind" so that we cling to God in order for His strength to sustain us during times of temptation and doubt. Thirdly, we must recognize that life's landscapes are replete with the shards and remnants of many who have worshipped their self-reliance and independence. Armed with the knowledge and understanding that we *need* God each and every moment of every day, because we receive God's peace when we trust Him in the midst of life's storms.

Questions

1. What are you biggest personal failures, and how have you chosen to deal with them?

2. Have you shared and talked about your personal failures with another person? If so, what affect did it have upon your consciousness, beliefs, and feelings about you?

3. How would you describe your relationship with God? Please include the ways and methods you draw yourself closer to Him.

4. I believe that repentance and forgiveness are pillars of our faith. Do you struggle with true repentance and if so, why?

5. Do you hold on to grudges and feel somewhat entitled to your feelings of hurt and/or anger? If so, please explain why.

6. Are you quick to judge and condemn the issues and sins of others and forgo Jesus's admonition to love others despite their lifestyle? Why do you feel entitled to judge?

7. Please talk about the sins you struggle with and how you have kept them a secret from your friends and family?

8. If your friends and family knew about your secrets, what would they say about you?

9. One definition of a "hypocrite" is someone who pretends to hold beliefs or who practices actions that are not consistent with their claimed beliefs. Please talk about your own hypocrisy.

Miracles

Your ways, O God are holy. What god is so great as our God? You are the God who performs miracles.
—Psalm 77:13–14

Are not two sparrows sold for a penny? Yet not one of them will fall to the ground apart from the will of your father. And even the very hairs of your head are all numbered. So don't be afraid; you are worth more than many sparrows.
—Matthew 10:29–31

And my God will meet all of your needs according to His riches in glory by Christ Jesus. To our God and Father be glory forever and ever. Amen.
—Philippians 4:19–20

When I initially heard from the Holy Spirit that he would provide a kidney for me and that a miracle would be involved, my mind could not fathom the degree with which I would be helped and rescued. As I look back, the odds of finding a stranger to donate a kidney are fairly slim. The fact that Millie's kidney was not only a match, but a perfect match was even more unfathomable to me. And, her kidney was a perfect kidney—meaning that if there were no signs of rejection, her kidney would last for my entire life. This was mind-blowing to me! It meant that I would no longer suffer with the afflictions and symptoms of kidney disease, replete with extreme fatigue, nausea, confusion and debilitating leg cramps. Instead, I was given a new life; a life to be used to bring even greater glory to God, my Creator, Redeemer, and heavenly Father.

You, the reader, might believe that miracles ended during the time when the bible was written. I know otherwise, not because I am smarter or more intelligent. I have heard the voice of God on several occasions and each time He spoke prophetic words which brought hope and assurance during times of crises. More importantly, His words have always come to fruition. I truly believe that God, in His mercy and grace set things into motion that would have prompted me to post my cry for help. He further orchestrated and put into motion all of the people and circumstances to save me from suffering and death.

I will admit that while miracles happen with greater frequency than we know, that are also more of an exception rather than the rule. Scripture tells us when we are in need of one, we should commit to prayer and if our prayers are in accordance with His will, He hears us. Why He chose to grant me this miracle, only God Himself knows. I have heard from many friends who have their own ideas, but I choose to allow myself to not question why lest I attribute human thoughts and presuppositions to my Creator. I am convinced that miracles occur more often than we realize. I sense that God has created miracles in your life that you are not perhaps aware of yet. Perhaps He performs miracles in everyone's life, but we are too busy with worrying and doing life that we fail to notice.

I do know that I will forever be a megaphone and with a loud shout, tell the world of the goodness of our God.

Questions

1. As in my story, one never knows who God will use to effect positive change in your life. You might also not know who He will use to bring about the miracle you need. Who do you count on for support, unconditional love, and encouragement during those times when a miracle is needed?

2. Is there a miracle you need right now? What is it?

3. According to your beliefs, what criteria does God use when He decides for whom He will perform a miracle?

4. If you sense that your faith is not strong enough to believe that God will perform a miracle for you, what should/can you do to strengthen your faith? Why do you feel these actions are vital to strengthening your faith?

5. Is your faith quickly weakened by unforeseen or unplanned setbacks? Why?

6. The Lord prompted me to write this book so that others might be encouraged by my overcoming tragedy, death, and trauma. Have you either heard from the Lord or sensed that He is prompting you to do something or take action which is out of your comfort zone? If so, what is He requiring you to do?

7. Miracles occur as a demonstration of how much He loves and cares for us, especially when we are in relationship with Him. Ultimately, God seeks to be glorified by us, His children. In what ways do you feel that God is glorified by your relationship with Him as well as with others?

About the Author

Jeffrey M. Rifkin, PhD, has been a licensed marriage and family therapist since 1986 and has devoted his life's work to helping individuals, families, and couples move beyond their emotional pain and dysfunction.

He was born and raised in the much-maligned borough of Brooklyn where he had witnessed many emotional traumas, many which were an integral part of his early childhood. In order to make meaning out of these traumas, Dr. Rifkin went on a lifelong quest in an attempt to understand the ways of God. He discovered that despite being raised Jewish, his many experiences with Jesus were undisputable, and he accepted Him as his Messiah in 1997.

In that same year, he learned that he inherited a family genetic disease which destroyed his kidneys, and while on dialysis, his wife left him as she did not want to take care of a sick man. Up until that time, his wife did not work, and Dr. Rifkin was the sole wage earner of his family. In 2016, God had led Dr. Rifkin and his current wife, Shar, into a relationship where they both received simultaneous messages confirming God's intentions of bringing them together as husband and wife. They married in September 2017, and their life together is quite challenging as she too has a genetic disease which manifests into cancer. They pray together daily and attend the Cove Church regularly, where they also volunteer their time to help others in need.

Dr. Rifkin is internationally published in his field and has additionally written three screenplays.

CPSIA information can be obtained
at www.ICGtesting.com
Printed in the USA
BVHW030219170519
548597BV00001B/14/P